D0193273

973.04924 B453
Berger, Joseph.
Displaced persons   26.00

MID-CONTINENT PUBLIC LIBRARY
North Independence Branch
317 W. Highway 24
Independence, Mo. 64050

NI

WITHDRAWN
FROM THE RECORDS OF THE
MID-CONTINENT PUBLIC LIBRARY

DISPLACED PERSONS

Growing Up American
After the Holocaust

JOSEPH BERGER

SCRIBNER

New York London Toronto Sydney Singapore

MID-CONTINENT PUBLIC LIBRARY
North Independence Branch
317 W. Highway 24
Independence, Mo. 64050

N I

MID-CONTINENT PUBLIC LIBRARY

3 0001 006220455 5

SCRIBNER
1230 Avenue of the Americas
New York, NY 10020

Some names and details have been changed to guard the privacy of
individuals not consulted in the writing of this book.

Copyright © 2001 by Joseph Berger

All rights reserved, including the right of reproduction
in whole or in part in any form.

SCRIBNER and design are trademarks of Macmillan Library Reference USA, Inc.,
used under license by Simon & Schuster, the publisher of this work.

Designed by Kyoko Watanabe
Set in Sabon

Manufactured in the United States of America

1 3 5 7 9 10 8 6 4 2

Library of Congress Cataloging-in-Publication Data
Berger, Joseph, 1945–
Displaced persons : growing up American after the
Holocaust / Joseph Berger.
p. cm.
1. Berger, Joseph, 1945– 2. Jews—New York (State)—
New York—Biography. 3. Children of Holocaust survivors—
New York (State)—New York—Biography. 4. Children of
immigrants—New York (State)—New York—Biography.
5. New York (N.Y.)—Biography. I. Title.
F128.9.J5 B43954 2001
973'.04924'00922—dc21
[B]   00-069606

ISBN 0-684-85757-X

Portions of chapters 13 and 31 originally appeared in somewhat
different form in *Newsday*. A version of chapter 31's circumcision episode
originally appeared in *Present Tense*.

For Marcus and Rachel Berger,
and the steady heroism of all the refugees

For Marcus and Rachel Berger,
and the steady heroism of all the refugees

ACKNOWLEDGMENTS

This book germinated more than twenty years ago when I first sensed that my immigrant family's struggle with America and with the unrelenting grip of the Holocaust was a story worth writing about. After I decided to tell the story as straight as I could remember it, and not disguise it as fiction, many people gave me invaluable help. Joel Fishman, my literary agent, helped me shape some stray chapters and an outline into something closer to a book. Eva Fogelman and her husband, Jerome Chanes, offered inspiration; Willie Helmreich, some necessary research; and Menachem Rosensaft, Sam Norich, Ben Meed, and Donna Cohen, the sense of a larger community. Friends such as the late Norbert Wollheim, the late Barry Kwalick, Esther Hautzig, Dan Cryer, Jerry and Eva Posman, Roberta Hershenson, Ira and Joyce Goldstein, Jules Bemporad, Nancy Albertson, Robin Gaines, Stacey Fredericks, Alon Gratch, Regina Schwartz, David Aftergood, Stuart and Susan Knott, and Ellen Abrams and my brother, Josh, sister, Evelyn, and brother-in-law, Ivor Shapiro, provided the needed cheerleading.

The book would have been poorer in every way without the passionate enthusiasm, literary sensibility, and plain good sense of my editor at Scribner, Jane Rosenman. Her assistant, Ethan Friedman, took care of important details with grace and cheer. Nancy Miller, my neighbor, friend, and editor on my first book, helped the book find its publisher and let me feel, as I kept on writing, that this was a project worth undertaking. Most of all, my wife, Brenda, gave me insight and understanding during long car rides and late-night talks and she and our daughter, Annie, were more than tolerant—they were loving and generous—in letting me take Sunday and weekday mornings to bring the story to light.

DISPLACED
PERSONS

INTRODUCTION

A few years after I joined *The New York Times,* its editors and reporters were asked to attend a presentation on the newspaper's future given by Arthur O. Sulzberger, Jr., who at the time was being groomed to become publisher. I arrived for work carrying a brown paper bag with a container of coffee and a seeded roll, thinking I'd have some time to enjoy breakfast at my desk before heading upstairs to the publisher's suite.

I've always enjoyed seeded rolls because when I was a child we would have them on Sunday mornings for breakfast, one of the few meals during the week that we shared together as a family. My parents were Polish-Jewish refugees who had survived the Nazi slaughter and immigrated to America, and throughout my childhood both of them had worked long days in dreary factories. A weeknight supper was usually a slapdash affair, with my father and sometimes even my mother absent. So Sunday-morning breakfast was a sanctified time.

Even at six and seven years old, I enjoyed walking the four or five blocks, savoring the warmth of the morning's sunshine, to the Cake Masters bakery on upper Broadway to fetch those rolls as well as a seedless rye bread and a few fruit Danishes that my nervously economical parents allowed themselves as a treat. Before entering the bakery, I would press against the glass display window and find myself hankering for one of the marzipan potatoes coated with a sprinkling of cinnamon and cocoa. Maybe next Sunday, I told myself, I would get my parents to splurge for one. Inside, the shop was snug and teeming, with the spirited air of men and women on the verge of indulging in some especially tasty food, in this case the bakery's rich confections, arrayed like the crown jewels in a sumptuous glass counter. I would wait my turn, and when the European saleslady in a white apron smudged with powder and jelly gestured to me, I recited my parents' order like the rote prayers I was learning in yeshiva.

"A round rye bread without seeds, sliced, four seeded rolls, and two blueberry Danishes," I would chant, anxious that I not forget anything on the list.

When I returned with the booty, we would sit around our table—I still remember the chill of its white enameled metal top—and devour our rolls and bread, perhaps some slivers of *schmaltz* herring and a cottage cheese salad with radishes, scallions, cucumbers, and tomatoes, and wash the meal down with cups of instant coffee. Sometimes we laughed, sometimes we bickered, but we were together. It was evident in their glimmering eyes that my orphaned parents relished the sight of our togetherness as a family as if there were no sweeter gift imaginable. And I reveled in their delight.

So this roll I was about to have at the *Times* would no doubt be made tastier by those pleasant associations. In the elevator I saw that my colleagues were already heading up to the fourteenth-floor suite and I realized I had gotten the time wrong. I would not have time for breakfast. I dashed to my desk, took off my coat, and, snatching the bag of roll and coffee, caught the elevator upstairs. Although by then I had worked for the *Times* for four years, mostly as a writer on religion and education, I had never been to the publisher's floor. I followed a stream of latecomers through the suite and up a winding staircase to a large and elegant penthouse lounge. I was struck by the stately cherry woodwork, the framed antique maps and sketches of ocean liners, the soft carpets. I did not want to spill coffee on these carpets. That would reveal that I really did not belong here.

The penthouse room was filled with more than a hundred reporters and editors, including management people like Max Frankel, Warren Hoge, and Dave Jones, who were sitting in the club chairs at the front.

I felt an air of formality unusual even for the distinctly formal *Times* of those years. Almost all the men had their jackets on. I spotted an empty seat two thirds of the way toward the back and, still holding my bag of coffee and the seeded roll, I slipped in.

Young Sulzberger, in shirtsleeves, crisply pressed trousers, and bright red suspenders, was talking about how the *Times* had teetered on the edge of financial failure in the early 1970s but had emerged gloriously by investing in a new printing plant and boldly starting several sections that invigorated advertising. The *Times* once again needed to expand. It was building a $400 million plant that would allow it to produce a bigger daily paper and use color for almost every section. When all the changes were in place, Sulzberger assured us, the *Times'* position as the best newspaper in the world would be enhanced.

I looked around and was glad to be part of this robust operation as it headed into the next decade, glad to be included among these smart, important men and women, glad to be a reporter on the world's best newspaper. But my smugness was interrupted by a panicked thought. I was holding my brown paper bag and it was tearing. Coffee had seeped through the lid, weakened the bag, and dampened the roll. It would be awkward to drink coffee in this group. I was hungry and thirsty but I would just have to wrap my fingers around the soggy container and wait until after the meeting to throw it away. Otherwise, as I had feared, my colleagues would surely realize I did not belong here. And that realization would be corroborated by the seeded roll, which would reveal that I was deeply rooted in another, incompatible world, a world not just of seeded rolls but of baggy suits, gaunt faces, and hollow eyes, a world of refugee parents who could not speak English and fumbled their way around American life.

This thoroughly trivial event—bringing a cup of coffee and a seeded roll to a publisher's pep talk—was like Proust's famous madeleine. It had triggered for me the kinds of associations that ripple subversively throughout my days.

Like many immigrants and children of immigrants, I have always lived in two worlds at the same time. There is my American world: jobs at prestigious companies, a co-op on the West Side or a house in the suburbs, evenings at the theater and summers in the Berkshires.

And there is the immigrant world that tinges all that comfort with a sense of raw peril, terror of imminent poverty, and, sometimes, an awareness of one's foreignness. To be sure, it also lives on in an ability to laugh at the pretensions of life and even, occasionally, in a kind of immigrant pride at how much we have accomplished. But its virtues are soon outweighed by the hovering fear that all will be snatched away by some malicious whim of the universe, for isn't that what happened to my parents and their generation of European Jews?

In me those immigrant feelings have been sharpened to a fine keenness by the fact that my parents were not simply immigrants, but refugees from the catastrophe that distinguished World War II from all previous wars—two of the more than 140,000 Jewish Holocaust survivors who immigrated to America between 1946 and 1953. These survivors did not come here just as foreigners seeking America's legendary opportunities. They came here because they had no place else to go. They had been stripped of their homes, their parents, their brothers and sisters, their villages and neighborhoods.

That occasional jolt of fear that I felt at the *Times* that day and sometimes still feel is part of my legacy. I am a refugee, and somewhere I will always be one. As a young boy, I thought entering the Bronx High School of Science and the Columbia School of Journalism would make those refugee feelings go away. Later, I thought marriage and a family would make them go away. I thought working for the *Times* would make them go away. Those successes did not make the feelings disappear. The refugee condition is a frustratingly hardy state, an indelible way of seeing the world.

I have come to learn that many people at the *Times* or in my generally comfortable circle feel much the same way, that having grown up the child of a janitor or of a shattered marriage or of a hardscrabble West Virginia backwater has made even well-spoken, long-rooted, stylishly tailored executives feel not quite deserving. Most people have their Rosebud. Mine was being a refugee. The major distinction is that the American world of the refugees—in contrast to their well-documented ordeals during the war—is not really very well known. But it is worth knowing because it was rich in its particulars, in its texture, in its colors. It was my world.

Refugee. That's what they called us when we arrived in America, and that's what we soon called ourselves, as if there had never before been such calamity-tossed exiles. No one called us Holocaust survivors. The word *Holocaust* had not yet been applied to the slaughter of Europe's Jews. The immensity of what had taken place had still not sunk into the world's imagination, nor even our own, still-reeling imaginations. Indeed, the refugees were so beaten down they did not think it their place even to complain, to merely let others know of what they had been through. Besides, there were more fundamental things they had to think about.

They were of a certain age—in their twenties or early thirties—because few of the very young or the old survived the concentration camps or could withstand the rigors of hiding or flight. Very few of the refugees had more than a meager education. Not only had the war robbed the survivors of their prime schooling years, but it is a bitter truth about the Holocaust that cunning, a capacity for bone-wearying work, and luck were more likely than intellectual prowess to have kept one alive.

They began knitting together as a community in the DP camps, the camps for "displaced persons" that were set up by the victorious Allies inside occupied Germany—a bitterly ironic location for their salvation. The survivors no longer had Jewish communities to return to and had little appetite for living under the emerging communist regimes of Eastern Europe. So they waited in the DP camps for three, four, sometimes seven years for visas that would admit them to Palestine, the United States, Australia, or the handful of other countries that, however grudgingly, were willing to absorb refugees.

While they waited the survivors began finding mates for their new lives and making the friends who would replace the families they had lost. The marriages were as often convenient as romantic. Men and women came together because they could no longer bear the solitude or because their mates had a knack for scavenging food or closing deals in the black markets that flourished in the occupied zones. The survivors also made decisions to have children, sometimes to recapture the families slain by Hitler, sometimes just to give themselves a source of pleasure and hope, a reprieve from years of privation. I was born in

Russia in the war's final months, but my brother, Josh, was born two years later in the Schlachtensee DP camp on the margins of Berlin.

The refugees came over to the United States in wobbling vessels that had earlier been used to transport the GIs to the European theater. Most of these remnants of European Judaism arrived in New York City, though others disembarked in places like Galveston, Texas. In New York, the survivors, weighed down with valises and duffel bags, were put up in shabby West Side hotels with names like the Marseilles and the Whitehall or as boarders in the tenement apartments of aging Jewish widows. The Hebrew Immigrant Aid Society and other Jewish agencies tried to find the refugees work and permanent apartments, but almost no one wanted their help for very long. They had been dependent for so many years—on the German guards in the concentration camps or on Allied relief workers—and they craved self-reliance.

Once settled, they began to work long hours sewing dresses and draperies, tending dim luncheonettes and Laundromats, reupholstering sofas or peddling door-to-door. When the refugees did find apartments they could afford, they stayed near each other, forming identifiable pockets in the South Bronx, in Flatbush, and on Manhattan's West Side. On Saturdays and Sundays they would take up a European custom and go for an afternoon *shpatzir*—a stroll—on Broadway or Riverside Drive, encountering faces they dimly recognized from the camps, be they concentration or DP. They found new friends by detecting a snatch of Yiddish on a passerby's lips or discerning the threadbare European cast of a topcoat. Or they would seize a chance for some pleasure, treating themselves to a Spencer Tracy movie at the Riviera Theater on Broadway followed by a hot dog at Rosenbloom's delicatessen.

Some survivors had relatives here who could help them get started. But just as often those ties were soon bruised by obligation and dependence. Nobody really was to blame. The American Jews were only one step up the American ladder. They may have scorned the reminders of their own squalid immigrant roots, resented having to share scarce resources, and perhaps felt a little discomfort at not having done more to save their imperiled kin. And, of course, just as the wave of refugees boasted a sprinkling of artists and doctors, it also had its share of freeloaders and connivers who made compassion difficult.

For the most part, the refugees went about trying to create the same prosaic lives for themselves that their working-class neighbors had. They had to find jobs, learn their way around the subways, choose schools, provide music and dance lessons, find summer camps, and steer their children into productive lives. The goals were quite basic, but not easy to accomplish. A remark a Vietnamese boat person, Vu Thanh They, made at a 1988 commencement is apt. "In fact," this refugee said, "surprising as it may seem, the daily struggle of making a living in America is more difficult to cope with than all of the events we went through in prison and at sea. The reason is that there is nothing 'heroic' about surviving the never-ending problems of daily life."

The Jewish refugees also had to deal with the questions that never ceased haunting them: Why did they survive and not their parents or brothers and sisters? Who was this God who closed his eyes to such suffering? What was his purpose in having them survive? They also had to cope with their children's questions about the horrors and humiliations of the war and with the children's shame at having parents with coagulated accents who were unfamiliar with baseball and pizza and seemed to have an inexhaustible well of grief.

In my world, there were Mordchale Weinberg and Moishe Granas and Simon Cooperman and Moishe Erlich and Sam Herling. There were Fela Herling and Saba Weinberg and Norma Cooperman and Shayve Erlich. They were all Jews from scattered parts of Poland, and for the most part they had met one another in the displaced persons camps. Motele Weinberg and Moishe Granas were tailors. Mr. Erlich and his wife were peddlers. Sam Herling was a barber. Almost all the women knew how to sew and soon used their skills to land jobs in the Garment District. They were not intellectuals or political activists, and none of them felt he or she had the station in life to register even the feeblest protest at what had been done to them, at all that had been taken away. Their task was to go on.

They were also young then, and that youth seemed to make them resilient even to their losses. You might think it strange to say, but when my parents got together with their friends, they laughed and joked with a gusto I rarely share with friends. There was also a certain excitement to their being in a new, bountiful place like New York.

They savored the stylish bustle of upper Broadway, the fresh rye breads and sweet butter and the American movies. They loved the open parks. They spread blankets on the grass and stretched out to soak in the sun and had picnics and taught their children to ride bicycles, and when they were especially merry, they dangled from branches and turned somersaults. They had parties. My mother would indulge in a drink of vodka and, with a friend, would laugh so raucously I would move as far away as I could to escape embarrassment. And they danced. Well, not my father. His feet moved to a jagged rhythm, as if he'd never heard music in his life. Given the fact he was raised a farmer, maybe he had not. But my mother danced, and men like Mr. Weinberg enjoyed sweeping her across the floor.

I point this out because the refugees or survivors are always portrayed as gloomy and bitter. They were that way at times. But they also lived lives that were quite full, lives of frivolity as well as mourning.

It is my desire to portray that fullness, largely through the story of my family, which, however particular, was emblematic of the stories of many of the survivors. I was a witness—a young and callow one, to be sure, but a witness. And I can report on what it was like being a child of people who survived the war and found refuge in America. It was a tangle of experiences and I never quite knew what to make of it. There was pride at the ordeals they had surmounted, but also embarrassment at their awkwardness in the American realm. And then my parents, like other refugee parents, lavished on their children volumes of attention that in a clan of grandparents, uncles, and aunts might have been dissipated. We were given a feeling of importance far beyond our feeble powers. We would provide the affection and entertainment that the dead no longer could. By our success as scholars and professionals, we would redeem those truncated lives. Like other immigrant children, I was expected to interpret the English world, to explain Con Ed bills and drug prescriptions and inquiries from the government. I was supposed to unravel the stock market, argue politics with my parents' friends, raise my brother, console my mother. Would it be surprising if such unspoken expectations of someone so young might result in a self-doubt or two? The children of survivors have been remarkably successful, but I sometimes wonder if we can savor our success or if we will always see it as insufficient. Perhaps we will always be children inadequate to the task.

The story of the refugees, it must be said, was not just the traditional immigrant story of newcomers wrestling with a strange language and the insults of poverty. For the most part, the Holocaust refugees had no families here to help them and, if they foundered here, they had no place to which they could return. The workaday realities of carving out a life in a strange country, in a wondrous but intimidating and not always welcoming city, produced its inevitable pathos and Nabokovian absurdities for them just as for other immigrants. But the refugees labored under an extra dimension: the inescapable shadow of their horrible past.

Yet, in setting down the story of a family of Jewish refugees, I have hoped to shed light on what other refugees go through. I know that despite my own experience, I spend little time thinking about the lives of Vietnamese or Cambodian or Salvadoran refugees. Sure, I wince at learning of furtive voyages on boats and of sweltering refugee camps. But I romanticize the great opportunities they have here, and that detached view misunderstands them.

Two decades ago my wife and I spent several weekends in a Catskills hotel that was populated almost entirely by Russian emigrants. I was charmed by the Russians' gold teeth, the same teeth that glinted in my parents' European mouths, and by the old-fashioned way the young couples took evening walks, just as my young parents had. But in my romanticization I had missed the kernel of their refugee condition. I remember seeing six men sitting at an outdoor table by a lake, huddled around a large cassette player that was pouring out Russian songs. Some of the men were in tears. How much they missed their homes. With all the oppression, discrimination, terror they felt there, how much they missed their homes. That pain, that homesickness, is universal among refugees. The Jewish refugees hated the countries they left, the anti-Semitic populations around them, but they missed their streets and towns and markets, even the particular smell of the air, and they longed for their lost families.

The life my family lived in America was a daily affair. The fact that my parents had survived the Holocaust and we were their children was a given. Life did not stop with that event. No one put us up on a stage and showered us with applause for having survived. The movies such as *Sophie's Choice* and *Schindler's List* came much later. We simply had to go on with our lives, day by day. This book is something of what those days were like.

It is not a story that can be told in isolation. Before the war, my parents led distinct lives of their own, and who they are was very much shaped by who they were, not just by the wartime trauma. My father, who has never been much of a talker, seems unable to summon the narrative spirit to re-create his early life for me. It may be the painfulness of revelation that locks him up, but I know almost nothing about his parents, his six sisters, the look and smell of his town. But my mother has always given me snatches of her life, and in recent years agreed to sit down for something of a formal interview. Moreover, in her late seventies, she has written an account in English of her early life before and during the war that she calls "A Legacy Given to Her Children by a Survivor of the Holocaust."

As I read it I realize how much of her character I had mistakenly attributed just to the Holocaust. She was shaped in large part by the years before the war. And I was shaped by those years as well. Her mother's death when she was not quite six robbed me of a piece of my mother. Her father's decision to send her away from home at fourteen so she could earn her own way sent me out into the world in ways that I was never ready for. It was perhaps no accident that I was hit by a car when I was six. Her panicked distraction has become my panicked distraction; her grief has, in some small measure, become my grief; her laughter, my laughter, whether I like it or not.

And there is one more reason why I have wrapped the story of her early life into my account. I feel an obligation. If we, the sons and daughters of those who survived, will not remember their vanished world, who will?

1

On Sunday mornings, my father would polish the family's
shoes. He would gather up his black wingtips, my mother's
high-heeled pumps, my brother's and my well-scuffed loafers, and line
them up over several pages of the Yiddish broadsheet *Der Tag* that he
had spread on the wooden floor of our narrow apartment hallway.
Squatting on his haunches in the boxer shorts and the sleeveless undershirt he had slept in, he slathered polish on one shoe after another,
black for his and my mother's, brown for my brother's and mine. As
the polish dried to a milky gloss, he returned to the first shoe and, with
his factory-honed shoulder muscles fluttering with each stroke,
brushed it to a fine shine. Each succeeding shoe seemed to require an
extra charge of energy, so he clamped his tongue between his teeth, the
pink mass of it glistening from his lips, as if that concentrated strain
would push him through the task. With each stroke of the brush, he
rocked back and forth on his heels, his bony buttocks almost touching
the floor. The exertion all seemed worth it when four pairs, and sometimes five, six, or seven, stood before him, gleaming brightly, ready for
another week of scuffing and rain.

I choose that picture, because in many ways it crystallizes for me the
image of my father as a refugee. My father is on the floor, squatting on
his haunches, a peasant attitude. Indeed, my father was born a peasant,
the son of a Jewish farmer in Galicia in the mountainous terrain where

Poland, Slovakia, the Ukraine, Hungary, and Romania all meet. But he is polishing shoes in a tenement apartment in New York. My father was not meant to be an apartment dweller in a polyglot, cosmopolitan city where people spend their summer nights lounging on stoops listening to baseball on portable radios and smoking cigars. Where are his vegetable patch, the cows, the barn, the hayrides, the hill town dominated by the Catholic church steeple where plain, unworldly Jews transacted their lives to the cycle of their holidays, asking only for a measure of tolerance?

And there are the shoes. My father has, in my mind, always been associated with shoes. He learned to repair shoes in the Soviet army, which is where he and thousands of other young Polish men wound up after the Soviets occupied eastern Poland at the outbreak of World War II. Not trusting the Poles to fight on their front lines, the Soviets confined them to military factories deep in the Russian interior, like the military boot factory where my father worked. Food in the Urals and Siberia was scarce and tens of thousands died, but my father survived by illicitly making extra pairs of boots for Russian officers and swapping them for food. Those bootleg boots allowed him to take care of the hungry, frail young woman who became my mother. Though my father is no longer a shoemaker, he knows and feels comfortable around shoes. He will gaze at my shoes from across a room and point out a cracked sole or slanted heel. He may ask me to take one shoe off and examine it, turning it over and peering inside, inspecting the quality of its leather and its craftsmanship. His interest is more than curiosity. I take it as an act of deep, inarticulate love.

In the Sunday-morning picture of my father, the newspaper on the floor is always Yiddish. My father could not then, could not for many years, read English. His children learned English long before he did and their Yiddish gradually faded. His Yiddish allowed him to get by in America's Jewish neighborhoods, with his boss and some of his colleagues. For the boy I was, though, his Yiddish was the mark of a conversational cripple. The Yiddish on my parents' lips declared how backward they were, how much they would drag me down in my quest to gain acceptance in this country.

I admired my father's muscular shoulders, but was sometimes

ashamed of them as well. They were the shoulders of a laborer, and I was going to school with children of businessmen and well-to-do merchants. There was also something threadbare about his undershirt and underpants. Why was he not in pajamas, even a robe? And why was he polishing our shoes? Where was his self-respect?

Finally, the Sunday-morning image of my father polishing the family shoes crystallizes the refugee experience because, squatting on the floor, my father is alone. I have always thought of my father as someone profoundly alone. He was unmoored from his large family when he was drafted during the war, and though that historical accident saved him, all those who were left behind perished at the hands of the Nazis in ways he still does not know. Neither his parents nor any of his six sisters nor anyone from the prolific colony of Berger uncles and aunts in his hometown of Borinya survived. He has no relative closer than a second cousin. Perhaps his consuming attachment to his wife and three children underscores his solitude. My father, an instinctively genial man, has a large circle of acquaintances in the Riverdale neighborhood he lives in now. Still, when I think of him leaving the orbit of his wife and children, I think of him as utterly alone.

An image of my mother: she is combing through the racks of boys' suits at Gimbel's while my brother and I are bored and irritated and would like to wander off to more exciting counters—the stamp collections on the ground floor, for example. But my mother is searching for the best suit in the store, riffling through the hangers and checking sleeves for size, price, and fabric. She is in a fever. The suit must not only fit as if it were tailored especially for me, but it must be 100 percent wool, priced reasonably if not on sale, and make me look, at ten years old, as dapper as Sinatra. I am, after all, not only her son; I am the bright, charming companion her rustic husband will never be. My mother is willing to have me try on every suit in the store, no matter how sultry the day, no matter how distressed I am, and then I will have to wait until she finds a duplicate my brother's size. If a salesman comes over, she will keep him at arm's length. She does not trust salesmen.

The image captures my mother at her finest and at her most exasperating. She is in Gimbel's suit department, which she considers a cut

above Macy's. Maintaining that edge of superiority is important to her.
She was born into a poor home in the resort town of Otwock, a short
train ride from Warsaw. Her mother died when she was not even six
and she suffered the bruising slights of a stepchild. She told us how her
family ate chicken only on holidays and what a rare delicacy an egg
was. In such privation, the distinctions kept her spirits up. She bol-
stered herself with the knowledge that she was a Golant, a family
whose erudition and style, she claimed, were respected far beyond the
unsung hamlets where they lived. Indeed, my mother made the Golants
seem the stuff of legend. Her father, Joshua Golant, may have been a
poor man who scraped a subsistence together by teaching young boys
Torah and leading prayers as a cantor on the High Holidays, but he
was tall, regal of bearing, a sage, and blessed with the voice of Caruso.
In short, he was a Golant, and so was she, and so was I. And though
she talked about our pedigree with a sly laugh at her own pretensions,
she somewhere believed that being a Golant made one a cut above
almost everyone else.

Sustaining that edge was important. A clever woman but one
whose education in Poland stopped at the seventh grade, my mother
did not study books or consult experts on what schools to send her
children to or where to buy her clothes. But she would hear names and
pick things out of the ozone. Florsheim Shoes. Horn & Hardart. Bronx
High School of Science. Juilliard. Columbia. Some matters she guessed
right, some matters not so right. But always she pushed for the finest,
wanted us to push harder, strive higher. With my father, we might have
led contented but plain lives in America. My mother gave us ambition.
Sometimes, however, her ambition overlooked us, failed to see what it
meant to wait in a hot store for the perfect suit.

For the image of my mother at Gimbel's captures another essence
of her during those refugee years. She was busy, frantically, frenetically
busy. She worked as a hatmaker for the first twenty years in this country, hunched over a sewing machine with her foot pressed to a treadle
doing the intricate needlework on straw hats for Easter. During the
season, she would come home at seven or later, trying to squeeze in as
much overtime as she could get. But she always tossed together a hot
and tasty supper. On Friday nights we had a Sabbath meal of chicken

soup, gefilte fish, and flanken. The floors were immaculately clean after my mother, squatting on her knees, pumped a washrag across the floor. Our clothes were always fresh, our shirts pressed, and except for a formal suit or dress, she never used a cleaner. Some people, I suppose, have mental pictures of their parents sitting tranquilly in an easy chair. I have no such picture of my mother. She could never allow herself the time to sit quietly in a chair, read a book, or, after we finally got a TV set, watch a show. Perhaps she did not feel she deserved a break. There were so many things to be done to reach some imagined plateau of safety that she could not rest. Often I think that rest was trying for her, that it forced her to dwell on the pain of her life, on her lost parents and brothers and sisters. Busyness was a magnificent escape and she busied herself until she dropped.

We came to America on a gray, chilly day in early March 1950. Our ship was a navy transport called the *General A. W. Greely*. I have remembered the name of that ship all my life because as a young boy I was hungry for distinctions, and a voyage on an oceangoing ship was indeed a distinction. I remember almost nothing of the voyage, although I retain a gossamer picture of moaning men and women throwing up, of my father standing perilously on a rung of the ship's railing and leaning out to glimpse the approaching harbor of New York, of my three-year-old brother's blond shyness, of my mother's panicked face. Indeed, I remember almost nothing of my life before arriving in America. Early memories seem to need a steady soil to flourish.

But on an inspired whim several years ago, I looked up the shipping news column for March 3, 1950, on *New York Times* microfilm. I found not only a listing of the *General A. W. Greely*'s arrival at the pier on West Twenty-first Street at 9:15 A.M., but a column-long story about its journey. It told how the ship had collided with another ship as it left Bremerhaven, Germany, in a dense fog, and of a tornadolike storm that sent the ship tumbling and lurching, knocking out its power for a time and delaying its arrival by three days. The story also had one lyrical detail: the day we arrived was Purim. Officials of the Hebrew Immigrant Aid Society, which we called HIAS, greeted the refugees off the boat with hamantaschen and coffee. I thought how tenderly symbolic that we should arrive on Purim, the day that commemorates the deliverance of the Jews of Persia from the tyranny of Haman. It was a time when I still tended to glamorize our journey as an adventure-filled rescue from the perils of Europe with a happily-ever-after ending in New York.

Our suitcases and duffel bags were piled into a van and we headed up Tenth Avenue as it flowed into Amsterdam Avenue toward the West Side hotel where we would be housed by HIAS (HIAS was a term in such common use among the Jewish refugees that into adulthood I thought it was Yiddish). My mother gazed out the window at the sullen tenements and shabby shops, at the lines of flapping clothes strung between fire escapes and alleyways, at the trash cans guarding the sidewalks and the clusters of loutish men gathered in doorways. My mother was thirty years old then. She had wavy brunet hair and blue eyes and cheeks that had somehow not lost their ruddiness. She was also a terribly nervous woman, and every surprise, every shift in fate in even the most trifling matters, seemed to jar her. As she peered out the window, her eyes flickered and trembled. Her heart sank. Was this the place for which she had forsaken the culture of Europe?

The possibility that she had miscalculated frightened her terribly. This would not be an easy error to correct. She had originally wanted to go to Israel, the country she had heard friends speak of with such hope and longing, a land in its infancy then but still a country where she could live among Jews at the tolerance only of Jews. Where would they get the money for the family's passage there now? They had spent almost all the money they had squirreled away in the displaced persons camps in Berlin and Landsberg on arrangements for the trip to America. Now they were stuck here for many years to come. Who knew what life would be like, how they would subsist, whether her husband would land a job, what kind of housing they would get, and whether they would find anyone they knew here or make friends? Would she need to go to work to put her children through a Jewish school? And if she went to work, who would take care of her children when they came home?

Such practical questions did not reverberate in her five-year-old son, but the dread seeped in through a kind of osmosis. Although I may not have been able to articulate it to myself, I already felt these alien streets would be a trial, filled with unfamiliar faces and unfamiliar tongues. How could I make a friend when I didn't even speak English? How could I understand a teacher or a classmate? And how could I rely on my perplexed, frightened parents to help me cope? I turned away from the car window and buried my face in my father's shoulder.

The hotel, the Capital Hall, was a dour, leaden building on Eighty-seventh Street between Amsterdam and Columbus Avenues. Our room was seedy, dusty, Victorian, with a large mahogany headboard and wardrobe that heightened the room's dark, oppressive feeling. A greasy armchair, a small enamel-topped table, a corner sink, and two fold-up cots for my brother, Josh, and me made the room feel cheap as well. My mother gazed out the window and her heart sank; the room looked out on an airshaft.

My father didn't take in the view. He dragged our large checked cardboard valise, which he had bound fast with strong rope, to the middle of the room, untied the knots and unfastened the latches, and pulled out a frayed white pillowcase. My mother bit into one edge of the cloth and ripped it in two, dampened both pieces and gave one to my father, and the two of them began scrubbing the room clean. They wiped the carvings of the headboard, the sides of the springs, the legs of the metal-topped table, the wardrobe, and the window frame. After washing the dirt out of the rag, they crouched on the floor and swabbed the linoleum clean. While this torrent of sanitation swirled around us, three-year-old Josh and I bounced up and down on the bed, delighting in the wonderfully springy coils. When they were done, my mother chased us off and covered the bed with a goose-down quilt she had brought in the duffel bags from Germany. The quilt had been made especially for her by an uprooted German couple more penniless than us.

It was time for lunch. Out of an inside pocket of his topcoat, my father produced a small bundle he had squirreled away that contained two drumsticks of chicken and two apples. They had been part of the last dinner on the ship. With a pocket knife he always carried with him, he cut the drumsticks into four pieces and peeled the apples, artfully keeping each peel to a single coil. We sat on the two chairs, my parents on the bed, and pulling the small table between us, we ate our first meal in the United States with great relish.

Ten years before, my father would have said a blessing before he ate and a lengthy blessing afterward. But he said nothing now. The anarchy of the war years had worn away many of the habits of my parents' pious childhood. They observed some of the rituals—Sabbath candles, the Yom Kippur fast, the Passover seder—but it would be many years before they made their peace with God.

The Capital Hall Hotel was one block off Broadway, and Broadway squirmed and palpitated with every sort of human life: shoppers, hawkers, idlers, connivers, and thieves. There were business executives in smart topcoats with their determined strides and Orthodox Jewish couples, the stout men in fedoras, the women starchily dressed, pushing pompous baby carriages with toddlers clinging to the sides. There were old women padding their swollen legs down the sidewalk for a trip to the grocery and Spanish-speaking men, newcomers also, clustering, smoking, laughing, and sometimes cupping their groins in a swaggering style at odds with the tame refugee men I knew. But the street was increasingly acquiring a European veneer, the product of the German, Austrian, and Belgian Jews who had come over before the war and the less decorous East European Jews who were coming over now.

The prewar refugees, many of whom had been able to escape with some money or had been able to use a craft to start a small business, had settled themselves into the formidable, thick-walled apartments on West End Avenue and Riverside Drive. The postwar refugees, who had only their brawn and a craving to finally start their lives, were living in the hotels or tenements on the side streets. The hotels included the Marseilles, the Whitehall, the Midway, and the Capital Hall, places that had once seen better days as residences for aspiring out-of-towners and were now down-at-the-heels enough to serve as way stations for the refugees. The Marseilles, on 103rd Street, had been bought up by HIAS and filled with survivors. Its lobby could seem like Rick's café in *Casablanca,* with refugees scouting for jobs or apartments or trying to make a little money by selling a watch or camera they had picked up cheaply in the black market of the DP camps. Everyone hunted for any information, any lead that could help locate a missing brother or sister or parent or even a hometown friend.

Passing on Broadway, the "greeners"—the recent refugees had adopted the Yiddish word for greenhorns—recognized one another as definitively as two men walking down the street in plaid kilts would recognize each other as Scotsmen. Maybe it was a hollowness in the cheeks, an intensity in the eyes, a timidity in the way they carried themselves, the European cut of their clothes.

The greeners and the prewar refugees gave to Broadway an urbane feel that enchanted my mother that first day. The bustling avenue reminded her of her teenage years in Warsaw. At fourteen, at the urging of her stepmother and the assent of her struggling father, she had been compelled to leave home to give her father one less mouth to feed. She spent two or three lonely, nomadic years in the city, but she managed to establish a settled routine for herself and began to savor the culture, variety, and savvy of a large metropolis. Here on New York's Broadway, there were appetizing stores that sold whitefish with gold sequinlike scales and sinewy herrings wading in sour cream. There were cafeterias where people lounged for hours over a roll and a cup of coffee, gossiping or nitpicking about politics. The Thalia was showing *The Bicycle Thief* by the Italian director Vittorio De Sica. The Riviera had *Father's Little Dividend* with Spencer Tracy and Elizabeth Taylor. My mother could not understand English, but she recognized the faces of the stars in the movie posters and stills. She had loved good movies in Warsaw, stars like Fredric March, Greer Garson, and Clark Gable. Indeed, the years just before the war had been the best of my mother's life, and the possibility of recapturing some flavor of those years gave her a needed lift that first day. Right then, she decided the neighborhood around Broadway was where she wanted to live.

But it was hard to hold on to the pleasures of Broadway because, as always, life kept reminding her of what she had been through and how tenuous her new situation was. Along Broadway, my parents ran into a couple called the Herlings who had arrived six months before us from Europe. Mrs. Herling was an affectionate and witty woman from Warsaw who had a citified tartness about her that quickly made my mother feel at home. Mr. Herling was a small-built barber with a brief mustache that set off a wry smile. They had a frisky, chunky boy named Simon about my age. But underneath the Herlings' air of cheer was an undertone of heartache that grew more plaintive the more we plumbed. Mr. Herling and his wife had been inmates at a Nazi camp, not a death camp but one where the Nazis relied on the Jews for grueling labor. Simon, they revealed to my parents' astonishment, was actually born in the camp two months before the war ended, one of only a handful of infants to have been born in the German camps. He had been allowed to live (as other newborns were not) because the Nazi officers had grown to like Mr. Herling's haircuts, or so the Herlings conjectured. The Yiddish newspapers had even done a story about Simon when the Herlings arrived in New York. What a miracle, what a triumph it seemed. Then, sometime after that first meeting on Broadway, the Herlings were to reveal to my parents that their war years had not actually ended in triumph. They had also had a daughter, a girl of four born before the war with a bashful, pretty face and blondish hair. When the Herlings were deported with their town's other Jews to the work camps, they had to leave the girl behind with her grandmother. They never saw her again. Not an hour went by when they did not recall that last picture as the German truck they had boarded drove off. There, standing alongside her grandmother, was their little girl, waving at them with what she and they thought was a temporary good-bye.

Everyone had stories like this, implausible, unimaginable stories, and my mother could barely listen. She could not summon enough sympathy for herself, let alone for others. All such talk of murdered children took her back to her own brothers and sisters, especially the three little ones, like her half-brother Shimele, who was eight years old when she left home for what she thought would be a short, exploratory excursion to Russia.

"He was such a *tayere neshome,* a gentle, dear soul," she would tell me many years later when she could first talk about him with some texture. "I imagine him starving to death in the ghetto and it pains me terribly."

What also made an impression on her in that first encounter with the Herlings was how rough it had been for them in this country. After six months in America, they had only just found an apartment off Central Park, and it was all of one room with a narrow stove and a midget refrigerator. Mr. Herling had just found a job in a barbershop on West Twenty-third Street. How long would it take my father to find a job, a man who had no skills beyond farming and shoemaking? Where would we find an apartment for two children? And how much longer would we go on squeezed into a single hotel room?

We walked home in a mood whose gloominess belied the old images of glowing European immigrants grateful for their American haven. My dispirited parents realized how much they had to do, how far they had to go to settle in. Whispering in Polish, they sniped at each other, frightening Josh and me. When they reverted to the Yiddish we could understand, I heard my mother raging at my father for persuading her to come to the United States.

"You were foolish," she snarled. "You grab. You don't think. We should have gone to Israel. Here, you have to have a trade and you don't have one. All you know how to do is fix shoes and here they have machines that do that. It would have been easier in Israel to find a job. In Israel we would have lived among Jews and they would make sure we were taken care of."

My father did not answer. My mother's quicker, keener mind seemed often to leave his tongue chained. He would fume and sputter, or laugh her off, but he did not seem to be able to fend off her arguments. She made him so insecure about his own views that often he sounded as if he did not know what he was talking about. I watched all this with rage and a kind of helplessness. I hated my mother's condemnation of my father but had to contend with the fact that she was so often right. Soon, my parents stopped talking altogether and we headed silently back to the hotel. When we got there, I noticed that my mother was quietly crying.

But weeping and a long, volcanic day did not stop her from cleaving to her duties. She undressed us, lay us down across the wide mahogany bed and sang us the lullaby "Raisins and Almonds." It is a doleful song about a widowed young woman rocking her son to sleep with a story of a snow-white baby goat who goes off to market, the place where she hopes her son will one day earn his livelihood. The song, I was to realize years later, was one that resonated with memories of a time when she had sung her little brother and two sisters to sleep. My parents' argument had spoiled the adventure of this first day in America. But pleased that my parents were no longer bickering, I nestled in the warmth of my mother's rich soprano and allowed the flotsam and jetsam of dazzling new images—of the towering ship sweeping into the Manhattan skyline, of the tumult of Broadway—to float across my mind until I fell asleep.

It is 1986 and I am covering the Statue of Liberty's one-hundredth-anniversary festivities for *The New York Times*. One of the articles I am assigned to do is a series of short interviews with famous immigrants like Louise Nevelson and Isaac Bashevis Singer about their memories of seeing the Statue of Liberty for the first time. The interviews touch many chords and I find myself feeling smugly proud that I too am an immigrant, one of the people this celebration is essentially about. I think again about our arrival in America and I feel energized, even heady, and I want to share this feeling with my parents.

When I see them in their tidy living room, I ask my father what were his thoughts as our boat sailed past the Statue of Liberty. He is mute and seems confused. I explain that I want to know if he was moved by a feeling of conquest and deliverance, by a surge of gratitude toward the United States?

"Who could think about such things? " he tells me. "I had two little boys I had to feed. I had to make a living."

His voice breaks and tears run down his face, tears he had not once allowed himself during those years of struggle.

2

We were alone in America; no one had invited us to come. But my father knew of one relative living in Brooklyn, his mother's brother, Morris Eisman. Morris had left Poland for the United States as a young man and had remained to work for a cousin. In Poland, my father's family would periodically receive letters from Uncle Morris. They would hear how he was prospering stuffing mattresses in a mattress factory. In the photographs he sent home, he and his wife, Tessie, looked flush, and that impression was fortified by the ten dollars Morris sent every few months and the bigger gift he sent when my father's oldest sister, Gittel, was married. My father had memorized the Eismans' address on Alabama Avenue, in the Brownsville section of Brooklyn, and he retained it throughout the war like someone might hold on to a frayed lottery ticket whose winnings he had only to claim. Now, in our first week in the hotel, my father decided to go and find Uncle Morris.

A HIAS worker had given him directions by subway, writing out in large, capital letters the names of the stations where he would have to switch trains. My father kissed my mother and brother good-bye. It was the first time the family was separating in America, and my parents, I could tell, were worried they might lose each other. The war had taught them how final partings could be. I was learning a lesson too. My father's trepidation, as we set out, was teaching me how frightening a city of eight million people could be, even on an hour-long trip by subway to the next borough.

Descending with my father into the Eighty-sixth Street station of the West Side IRT, I found myself transported into an eerie underground kingdom, enchanting and daunting. The colossal columns running in a line to the end of the platform, the glimmering steel tracks, the light splintering through the street gratings overhead, all spoke to me of both grandeur and menace. When the train roared in, ballooning ever larger, I pressed against my father's leg in fright. Inside the car, the plump yellow rattan seats were warm from the heat seeping out of the radiator underneath. People seemed lost in themselves. If you looked at them they looked away.

Standing on tiptoes, I looked out the front window all the way into the depths of Brooklyn. I was the engineer, propelling the train through the shadowy tunnel, making it careen and lurch around the bends, heeding the red and yellow signal lights. I could see a small field of light beckoning ahead, growing larger and larger until it became the next station, and I yanked hard on the brakes to slow the train with a screech. I liked this feeling of power and control. Right then and there I decided that what I would do with myself in America was become a locomotive engineer.

Somewhere near the end of the ride, the train rose up out of the darkness and barreled into the sunburst of Brooklyn. We were on the elevated stretch of line, cutting a swath through shabby tenements and frail row houses, and I could look right into people's apartments and glimpse them frozen unawares. Soon my father joined me at the window. The HIAS man had written the name of the stop *Pennsylvania* down on the slip of paper and told him how many stations it would be. My father had been counting all along our journey, anxious that he not miss this stop closest to Alabama Avenue. I fretted whether he would find it, so often had he blundered his way to unfamiliar destinations before. But this time, the right combination of letters appeared and we stepped through the doors onto the elevated platform and down the stairs to the street.

A stranger to whom my father mutely pointed out the word *Alabama* on the HIAS note directed us toward Morris's house. My father hurried, tugging on my arm, coaxing me to pick up the pace. He was growing more short-tempered, frenzied, muddled. He seemed not to know where he was, bewildered by the English street signs he could not read, and as I think about it now, he also had several formidable matters weighing on his mind. He certainly nurtured the hope that Morris would be his salvation, provide him with help toward securing an apartment and a job and maybe some money to tide him over. He must also have wondered how he might report to Morris what had happened during the war to his sister, my father's mother, and to his nieces, my father's six sisters. Perhaps my father felt personally accountable for the loss of the family, as if he should have taken better care to see they survived. Perhaps he was afraid of the emotion he might feel looking at Morris's face and discerning remnants there of his own mother and his sisters.

The neighborhood was made up mostly of flimsy, shingle-sided two- and three-family row houses, with larger brick apartment buildings at the corners. The hedges trimming the buildings were bare and forlorn in the lingering chill of winter. On the sunny side of the block, old men and women sat on gaily striped aluminum chairs, bundled up in coats and scarves but savoring the sunshine. My father sensed a familiar Jewish flavor about the group and, chancing a few words of Yiddish, asked an old man whose cane was dangling over the arm of his chair for 780 Alabama.

"Who ya looking for?" the old man asked, also speaking Yiddish.

"An uncle of mine, Morris Eisman," my father said. "He came to this country from my town in Poland and was supposed to live at 780 Alabama Avenue with his wife and sons."

The old man listened, but his startled face suggested he had an answer my father had not expected.

"Morris Eisman?" he said, shaking his head. "Morris Eisman died maybe three years ago. Nobody told you?"

My father looked dazed. It was not as if he remembered Morris all that well. But all his anticipation about what might happen at his meeting with Morris was now unraveling. There would be no salvation. There was only the awkwardness of this encounter with an old man on a sidewalk, one that his son was witnessing.

Heartsick, yet feeling a need to explain, my father told the old man that he was a small child when he had known Morris and that after the war, he had written to him just once: a letter from Russia asking if Morris may have heard something about my father's parents and sisters. My father had searched the printed lists of survivors published by the Red Cross and had not been able to trace a single relative. Morris had written back that he too had heard from no one.

"How come Morris died?" my father asked. "He wasn't so old."

"It was a coronary," the old man answered. "In his fifties, definitely not sixty years old. He smoked too much. Or maybe it was the mattresses that killed him. Breathing in that stuffing all day. After he died, his wife, Tessie, moved down to Florida with the two boys. Maybe you can find them there."

"I was hoping," my father said, "to meet him, because we don't have nobody in this country. We came over from Europe on the boat two days ago."

My father tried to push down his disappointment, lingering among these strangers, waiting for some deliverance. The uncle in America had been one of the arguments he had used for choosing America over Israel. His wife would surely remind him how foolish he had been.

A middle-aged woman had been eavesdropping on the conversation, my father's visit probably being a highlight of the day for this flock of idlers.

"You know, mister," she said. "The widow, Tessie, has a sister. She lives the next block over, on Sheffield Avenue. Maybe she can tell you how to get in touch with Tessie and the boys."

The old man, taking personal responsibility for us, pushed himself up from his chair on his cane and motioned us to follow. Shuffling resolutely, he led us around the corner to a run-down wooden house and rang the bell. The door opened and a slight, balding man with steel-rimmed glasses squinted at us. Our old guide introduced my father as a relative of Morris Eisman's, and my father explained that his mother and Morris were sister and brother. When he absorbed this, the balding man bounced down the steps of the porch and extended his hand to my father with generous verve.

"So you're Morris's nephew," he said in Yiddish. "Morris told me he had a nephew on the other side who made it out of the war alive.

My wife, Fanny, is a sister to Tessie. You're not exactly a cousin, but you're something they don't have a name for in English. But you're a relative for sure. And that's your boy? What a smart-looking boy! Come, come on in the house."

He rushed inside, shouting excitedly, "Fanny! Fanny!" in a high-pitched voice that seemed quickly to run out of breath. My father and I followed and, in a small dining room whose four walls snugly girdled a round Formica table and four plump chairs, we saw Fanny. She walked in, wiping her small pudgy hands on a stained apron. The curls of her dark, graying hair seemed to have been whisked and churned by the effort of cooking. Her eyes appeared startled.

"Fanny, this is Morris's nephew," her husband said. "He's just come from Europe."

"Nephew? A nephew? I didn't think anyone made it out alive with that butcher." She spoke with a slight accent that betrayed her immigrant roots. "What's your name? And your boy's name? But first sit down. Take their coats, Sidney. You want something to eat?"

My father sat down in his gawky fashion. Shy by nature, he seemed particularly uneasy in this house, as if his presence might stain the upholstery or break the china. It had been more than ten years since he had been in an orderly home furnished with a faith in stability, and that had been his parents' weather-beaten farmhouse. The apartments in the Soviet Union and the DP camps contained only the sparse furnishings of a transitory life. This home, while modest, had a sofa and armchairs, prints on the wall, a phonograph player, and a collection of 78s. Moreover, these people were not his blood relatives, would not understand who he was and what he had been through. They probably looked upon him as an intruding freeloader. If I was embarrassed by his awkwardness, I also had absorbed it. I sat stiffly, overpolitely on an armchair. I was hungry but I did not dare ask for food. Besides, my mother had warned me that at other people's homes I should never eat too much. It would make them think we were needy. Luckily, Mrs. Lessen—for Lessen was Sidney and Fanny's last name—didn't wait for my father to finish explaining his relationship with Morris Eisman. She rushed off to the kitchen and came back with rye bread sandwiches thick with white chicken and lettuce.

"I always remember Morris telling me nobody from his side survived," Mr. Lessen said in his reedy voice. "Tessie too. She lost everybody over there. And then he said he got a letter from a nephew. How did you make it?"

My father unfolded his story. This was the chance I always waited for, the chance to imagine my father in a swashbuckling saga, surviving the perils of the Soviet army and Soviet life. The emotions, though, were lost on me then and would be for many years afterward. What did I know of what it was like to say good-bye to a mother, a father, and six sisters in the belief you were heading off to a brief adventure?

Sidney Lessen listened with a keen attentiveness, not just for the flow of the tale but for the history and politics he could soak up. As we came to know him, we discovered what a passion he had for public affairs and social currents. Cruelty and injustice left him indignant. He was a victim of injustice himself. During the Depression, he had been blocked from becoming a teacher by an examiner for the board of education who disdained his Jewish accent. He went to work for the Workmen's Compensation Board as an investigator and never left. But inside he remained a teacher—a frustrated one, but a teacher. That was to become a blessing for me. As soon as I learned a smattering of English, he began to teach me about America, its geography and history and legends, its triumphs and disgraces.

"If you're Morris Eisman's nephew, I feel like you're a nephew to me," he told my father. "Because Morris was like a brother to me."

We spent several hours with the Lessens that afternoon. Mr. Lessen and Fanny told us about the hard life Morris endured as a teenager on the Lower East Side and the work in the mattress factory that damaged his lungs and stressed his heart. But life in America, they said, could be more than comfortable, if one was willing to work hard and save some earnings.

"This is not like Europe," Mr. Lessen said, proud of his grasp of the international realities. "There are no laws here that make it impossible for a Jew to make a living. There are plenty of people who don't like Jews, but the laws are fair."

Before we left, Mr. Lessen—for that was what I, with European-bred formality, continued to call him even into adulthood—pulled out his wallet and gave my father a twenty-dollar bill.

"I want you to have this," he said. "Everyone needs help when they come over."

My father resisted, but Mr. Lessen insisted and my father succumbed. We left with Mr. Lessen asking us to telephone as soon as we had a permanent address and promising to remain in touch with us. It was a promise he was to keep. In a squat gray Mercury whose balky steering wheel dwarfed his short arms and left him panting with exhaustion whenever he parked, he struggled to visit us wherever we lived, bringing his wife and daughter along on the tiring drive from Brooklyn's Brownsville. They came not just out of kindness, but perhaps a longing for relatives, seeing in my parents a silhouette of their own immigrant parents. Of course, they were not relatives, did not have the inescapable pressure of relatives, which may have made them more pleasant to be with but also meant we could not count on them in the same duty-bound way we might have counted on Morris Eisman. But they became a reassuring landmark in the wilderness that was America in those first years.

3

As a child I saw my father as a quiet, sometimes sheepish man, uneasy with his friends, let alone strangers. He was unsure of his own thoughts, and his sentences sometimes withered before they left his mouth. I was also aware of darker forces seething inside him. They would peek out at moments when his frustration boiled over and he seemed not to know what to do with his rage. His tongue would suddenly appear rolled up and clenched between his front teeth and his eyes would quiver in fury. We were terrified of this demon inside him. But, outside the family, he so often exhibited a good-natured tolerance that we longed for the demon to appear. How sweet then when it would finally rear up and show itself.

That happened in our last days at the hotel. After we were there for two weeks, two workers arrived at our room to tell us we had to move that morning. The hotel's contract to house the refugees was up and it wanted to be rid of them.

"What am I supposed to do?" my father asked. "Live on the street with two children?"

"I got my orders," the larger of the two men replied. "You need to be out right now."

When he lifted a valise and moved it out to the corridor, something seemed to snap in my father. His response was out of all measure to what the man had done, as if injustices had been mounting inside him like fissionable material waiting to reach critical mass. He pounced on the man from behind and wrestled him to the floor, sprawling on top of him and pummeling him wildly while my mother circled the scene in panic.

"Marcus, what are you doing?" she screamed. "Get off him. They'll throw us in jail."

Hiding behind her, Josh and I watched this scene with something like awe. We had never seen my father fight before.

The smaller man pulled my father off and calmed his companion down, talking him out of retaliation. They walked off, warning us they were going to call the police. They never did and instead we were given a day's reprieve that allowed HIAS to find us somewhere else to live— a room as boarders with a widow in the South Bronx. Still, the memory of my father rising up in fury, unloosing the accumulated rage of so many years, remained fresh in my memory for years afterward, there whenever I wanted to glorify him as the courageous man he sometimes could be.

For three months, we lived as boarders with Mrs. Scher, a nervous, nasty-tempered woman, in her dark ground-floor apartment on Cauldwell Avenue. My father spent most days traveling down to HIAS to ask about work. With his only experience farming and shoemaking, he did not match any of the jobs the agency had to offer. He did not want to join one of HIAS's job-training programs. He needed to make a living right away. On days my father stayed home, my mother went looking for apartments. New York was still in the grip of a postwar housing shortage and HIAS had little to offer. So my mother roamed the streets of Manhattan's West Side, pausing at tolerable buildings in the hopes she might find a Yiddish-speaking tenant or a Polish-speaking superintendent who might have some information about a soon-to-be-vacated apartment. Sometimes she paused at buildings she knew were way beyond her reach, grand Central Park West temples like the Eldorado, the Bolivar, and the Beresford, and imagine wildly that some stroke of fortune, some inspired move on her part would land her in such opulence. But it was only a fleeting thought, for what resources did she have to even dare to imagine such possibilities?

Day after day, either my mother or my father came back disheartened. When the frustration of living in the ground-floor apartment got to her, my mother again lashed out bitterly at my father for bringing her to the United States.

"You grabbed without thinking," she said. "We should have waited for Israel."

"Then every day we would be worrying if the Arabs would attack us," he retorted, chuckling so as to defuse the force of his remark.

There were days when my mother would not talk to my father, except for the bare conversation necessary to care for my brother and me. An iron gloom pervaded our room in Mrs. Scher's flat, a gloom that fed on itself and deepened because there was no other room to which any of us could escape.

But then my mother found us an apartment in Manhattan. It was at 62 West 102nd Street, one block off Central Park in a shabby quarter that bordered on Harlem. Yet it was on the West Side. The rent was forty dollars a month and, since there was a citywide apartment shortage, bribes were the order of the day and my mother had to make an additional fifty dollars payment to the superintendent in "key money" on the pretext of our buying the flimsy furniture left behind by the previous tenant.

The building was a corner tenement, gray in color with castlelike adornments on the roof in some feeble attempt to add a touch of elegance to a building crisscrossed by fire escapes. The entrance was one flight above the street at the end of a high stoop with a handsome balustrade. That stoop, together with a kind of trench that hugged the building's basement and was used for receiving monthly shipments of coal to fire the furnace, seemed to me to pose all kinds of lively possibilities for adventure.

On the day we moved in, I watched my father, his face taut with strain, lug two valises, a trunk, and two duffel bags up the stoop and into the apartment while my mother shouted directions. Once he paused to catch his breath and suddenly broke out in a fit of caustic, almost devilish laughter as if he realized the absurdity, even maliciousness, of a fate that had taken him from a homespun vegetable farm in the craggy mountains of eastern Poland to a pile of apartments in the middle of the most seething city in the world.

It was to me, though, my mother turned for an evaluation of our new home.

"Joey, you like it?" she asked.

I was not yet six, but somehow, she was already beginning to consult me. She did not trust my father's taste or sensibility. I was probably heady with the authority she gave me, with some primitive appreciation that I was being chosen over my father. But it became a bad habit. As I grew older, she asked me to evaluate more difficult matters—whether she should buy a Laundromat or invest her savings in stocks—and more sensitive matters—her relationships with her friends and her relationship with my father. By that time, I felt obligated to make a judgment, felt it had become my role. And when I misjudged, which I sometimes did, I began to shrink from making judgments, a trait that did not always serve me well when I grew up and had to make my own decisions.

Right away, my parents began unpacking. They filled the wardrobe we inherited with our winter coats, my father's navy-blue wool suit, and a Prussian blue suit of my mother's that she had acquired in Berlin. Out of a black trunk they took heavy cast-iron pots and our dishes, all of which had not been opened since Europe.

What captivated me most was my father's chunky iron last, the molded leg and foot on which he used to mend shoes in Russia. That last had been first his salvation and then later my mother's. He had not taken it out since we arrived from Europe, but whenever he worked on it I would watch with enchantment. Sitting on a hard, wooden chair, he would grasp the iron post between his thighs and fit a shoe over the foot and draw the outline of its sole on a thick piece of leather. Then he would pull the knife—a broad six-inch blade that he kept in a leather sheath—toward his chest and shave off slices of golden fresh leather until he had duplicated the sole of my shoe. As he worked, his tongue was again clamped between his teeth, a little pink sliver gauging his every exertion. I would sniff the manly, sweet-acid odor of the leather and try to salvage the shavings. He would toss some nails into his mouth, spit one out, push it into the sole, and, with a swift stroke or two of the hammer, pound it in. I loved seeing my father at this last because I needed such confirmations of his competence.

My mother, meanwhile, reached into the trunk and gently pulled out three porcelain figurines she had bought off a peddler in the displaced persons camps. Two were of dark-haired ballerinas in short green dresses frozen in midpirouette. The third was of a lace-collared and bewigged Hapsburg couple playing chess. So fine was the work that even the chess pieces were recognizable as knights, bishops, and kings. Who knew where the peddler had gotten them? Perhaps they were from some Nazi bigwig desperately selling off his treasures at war's end for some cash or from some bourgeois Jewish family whose belongings were plundered just before they were sent off to the gas chambers. Whatever their pedigree, the figurines were a lovely touch of brightness among our possessions, the only frills we had. For me they were something that gave my family a touch of refinement, and I watched as my mother handled them with an uncommon tenderness and laid them on a bright windowsill.

We had some lucky breaks in the new country, but my father's finding a job a week after we had moved into 102nd Street was a lucky break that proved to be a mixed blessing. There was a couple down the first-floor hall from us by the name of Levy. They were German Jews who had escaped Hitler just before the war and, as refugees, had a leg up on us of a few years. Fred Levy was a portly, gregarious man with a thick-lipped smile. His wife, Gerta, was also heavy-set and cheery, with a trace of a busybody's curiosity about all of her neighbors' goings-on. In middle age, after the turmoil of war and flight, she had given birth to a daughter, Susan, who was a year or two younger than I and was the marrow of their lives. In general, the refugees treasured their children to an extreme. They were, in many cases, the only family that fate had left them, and the refugees had learned firsthand and bitterly how ephemeral family could be. But the Levys pampered Susan to a fault. Even when she was six, they tasted her food before she ate it to make sure it was neither too hot nor too cold.

Still, they were caring people and they had a palpable sense of how tenuous our situation was. When my parents ran into them in the hallway those first few days, Fred, puffing on an acrid cigar, asked a stew of questions about what my father might be willing to do, then promised to see if his boss could use another worker. The next day he knocked on our door and told us my father could start the next morning. The factory Mr. Levy worked in, General Textile, made the asbestos covers used on ironing boards. It was as prosaic an item as one could imagine but necessary for the running of an ordered home. The factory needed another hand to help lay out and cut the asbestos cloth. Mr. Fefferman, the boss and owner, was a son of immigrants and liked employing immigrants. They worked harder, came on time, and gave you less trouble. They also didn't demand American-sized wages. The pay for the job my father could have was a little more than thirty dollars for five days, but with a sixth day of overtime on Saturday, compulsory if my father wanted to have the job, the pay could amount to almost forty dollars, enough to pay the rent in a week. There was one major drawback: the job was in Newark, which meant almost an hour and a half of travel each way. But Fred made the trip every day, and immigrants, he implied, could not be choosy. My father, Fred said, could take a subway with him down to Canal Street. There they would meet some coworkers traveling from Brooklyn who would give them a ride through the Holland Tunnel to the factory.

My mother and father set up the two olive-green canvas army cots that my brother and I slept on—relics of the DP camps that could be stretched tight by poles inserted at each end—and struggled all evening with the decision about taking the job. As I lay on my cot, I could hear them whispering in their bedroom, their voices sometimes rising to a shout. The pay was low, my mother said, lower than other refugees they knew were getting. It was a job that required no skills, offered no training in any useful trade, and so held no prospects. My mother pointed out that my father would have to work on Shabbos. She had hoped that once she found a stable home she could resume the religious life she had led in Poland. Besides, traveling to New Jersey would eat up his free time, leaving him no time to learn a trade or, just as important, study English, a facility he would need if they were to move in the more cultured circles of my mother's outsized aspirations. My mother made all these points and my father agreed.

"I'll let the job go," he said. "I'll wait for something else to come by."

There was a pause and I could feel the tension mount to the breaking point.

"Maybe another job won't come along so soon," my mother said, a taut edge to her voice. "What are we going to do in the meantime for money, for eating, for rent?"

"You are right," he said wearily. "I'll take the job. Maybe something better will come along in a few weeks. Meanwhile, we'll have some money in our pockets."

"We won't have money!" she said. "Thirty dollars? Forty at most? That will be barely enough for the rent. And when will you have the time to look for a good job? You think one will come flying in through the window?"

And so it went until I fell asleep. I didn't find out what the decision was until morning, when I woke up and saw that my father wasn't home. He had gone away with Freddie Levy at six-thirty.

Thus began a job that my father was to have for twenty-five years, a quarter of a century. Every morning he would leave the house at six-thirty while I was still fast asleep. He would return around seven-thirty, hours after I had returned from school. He would gaze with pleasure at me, at my brother, at my mother as we stood at the door to greet him, but his eyes would drift away with fatigue and maybe with shame at the punishing strain of his day. As he gave me a wet kiss on my cheek, I caught the scent of salty sweat. That became his smell for me. Then he would sit down alone and wolf down the dinner my mother had prepared for him. The rest of us had already eaten. Sometimes, though, Josh and I would join him at the table, picking a fried potato or a crisp piece of chicken off his plate. My mother often shouted at us to "let Daddy eat his food," but he seemed to enjoy our eating off his plate. He could not give us toys and comforts and had little to teach us, but he could give us food off his plate.

We listened to my mother tell him about her day or some problem that needed solving. Often she would goad him to ask for more pay or find another job. He always inquired how we were feeling, but in contrast to my mother, he was not especially curious about how well we were doing in school, what triumphs or fiascoes we had there. He cared that we were healthy and happy, and if we were, that left him content.

After dinner, he would sit down in an armchair—when we finally acquired one—and within minutes his head would drop back and he would fall fast asleep, his mouth agape, his snore rasping and snarling across the room. At some point, my mother would shake him and urge him to go to bed. He would startle awake and, still in a dreamy state, mutter in Yiddish that he was just *"khapping a djim"*—catching a nap—and that he would go to bed in a minute. But as soon as she left, he would fall asleep again.

Some mornings, I would wake up early and hear his scurrying footsteps. A closet door opened then shut. A faucet gushed. A boiling kettle whooshed softly. I would prod myself awake and pad into the kitchen, anticipating my father's delight.

"Joey, what are you doing up so early?" he said, with a smile that belied his scolding. "Go back to bed!"

"I'm not sleepy," I said.

He would make me a cup of instant coffee and butter a slice of rye bread. I sat down catty-corner to him at the small table with its white metal top and watch him bolt his bread and slurp his coffee. He said nothing to me. He seemed preoccupied with getting out of the house in time to catch the subway train to Canal Street, where he would meet his ride to Newark. But I didn't mind his silence. As I held the cup in my hands, feeling its warmth, savoring the steamy, sweet smell of the coffee, I felt I had somehow been initiated into the hermetic world of working men, a world that to my boy's callow imagination seemed profoundly heroic.

I didn't know what exactly my father did at work. But in my imagination it wasn't different from the work I saw him do at home: hoisting, hauling, shoving, yanking, hitching, hammering. I knew he used the raw strength of his body rather than the powers of his mind. I knew he sweated a lot. And I knew when the tasks exasperated him, his tongue would be clamped furiously between his teeth.

4

I cannot remember a time in America when I did not speak English, but of course there was such a time. When we lived as boarders with Mrs. Scher in the South Bronx, I went to a neighborhood kindergarten and could not speak English, and I still could not speak it very well some six months later when we moved to 102nd Street and I started first grade in a public school. All I remember of that school at 102nd Street, which I attended for just a few months, is a warm, honeyed smell drifting up the stone staircase from the cafeteria, the aroma of baking white bread with a whiff of peanut butter mingled in. In the classroom, I watched the children gabbing easily with one another, showing off a gadget from home or a funny picture they'd drawn, and I felt invisible. No one seemed to know I was there, and somehow I felt that making my presence known would not have roused a soul.

That is why I liked the circle games we'd play in the large gymnasium on the ground floor. We'd sing "A Tisket, a Tasket" or "Skip to My Lou" or "What Can the Matter Be?" We'd all hold hands, and one child would pull me and I'd pull the next child and we'd shriek with laughter and I'd see the children across from me laughing and sometimes, as our shouts and footsteps echoed off the walls, I would think we were laughing together.

Then just as I was beginning to feel some comfort in the school's routines, my mother pulled me out and enrolled me in a yeshiva. My

mother wanted my brother and me to have a Jewish education. Her
father had studied a page of Talmud every day of his life and one day,
God willing, perhaps we would do the same. My mother had heard
that the yeshiva reduced its tuition for poorer children. She heard this
from the one refugee woman we knew who was on welfare. If a
woman on welfare could send her son to yeshiva, so would my mother.
She made a forceful, histrionic appeal to the principal, Dr. Herman
Axelrod.

"I don't want my son believing in Jesus Christ," she told him.

It worked. She got me in for a tuition of one hundred dollars a year,
payable in monthly installments of ten dollars. For me it did not seem
such a bargain. Not only did I have to acclimate myself to a new locale
and a new set of classmates in the middle of a school year, but, just
beginning to understand some English, I would now have to learn
Hebrew as well.

Manhattan Day School was a redbrick, fortresslike Victorian institution graced only by a wide stairway at the entrance. It was in the same
raffish area I lived in, but it drew most of the children from the stout,
middle-class apartment buildings on West End Avenue, Riverside Drive,
and Central Park West. I would walk to school and when I arrived the
yellow school bus would pull up and out would pour children, yam-
mering with excitement as they lugged their book bags up the stairs,
genial, breezy, clubby with one another, or so I saw them from my newcomer's angle. On rainy days, having no raincoat, I would arrive at
school with wet hair and damp clothes and see my schoolmates come
dashing off the bus in slick yellow mackintoshes with those reassuringly
sturdy clasp buckles, their heads kept dry by sou'wester caps. They
lived no more than a mile or two from my house, but they might as well
have come from another planet.

Of course, much later in life, it dawned on me that not all the children in my class were that much better off. Many, if not most, of the
students were also children of refugees, though their families had
arrived before the war, fleeing Germany during the rise of Hitler, or
Austria after the Anschluss, or Belgium just before Hitler marched in.
A few had been able to rescue much of their European prosperity; others came over penniless but capitalized on a professional skill, like dia-

mond cutting. They had a few years' head start on my family, not a negligible advantage but not as much as my deep sense of disadvantage made it out to be.

On my first day of class, the teacher, Mrs. Martin, asked me to bring in a supply kit—pencils, crayons, glue, scissors, an eraser, a ruler, a sharpener, Scotch tape—all the supplies my classmates had already assembled. When I informed my mother that afternoon, the expense distressed her, but she took up the challenge. From the cookie tin that was her sewing kit, she pulled out an old pair of black-handled steel scissors that were a little unwieldy for my small grip but which she said would have to do. Then she led my brother, Josh, and me around the corner to the five-and-dime on Columbus Avenue. The counters were heaped with more goods than I had ever seen in one place—a lush rainbow of thread spools; a latticework of red and pink lipsticks; envelopes bulky and thin and several sizes in between; tanks of flitting goldfish; cages whistling with parakeets and canaries; eggbeaters and spatulas and aluminum pots; bobby pins; picture frames; electric fans; screwdrivers; house plants. Dazzled by this American cornucopia, we had to remind ourselves that we were here for school supplies.

My mother picked out the smallest box of crayons—the one with ten inside—searching the box for the price tag before agreeing to buy it. I found a six-inch-long ruler, a fresh eraser with a pleasing acrid rubber smell, a red plastic sharpener, a package of three pencils, and a bottle of whisky-colored glue that I tilted and turned to see the air bubble float from the rubber top to the bottom.

"For what do you need three pencils?" my mother said irritably. "Buy one and when you finish it, I'll buy you another."

Josh took this expedition in with delight. In those days, nothing seemed to make him happier than being alongside his older brother, joining him in whatever he had to do, helping him take care of his life as if he did not need to tend to his own. With good humor, he gathered up extra rulers and erasers and packages of pencils until my mother forced him to put them back. Before something else could beguile us, she dragged us over to the cashier. I could see it hurt her to turn over the two dollars she fished from her clasp purse, dollars my father had worked two hours to earn. But I walked out of the five-and-dime puffed up, the brown paper parcel of school supplies pressed to my chest. After all her resistance, my mother seemed pleased as well.

"I don't want you to feel inferior to no one in class," she told me as we headed home.

Just before we reached our building's stoop, she darted around the corner into Mr. Zlatagorsky's basement candy store. Mr. Zlatagorsky, a thickset, ruddy-cheeked Hungarian Auschwitz survivor, had only recently purchased that narrow, cluttered basement space with a refugee partner. Now he was chained to the long, tedious days of a busy shop. He was at the store at five-thirty every morning to haul in the twine-lashed bundles of morning newspapers—there were four morning and three afternoon papers in those days—so he could start selling them to his customers as they headed off to work, and he remained behind a counter, sheated in a white apron, dispensing seltzers, cigarettes, and Mary Jane peanut brittles, until seven at night. But he was not too tired to help us out. Grinning with mischief, Mr. Zlatagorsky provided the coup de grâce to my supply kit: he picked out an empty cigar box from the glass shelves above the candy jars, blew the lingering shreds of tobacco out, and handed it to us.

"There!" he told me with a sardonic laugh. "Now you got a fancy box for school."

How laughable, indeed, this fuss made over a supply kit must have seemed to him and my mother, people who were glad, as children, to have been able to afford shoes with which to walk to school. But to me this was a momentous assignment and I rushed my mother home so I could assemble my school kit. I was intoxicated first by the cigar box with its vintage portrait of Dutch burghers and its masculine smell of tobacco, and then by the crayons, the ten basic colors lined up trimly, their shiny funnel points at attention like soldiers in a regimental parade. I enjoyed arranging the crayons and glue and ruler and pencils and scissors inside the box until they formed a pleasing tableau, then closed the box and fastened it with a rubber band. This box was mine. These tools were mine, tools I could use to take on the world, just as my father had his last and leather knife for fixing shoes and my mother had her tin of needles, threads, and thimble.

But the next day, which I had hoped would be triumphant, turned into a debacle. Seizing the opportunity of a new student to check on her pupils' tidiness, Mrs. Martin asked all students to take out their kits. I pulled mine out proudly, knowing I had everything on that list, aching for the reassuring nod of her approval. But, as she weaved through the aisles on her inspection tour, I glanced over to the next row and saw my classmate Joycie showing her supplies to the girl sitting alongside her. She not only had a packed cigar box but a separate box of crayons, sixty-four of them. This box was open and I could see the crayons, arrayed in tiers, in such exotic and subtle shades as lavender, salmon, apricot, mulberry, flesh, olive, silver, gold, melon, copper. I could never hope to match her assortment. My regiment of soldiers felt like a ragged platoon.

My mother paid the yeshiva's monthly tuition by stopping off at school and handing a ten-dollar bill to the school secretary. There came a time, though, when she felt she could trust me with this task, and she handed me an envelope with the money to give to the secretary.

"Don't tell anyone what's in the envelope!" she warned me.

This was another responsibility I would have to take on. By this time, I was already taking care of my brother. My mother had gotten a job, in a downtown hat factory, sewing trim on straw hats. During the twenty-week season before Easter, no one was home when Josh and I returned from school and, at seven years old, I unlocked the door and walked into a house that had a stony emptiness to it, as if the inhabitants had died. In the two or three hours until my mother came home, I felt a recurring current of dread. Something would go wrong. I would do something wrong and there would be no one to help me right it. I had to keep an eye on Josh and he felt like a heavy sack on my back. In my frustration, I was not always kind to him.

It was scary now to be trusted with the tuition, a sum I knew it took my father more than a day to earn. So I carefully placed the envelope with the ten-dollar bill in a schoolbook, telling myself I would drop it at the office during lunch period. Somehow over the morning I forgot about the envelope and never gave it a thought for the rest of the day. I did not remember the envelope until my mother returned from work that evening and asked me, "Joey, did you pay the ten dollars to the office?"

Terror roiled through me. I had not paid it, but I also could not remember where I had put the schoolbook with the envelope. Was it in my book bag? Was it in my cubbyhole? Had I taken the envelope out of my schoolbook and put it inside my pocket?

"I forgot to, Ma," I said, stalling for time.

"Why didn't you? They get upset if you don't give it to them on time. Give me back the envelope."

I dashed over to my book bag and riffled through the books stuffed inside. The envelope was not there. I must have left the book with the envelope inside my cubbyhole.

"Joey, what did you do with the money?" my mother demanded, her voice shrill now and edged with panic.

"I can't remember, but I must have left it inside the cubbyhole. I'll find it tomorrow."

"Tomorrow? No! Someone will take it before then," she said. "Let's go right now. You don't put money in places like that. Anyone can steal it."

I tried to persuade her the school was closed, but she was adamant that we go; there might be a cleaning person there who would let us in. So, with a sense of futility, I buttoned up my winter coat and we ventured out. It was a damp, chill night—November or December, it must have been—and we walked the three blocks to the school rapidly and in silence. My mother was angry that I had burdened an evening she needed for cooking and cleaning with this expedition. She walked in hurried long strides and I raced to keep up with her.

There was no answer at the school's front door so we walked around to the delivery entrance and, for several minutes, rang the night bell. A squat Puerto Rican man in green overalls brandishing a tall broom finally opened the door, grimacing at us in annoyance. Looking at his sweating, unwelcoming face, I felt we were engaged in some kind of intrigue, probably illegal, that would surely get us in trouble. We had no right to invade the school at night. There would be a price to pay in the morning. So conscious was I of our modest position in the world that I invested even this janitor with the imposing mantle of authority.

My mother explained our predicament in her fractured English and a ballet of hand gestures and the janitor replied in a similar code. Although neither could understand each other, it was clear he did not want to let us in. But the improbable sight of a woman speaking little English with a seven-year-old boy at her side melted his resolve. He led us up two flights of stairs and guided us through the dimly lit, dungeonlike halls, the small pools of light on the newly waxed floors reflecting the few bulbs that were on. I had never been inside the school when it was so deserted. I felt like a thief.

I pointed out our second-floor classroom. The janitor switched on the lights. The room was pristine, the blond wood chairs neatly turned upside down on the oak desks, the aisles swept of paper, the blackboard erased, the wooden floor glistening brightly. I rushed over to the bank of cubbies and bent down to my compartment on the bottom row. There were three books and a composition notebook and I searched them thoroughly. But the envelope was not there.

"Let me look," my mother said, snatching a book from me.

She turned the pages, leaf by leaf, then did the same with the other books and the notebook.

"You sure this is your cubby?" she asked.

"Yes," I said. "These are my books and my notebook."

"Maybe you put the envelope by accident in one of the other cubbies?"

She ignored my answer and began poking through my classmates' cubbies, disregarding the janitor's timid protests as well. She dragged the entire cubby unit away from the wall and looked behind it. She checked the teacher's desk and the file cabinet and glanced at each of the children's desks. Finally, she implored the janitor to check the day's garbage collection, but this she could not persuade him to do, and when he brought her downstairs and showed her ten cans of garbage in two tidy columns, she stopped imploring. Without thanking the janitor, she left the building, looking tired and deflated. She would not speak to me or even look at me.

Halfway home along the lamplit streets, she finally burst out, "The janitor took it. He found the envelope when he was cleaning the room and he took it."

"Maybe he didn't," I said. "Maybe I didn't put it in the cubby."

"He took it, but it's still your fault. When I give you money you have to watch it like your life. Daddy has to work almost two days for that money and you threw it away."

The image of my father struggling to earn the money I lost made me feel the enormity of my crime with an extra keenness. I had done it not just to us, as a family, but to him, our family's most burdened member.

I am sitting on the living room couch watching the Yankees game and my daughter Annie, who is not even two years old, is frolicking around me, a moon to my planet Earth. It has not been a contented day at work. Not a bad day, but an accretion of too many frustrations has made it unsatisfying. Annie, though, forces my attention. She is playing with plastic blocks and is building a tower on the coffee table, piling first three, then four, then, to my astonishment, seven.

"That's terrific, Annie!" I shout.

She is screeching with joy, swinging her arms, distinctly aware she has journeyed into uncharted territory and survived. She climbs onto the couch and leans back, her shock of blond curls framing a triumphant smile.

I find myself drifting to thoughts of my parents when I was growing up. In our early years in Manhattan, when they had to find jobs and apartments, aware there was no home to which they could return, what curiosity and excitement could they spare for my brother and me? With all they had been through, did they not have something more on their minds then slights and frustrations? I have never asked them such questions, partly because I am sure it would make them defensive and partly because my mother would probably laugh off such an inquiry. "Psychology, shmuckology," she would shrug. It is that refusal to lament her life or pity herself that, I guess, has given her the strength to endure what she has been through. But steel she is not. She reveals herself in her own time.

Several years ago, she told me of going to school to visit my first-grade teacher, just about a year after we had been in this country. The teacher, Mrs. Martin, had informed her that I was doing very well in school, that I was an intelligent boy who was more than mastering English and Hebrew. My mother remembered how she had broken down in tears.

"Nothing good had happened to me for so long," she explained, weeping now again, "that, when the teacher told me that, I started to cry. I couldn't believe that I could have anything good happen to me."

5

My mother's Bronx kitchen is snug and narrow, two banks of walnut-stained cabinets broken by a stove, a sink, and a refrigerator. And yet out of this dim, cramped space will flow a Passover banquet for twenty people of gefilte fish, matzoh ball soup, brisket, roast chicken, the sweetened carrots known as tsimmes, a compote of dried fruits, and a nut cake. That my silver-haired mother can produce such feasts from this space is no more remarkable than a beaver's ability to dam a rushing stream. Steady work is the secret.

There is an equally narrow dining alcove leading to the kitchen, but it is bright, its white walls adorned with enlarged snapshots of our clan gathered on my parents' fiftieth wedding anniversary and a few faded decorative plates purchased in Israeli tourist shops. It is in this alcove that we—sometimes eight adults and my parents' seven grandchildren—squeeze into to hold our Friday-night dinners and Passover feasts.

It is also in this alcove, sitting catty-corner to her at the dining table, that I interview my mother about her memories. It is uncommonly quiet now with just the two of us in this room and my father at work. I keep my distance by acting the dispassionate reporter, recording her words on tape and scrawling notes on a yellow legal pad. I think not only of the family that gathers in this kitchen on Passover but of the family of eight children that once filled my mother's home in Otwock,

Poland. As my mother spins her story, I clamp down whatever emotions I am feeling because I have a mission: after fifty-one years, with my mother in her late seventies, I want to know the entire story, not just the sketchy, sanitized version she has doled out over the years. And perhaps because I am fifty-one, my mother may feel I am finally ready to hear the full story.

In the clinical voice of a bureaucrat, I ask questions about the grandparents I never knew and the children who, had they been allowed to grow up, would have been my uncles and aunts. I am afraid that if I let her pain pierce me, I will not be able to go on with the collecting of facts. My mother is better than me. In the final years of her life, she is finally willing, even eager to talk. But I am also afraid that if she senses my sympathy, the wall I have built up that has kept her at a distance, that has let me grow into my own person, will come crumbling down. She will invade, take over in her relentless, flailing way. But her story eventually lets me understand why she requires such control.

For years, my mother spoke of her town of Otwock as a village in a fable, a place where chestnut trees bloomed in spring and lilacs sweetened the pine-scented air and where Jews from all over Poland came to summer and heal their tuberculosis. The Jews were poor and downtrodden, but they took care of one another. Her father, she often said, was not just the town's star cantor, sought out by each of Otwock's half-dozen synagogues, but a Golant, a name she accentuated as if it had the aristocratic gravity of *Roosevelt*.

It was the Holocaust that destroyed that shining idyll of my mother's childhood. But as she starts to spin her tale, my mother seems less inclined to prettify the facts about her town and family. It seems that the five years of the war and the squalid years that followed in the refugee camps may have had less to do with shaping my mother than a childhood deficient in love and food.

She tells me, for example, how much it meant to her as a teenager when her older brother, Simcha, who had been earning an appreciable amount of money peddling damaged lingerie in Warsaw, came home on a visit and treated her to her first professional haircut in a genuine beauty parlor.

"Believe me, I remember this haircut," she tells me. "The bangs were so straight and it made me look authentically pretty."

Until then, she says, her haircuts were given by someone distinctly unprofessional—an old man who came to her home to repair her family's grimy winter coats. The old man's special skill was turning a coat's cloth inside out so that the cleaner side faced the world. Thus the coat could be worn for another winter or two. In the poverty that prevailed among Poland's Jews, such was this old man's remarkable occupation.

"And this man also cut my hair," my mother says, laughing heartily at the absurdity of such deprivation. "You can imagine how good he cut."

My mother is no longer holding back stories that might let me sense the humiliation she experienced.

"So I'd like to know more about your father," I begin. "What did he look like? What did he like to do?"

"I remember a lot of things about my father," she replies. "He was a scholar of the Talmud, a very learned man. He was tall, slim, intellectual-looking. His back was straight and proud. He had a beard. It was graying at the end. Joshua is the spitting image of him. He was a very cheerful person. He was very well liked by the neighbors. I remember he got up in the morning and the first thing he made was the fire and then he peeled the potatoes so when Bluma, my stepmother, got up she would not have to work too hard. Then he sat down and learned the Gemara. I can still remember the sound of the music that he used to express the Gemara."

She tells me how he would dress simply—usually a black caftan and a plain workman's cap. Yet everyone who met him seemed to have been affected by him. Whether he was discussing the news of the town or bargaining with a peasant over a sack of potatoes, there was a zest to his personality. His resonant voice, his perpetual humor, his genial demeanor seemed to earn him everyone's affection.

"He knew how to bring the arrogant to his level," she says. "Yet he could humble himself to make the humblest person feel good."

The central struggle of his life was simply to feed, clothe, and house his family, and pray that the Angel of Death stayed far away. His first wife, the woman he married before my mother's mother, died of tuberculosis, and left him a son, Yosef or Yussel, who grew quickly into a yeshiva scholar. His second wife bore him two children, my mother and her brother, Yasha, until she too died of tuberculosis. He then married for a third time, to Bluma, the woman who largely raised my mother.

"In general, the majority, the masses, were all poor," my mother says. "My father was one of them. Basically he made a living out of being a *melamed,* a teacher. I remember him having a school at home. You know the song *'Oyfn Pripetshik'* ['At the Fireplace']? We didn't have a *pripetshik*. We had a big room and a kitchen. He would have about twenty children. They took along a little lunch and he taught them, starting from three until eight, nine, ten years old."

As she speaks, pictures of faces spring up in my mind, pictures of pale-faced boys with moist, globular eyes. The scruffy boys happily did the bidding of their fathers, sitting at worn wooden tables in dank basements or ramshackle cottages studying the sloping, sinuous black letters of an ancient language with the same zeal we see in boys today playing with their Nintendo Game Boys. Some of my first memories of my mother are of her singing songs like *"Oyfn Pripetshik"* to me or Josh as she put us to sleep. To us, they were consoling melodies that softened the blows of the day and let us slacken and sleep. To her, these melodies were touchstones to that vanished world, a world that included her cherished father. I was too drowsy, or perhaps too young and afraid, to ever notice the tears that gathered in her eyes.

"What do you remember of your mother?" I ask.

"My mother? I have only one memory. From almost the time I was born she was sick with tuberculosis. They wouldn't let me close to her. I don't even remember her kissing me or embracing me. I remember a scene where my father and mother bought lace cloth and they said, 'See, we're going to make out of this nice, pretty dresses for Passover.' That's all I remember about my mother. They both stood and they both had such a nice smile on their faces. They were very young—in their twenties, probably—and they showed me—and my sister Freyde Leah stood next to me—and they said, 'We're going to make pretty dresses for Passover.'"

She pauses and looks away, lost in a transitory thought.

"I wrote something about my mother's death. I will read it to you. I could write it a lot better, more details, better words. But who has time? I never have time. And my English, Joey, is disappearing. I still remember Polish and Yiddish, but my English—I can't remember anymore the words. I forget the simplest words that I used to know perfectly."

"I'm sure it's not as bad as you say. Can you show me what you have written?"

With her brisk walk, she dashes off to her bedroom and returns moments later with a schoolroom composition book with a mottled black-and-white cover. I open it and on the first page, in her spidery Europeanized English script, is the title: "A Legacy Given to Her Children by a Survivor of the Holocaust."

As she reads to me, I look at my mother, her body thin and shrunken, her bony face a wisp of the robust face I remember from my childhood. But her eyes are as lively and opalescent as ever and she still dresses and walks with a young woman's sense of her own attractiveness. When she talks of her parents, she is talking about people young enough now to be her grandchildren. But the tremor in her voice tells me that her parents could have died two months before, so raw is the memory.

～ Spring arrived softly in March 1925, bringing to the residents of Otwock its long-awaited relief from the bitter cold of winter. The sunshine thawed away huge plates of icy snow and the dark earth in our small villa on Lesna 17 seemed to stir with life. Already, tiny clumps of new grass peeked out from under the tall, old pine trees. Here and there, young and old came out from their crowded homes and the streets of Otwock were animated with the voices of Jewish children and stray dogs.

I was peeking across the broken fence that divided our villa from our neighbor's, listening to Chaya Leah scolding the four youngest of her ten children, when I turned and saw my Bubbe—my grandmother—in her broad white apron and white kerchief come hurrying over. There were tears in her eyes. Something was terribly wrong.

"Come here, Rochele," she said. "I have to tell you something. Your mama is very, very sick, and we have to pray very hard to God and ask him to help her get better."

Children were running down the street, shrieking with laughter. My best friend, Esther, Chaya Leah's six-year-old daughter, was jumping rope in front of my eyes. I wanted to join her, but my Bubbe insisted I stay put. She wanted to show me how to raise my arms toward the sky and say *Shema Yisroel* (Hear, O Israel), asking God in my own words to make my mother well. In my Bubbe's desperate embrace, I slowly raised my hands to the sky and mimicked her words.

"*Shema Yisroel*," I murmured.

When my Bubbe released me, Esther hurried over and implored me to tell her my secret. Why was I lifting my hands toward the sky?

The next morning my father left earlier than usual to catch the morning *minyan* at synagogue. The grown-ups and my older sister, Freyde Leah, whispered that he had gone to ask for a *Mee She-beyrach,* the blessing for the sick that is recited during Torah readings. I was sitting on the floor with my little brother, Yasha, using scissors to make paper cutouts. From the corner of my eye I saw my grandmother squeezing a tube of a white medicine into my mother's mouth.

Suddenly my grandmother let out a sharp cry. Freyde Leah too began screaming and, in fright and confusion, I cried. When I saw my grandmother covering my mother's face with a white sheet, I sensed that my mother was gone.

The news spread quickly and the single room we lived in soon filled with neighbors and friends, most of them women who wept together in what seemed like a chorus of lamentation. My Bubbe sat on a low stool that one of the neighbors provided and sobbed inconsolably for her daughter. When my father returned from shul, his head was bent in sorrow and he looked at me with tears in his eyes.

"You are an orphan now," he said quietly.

Chaya Leah, Esther's mother, her face red and damp with tears, tried to reassure me. Mama was a good person, she said, and would return when the *Moshiach* (the Messiah) arrived. I took some hope in this. But my sister Freyde Leah, overhearing the conversation, pulled me over and gave me the unvarnished truth.

"Don't believe them, Rochele," she said. "Our mother will never come back. Never!"

A group of men in long black frock coats arrived. I had sometimes seen them gabbing with my father in the synagogue. They picked up my mother's limp body off the bed and stretched her out on the hard floor, her legs reaching toward the door. They covered her with old black garments, then placed candleholders on each side of her body and lit the candles. There she lay for the rest of the day as men and women streamed in and out of our home. At nightfall, Chaya Leah took me and my younger brother, Yasha, to her home to spend the night.

In the morning, in the middle of the clamor of her ten children, Chaya Leah served Yasha and me fresh rolls and cocoa for breakfast. But something kept drawing my attention across the fence. When I heard the sound of hammering, I ran away from the table back to my house. The front yard was filled with men and women and among them I saw several men nailing together a long wooden box. I entered the house and again I saw my mother's lifeless body stretched out on the floor with flickering candles at each side. Behind her, standing in a corner, was my grandfather, Israel Zelig. He had come from his hometown of Parysow, a day's journey by horse cart. I wanted to run swiftly to him, as I always did, but this day I knew from his face I must not do that. When he saw me, however, he pulled me toward him and clasped me to his body so tightly I could feel the warm emanations from his tear-covered cheeks.

Soon, the wooden casket emerged, the men barely straining under its meager weight. They placed the casket on a horse-drawn carriage and the funeral procession began. Two of my mother's woman friends urged me to stay with them and not follow the funeral, attempting to bribe me with chocolate candies. I resisted even though they were my favorite candies. But a tall, lean teenager appeared out of the crowd and goaded me into taking the candies. There was something instantly compelling about him. In the days ahead I was to learn that he was my half brother, Simcha. He was fourteen years old, my mother's son from a previous husband, and lived with my grandparents in Parysow. I gave him the candies and ran off to catch up with the procession.

I pushed myself through the crowd of men and women and found my grandmother and sister walking behind the casket as it rocked atop the carriage. They were moaning and wailing and grasping urgently on to the casket as if doing so could hold off her burial. My father, his head bent, was walking alongside them, his hand clutched tightly to an edge of the casket, as if he were striving to hold on to a remnant of my mother. As the carriage moved along the streets, men and women came out of their houses or peeked over their fences, gazing at this tragic procession of a young woman's funeral.

"How old was she?" I heard someone asking.

"She was thirty-two years old," someone else answered. ❧

As my mother weaves her stories, in our talk and in the words of her composition book, I find myself touched by the picture of a little girl drifting about her mother's funeral in bewilderment with seemingly no one to comfort her, but I do not probe. Instead I seize on facts I had never solidly grasped before. My mother was not even six years old when her mother, Peseh Tutel Olszewski, died. In her short life, my mother's mother had married twice—the first marriage ended in divorce, something that seldom occurred in that community—and she produced four children: Simcha and Freyde Leah from the first marriage and from the second my mother and Yasha. I wonder what strains led to the divorce, what impact her divorce had on her first set of children, what it was about this divorcee that attracted my grandfather. But I resign myself to the fact that because my mother scarcely knew her, I too will never know very much about my grandmother.

My mother tells me that a few weeks after the funeral her father came home with a new wife. Her name was Bluma and she was a first cousin of Peseh Tutel, his dead wife. In the unsentimental pragmatism of those times, the marriage had been arranged while Peseh Tutel lay dying of tuberculosis. Bluma was twenty-nine, plain and scrawny, as my mother tells it. She too lost her mother, when she was just eleven, and soon after began working as a maid in Warsaw. The hardships of her life did not make her any more benevolent and there was, my mother suggests, a biting, resentful edge to her stepmother's personality. At the time, my mother lived in an apartment in a "villa." The word echoed Italian grandeur, but the house was actually a weathered frame dwelling cut up into three spare apartments. Her stepmother kept the apartment orderly and meticulously clean and made artful dishes from the scant provisions she could afford.

"Our main food was bread and potatoes—aside from that there was almost nothing else," my mother tells me. "We never bought potatoes by the kilo. We bought them by the bushel. My stepmother used to cook every day something from potatoes. There was boiled potatoes with a little onion or there was a soup from potatoes. Either she made the soup with *kliskelech* [potato dumplings] or she made an *ugebrente* soup [soup with scorched flour]."

From what my mother tells me, the family seemed to spend the whole year looking forward to Rosh Hashanah and Yom Kippur. Her father was widely known for his pealing baritone and the passion of his praying, and on the holidays, the town's ritziest Jewish hotels as well as its half-dozen synagogues would vie for his services.

"You couldn't live from what you made as a *melamed*. The High Holidays, that's when the money came in. He got paid for the holidays 350 zlotys. That paid the rent for the rest of the year."

~ In the late fall, my father took me along to Otwock's central market to buy a 100-kilogram sack of potatoes that would tide us through the winter. At the market, peasants eager to sell off their harvests stood next to their wagons, the horses' breath turning to fog in the frosty morning air. I watched my father bend close to the ground and let a peasant settle a sack of potatoes on his back. As I scurried to keep up, he carried that 100-kilogram sack a half mile toward our home, brought it down into our cellar, and found a cool spot where he stored it for the winter.

"Bluma, we won't starve this winter, that's for sure," he said with a look of accomplishment.

"With the help of God, you will also find us enough coal," she answered with a gloomy smile.

On Fridays, my father did not teach but he still rose early to help his wife do their shopping for Shabbos at the market. They needed time to find a peasant who would give them a good price for a chicken. They had to find the inexpensive varieties of fish my step-mother preferred for gefilte fish. They had to find soup greens, two or three carrots, a couple of eggs, a half kilo of flour, some oil, and the prunes that my stepmother would cook and blend with rice as a dessert. They calculated each purchase carefully to make sure they would not go beyond the few zlotys they had brought with them. Burdened by heavy shopping bags, they would head home in plenty of time to prepare the Shabbos meal, my father taking long, sure strides, my stepmother scurrying to keep up behind in the deferen-tial custom of the time.

When my stepmother cooked, she scattered all the children out of her way. Only my father stayed. He peeled and chopped vegeta-bles, sharpened the knife, kept the wood fire burning in the potbel-lied stove, fetched water from the pump we had in the backyard, dumped out the dirty water, and peeled the potatoes for the cholent—a stew of potatoes, beans, and a little meat that would be set in a baker's oven before the Sabbath and simmer overnight so that we did not violate the Sabbath prohibition against lighting a fire.

While my father brought the cholent to the baker to be cooked overnight, my stepmother tidied the apartment, spread a snow-white tablecloth on our table, and set up two tall silver candlesticks. She took a bath and put on a special Sabbath dress with a clean apron and a matching kerchief over her hair. My father, having returned, planted two candles in the candlesticks and placed a decanter of wine in front of his seat. The children, now neatly dressed, joined my par-ents at the table as my stepmother lit the candles, covered her eyes, waved her hands over the candles, and murmured a blessing as if she were saying a magical incantation.

As poor as we were, Sabbath in our home was a celebration in which we expressed our gratitude for the abundance of food we could enjoy that day, for the beauty of Sabbath rest, and for our togetherness as a family, something we could not take for granted. Our spirits were lifted as we stood up to listen to my father, in his rich voice, bless the wine and the challah. We listened quietly, respectfully, and then merrily joined in the Sabbath songs that we sang between courses. Bluma too took pride in being part of this way of life and she seemed to gain the encouragement to pursue her duties as a housewife for another week. ✎

As we sit in the kitchen, my mother tries to impress me with her father's dignity and force of character. But I also realize in what she tells me that her father was not a saint. As poor as he was, he often treated himself to cigarettes. He and his stepson, Simcha, fought so bitterly that he once threw Simcha out of the house. My mother also tells me, to my amusement, that her father had a weakness for a pretty, charming woman. He was human, I realize with pleasure.

"He had a little affair," she says coyly. "I would say a romance, not an affair. Here, in an affair you have sex and everything. But he had a romance with somebody who was the wife of my stepmother's brother. She also had tuberculosis. She came to Otwock and stayed in our house. She was a very gentle, good-looking woman and he romanced her. He didn't realize that I sensed something was going on. Children sense a lot of things that we don't think they do. I didn't know anything about sex. What did I know? But I knew there was something going on. There was nothing wrong. I was happy for my father. I didn't think there was anything attractive about my stepmother to love."

If anything, it seems clear to me from her vignettes, her father heeded Bluma too obligingly.

"My father was always making things. Something like this table, this is nothing for him to make. There wasn't a thing in the world he didn't know how to do. One time he made some kind of cabinet for the kitchen. To hold my stepmother's meat and dairy dishes. He asked me to hand him tools from the toolbox. I was six at the time and my stepmother had just moved in with us. So I handed him something, and

I don't know what it was he told me. 'Rochele, you're such a pretty girl, I love you so much.' "

My mother whispers my grandfather's words. After all these years, her father's affectionate words are still too intimate to share with the world.

"Just then, my stepmother appeared with a red face, and she started screaming. I still get goose pimples when I remind myself of that scene. She said, 'Don't you ever do that! You're spoiling her.' At that time, even though I was only six, I realized she's jealous of me. She wasn't a good-looking woman. I was always pitying her. She looked so homely. She was small and had a big nose. He never told me anymore, '*Rochele, ich hub der liebe*'—Rochele, I love you. He never told me again, '*Du bist a sheyn meydele*'—You are a pretty girl."

"Why would she treat children badly?" I ask.

"Because they weren't hers."

✎ During the week my stepmother would often ask me to run to the store for a quarter kilogram of sugar or to the baker's for bread, and I went happily. But sometimes she would ask me to run an errand after it got dark and then I would be afraid. I could not tell her or my father why I felt this way. But when I walked outside in the dark, every tree in my path became a person who had returned from the dead and was out to frighten and hurt me. Sometimes, among the menacing trees, I even saw my dead mother. I could not stop my mind from conjuring up such ghosts. The more I kept running, the more they followed. ✎

I lay down the composition book.

"This is very vivid, Ma," I say. "The whole memoir is very well written."

She welcomes the compliment, but she has something more pressing she needs to say.

"It had an extreme impact on me, my mother's death," she tells me. "How I suffered."

6

"You've never told me very much about school, Ma," I say. "The sense I've gotten is that school was where you had a chance to shine."

"School? I was very good in school, in Polish grammar, in analyzing sentences. I finished seven grades. If my father had money I would have gone to gymnasium—what you call here high school. But school was a different ball game there. It was not what you have here. Here you worry every child should feel good, should have what you call self-esteem, no one should feel insulted. There they gave you to learn grammar and geography and mathematics and you had to know it, and if you didn't they ignored you. Who cared whether you had troubles at home? Besides, in Poland everything was anti-Semitic. You don't know about such things. Thank God you don't."

I pick up her composition book and, as I read, try to imagine a scared, motherless, but ever-hopeful girl starting school.

In September 1926, my father handed me a brown paper bag with two slices of bread and a pear and asked me to tag along with an eleven-year-old neighbor to school, which was three kilometers from my home. I was starting first grade.

When we arrived, the neighbor ran off to her class and I blundered around trying to find mine, so when I came in late the teacher gave me a displeased look.

"What's your name?" she asked in tart Polish.

"Rochele Golant," I answered timidly.

"And what's your father's name?" she asked, her voice louder and more intimidating.

"Yehoshua Golant," I said.

I was afraid that I had somehow given the wrong answers.

Although all the children in my school were Jewish, my first-grade teacher, Pani Zarowska, was a Gentile, as were most of the teachers. The Polish language she spoke was strange to me, as it was to most Jewish children, who grew up in neighborhoods where everyone spoke Yiddish. Not only did we have to speak Polish in school, but we had to begin the day by standing in formation alongside the school's athletic field and singing a prayer to God that seemed quite Christian to me.

I was full of curiosity that first day and enjoyed everything about this unfamiliar world except for the sternness of my teacher. But on my way home, I realized I faced something more frightening than any homework assignment. How would I ask my father to give me money for a first reader, a notebook, and a pencil? It was like asking him to let the family go without bread for a week. My father's eyes looked shamed and saddened as I told him about the supplies I needed. Buying a new book was out of the question, he said. But he had an alternative. He took me down the street to a neighbor whose child he knew was starting second grade and asked if he could purchase the first reader that child had used the year before. The neighbor agreed and my father reached into his threadbare brown purse, counted out seventy-five groschen, and we brought home that battered first reader. After supper, my father stayed up late into the night with a needle and thread binding the book's tattered pages together. This was a book that had changed hands many times before.

In October, when the ground was thick with fallen leaves, it was fun to walk the three kilometers to school. I enjoyed dragging my feet and kicking the leaves, listening to their crackle and rustle, as I strolled along narrow streets, over the train rails, into the woods, and out into the open again, all the way toward Warszawska Street. By November the weather was wet and chilly and I was often cold and, after my skimpy breakfast, sometimes hungry. More than once I opened my brown paper lunch bag on the way to school and ate the pear my father had given me. That left me only two pieces of bread for lunch. But the pear stirred my appetite and I began to pick at the bread inside the bag until it too was gone. Days like those seemed excruciatingly long. There was nothing to look forward to.

After school, I did not especially look forward to the first hours at home either. My father did not arrive home from teaching Talmud Torah until four or five and Bluma was still something of a stranger to me. I didn't dare ask for a piece of bread. I felt such a request would get me in trouble. So I sat quietly on a chair and waited restlessly for supper, watching Bluma cook the potato soup that I knew would finally slake my craving. ◥

As I read my mother's story about her school days, I am struck by some of the parallels. She had to learn Polish from scratch. I had to learn English and Hebrew. She was ashamed of her books, I of my crayons. Growing up, however, we each had a parent who took time from the pulls of the day to try to make sure we went off to school with one less source of shame. But the parallels stop. I never remember being hungry, nor having a mother who resented the stirrings of my appetite.

"It was a different world, Joey," my mother says. "You can't imagine. Every few months we had a visit from the hygienist. She came to check on lice. If she found no lice in your hair, she made you undress and inspected your clothes. Whenever she checked me over, my heart pounded like a hammer. If she found lice, the teacher would announce your name to the entire class. Children would point at you. Gone was your dignity. Those with lice had to march in a row through the streets of Otwock to the public bath. You tried to hide your face so nobody in the street would see you. But they made you sing a marching song that was written especially for this humiliating parade."

I laugh at these indignities, but I realize we're racing ahead, and there is some basic information I haven't gotten. I've learned nothing yet about the three children my mother's father had with his new wife.

❧ On a cold February night in 1927, long after I fell asleep, I heard a loud commotion. Bluma was moaning and crying. Barely awake, I glimpsed a neighborhood woman hurry into my family's one-room apartment carrying a small suitcase. I had no idea what was going on, but from my bed, with Yasha sleeping on the other side, I saw the neighborhood woman quickly take off her coat and wrap a white apron around her waist. She ordered my father to prepare boiling water and hand her a basin. My stepmother's moans turned to screams of pain and desperation.

"Spread your legs and push," the woman told my stepmother.

Bluma pushed and shrieked. My father stood at her side murmuring Hebrew prayers. I slid under the feather quilt and pleaded to God for the pain to end. It took a long time, but her shrieking subsided and I peeked out from the quilt and watched with bewilderment as a baby emerged from a pool of blood and the neighborhood woman snipped the umbilical cord with a scissors and tied the remnant into a knot.

"It's a girl!" she said.

I slipped out of bed and tried to draw closer.

"Go back to sleep," my father commanded in a sharp whisper.

The midwife shook the baby up and down until it let out a small, sweet cry, the sweetest sound I had ever heard. But I was still anxious.

"Is Bluma dying?" I asked my father.

My mother's death a year before was still fresh in my mind and I was terrified of blood and sickness. How could a baby come out alive from such a pool of blood? I asked my father.

"Go back to sleep, Rochele," my father ordered. ❧

"What was the name of that baby?" I ask.

"That was Esther," my mother answers.

I am slightly embarrassed to be asking this question. Esther, after all, was my aunt, and in my fifties I should know the name of my aunt. But this is part of the Holocaust backwash. The survivors' children were left with a roll call of dead relatives they never met and with parents who found it too painful to bring these dead to graphic life. For many of the children the relatives became a list of names, as easy to forget as the names of the first ten American presidents or the Seven Dwarfs.

"Esther," my mother tells me, "brought some sunlight into our lives. She was the first person I looked for when I woke up in the morning and the first I looked for when I came home from school. I talked to her and smiled at her and watched her grin. I couldn't wait for the chance to put her to sleep and sing her all my favorite Jewish songs.

"I loved putting Esther to sleep. I even wanted to feed her but I couldn't because my stepmother nursed her. I'll tell you this cute story. One day—it was summer and warm—my stepmother asked me to take the baby outside so she could straighten the house and cook the potato soup. I decided to do something I was plotting for a long time. I tied the baby tight to my body with my stepmother's shawl. I stole a chipped blue cup from the cupboard and I took the baby to the villa of the butcher a few houses down the street. The butcher had a fat milk cow. I put the baby on the grass and I milked the cow the way I had seen the butcher's wife doing it. Soon the cup was full of milk and I gave it to the baby. She sipped it eagerly. I felt a sense of real accomplishment.

"That was one of the last summers I spent at home. My father began to send me away for the summer to stay with my mother's parents in Parysow. Maybe thirty miles away. I didn't like leaving my father and I didn't like leaving Otwock. But my grandfather proposed the idea and my father and my stepmother wanted one less mouth to feed."

"Your grandparents were better off?"

"They were considered rich. Ha! People on welfare here are richer than they were. But my *zayde*, Israel Zelig Olszewski, had a good business. He made shoes for the army. He was quite a handsome man, tall and erect with a nicely trimmed beard. I'll never forget how he ate his breakfast. It was a piece of dark pumpernickel smeared with a little butter and some salt, and maybe a few pieces of herring. Before he took a bite, he went over to the closet and took out a bottle of pure spirits. Not like the vodka you get here. He put me on his lap and let me take a sip and then he drank the rest. Then he ate his breakfast. That was the best part of those summers away. Being with my grandfather."

"Sounds like your family made all their decisions, like whether to send you away for the summer, around getting enough food."

"Food was the main preoccupation. But my father didn't just think of food. He was a very cheerful person. He was very well liked by the neighbors. I remember the winter of 1929. It was unforgettably cold. They closed the school and *cheder*, and my father stayed home with us. The house felt warm just because he was there. He kept putting coals in the stove and he put little round potatoes in the coals. And when those potatoes were brown, Joey, I'm telling you, nothing was more delicious.

"There was nothing to do in the cold evenings, so he used to read us stories, something like Isaac Bashevis Singer, stories about devils. He called in the next-door neighbor, who was a shoemaker, and another neighbor, and another. People came in. Just like we are watching television today. That was their entertainment. My father was reading to them. When he talked, he talked in such a legible way—articulate, articulate. He spoke a Litvashe Yiddish—how you say, Lithuanian Yiddish. This was more refined than a Warsaw Yiddish. My father spoke with a nice voice. He had a natural tenor. So when he talked it kind of rang."

"He sounded like a generous man," I say.

"He was very kind, very generous. On Passover, before he went shopping for himself, he took twenty zlotys—that was his weekly pay, more or less—and he went around to important personages that he knew—he knew everybody and everybody knew him—and he asked them to give. He took the money he collected and went to the other side of the railroad. There lived there a shoemaker. I remember that little room that he lived in. So poor. His wife used to *tzip* feathers for pillows to help him make a living. She *tzipped* the feathers and he was sitting cobbling. And my father had a good relationship with him.

Because my father always needed to fix the shoes of his children. You didn't throw away a pair of old shoes and buy a new one. You fixed them. My father took his twenty zlotys and the other money he collected and gave it to that shoemaker for Passover because the shoemaker didn't have enough for the holiday. Maybe it was just *rakhmones* [pity]. Twenty zlotys was a lot of money for a poor man to give. But my father was a charitable person. Here, Joey. My voice is getting tired. I'll find you in the notebook what I wrote about Passover."

No holiday seemed as majestic as Passover. The preparations began weeks before. Everything was cleaned, even the straw mattresses, all to make sure there were no traces of *chametz* [forbidden products of grain]. My father used to take his Talmuds, the size of world atlases, and other religious books outside the house and spread them out on long benches and dust them and give them air. Across the fence we could see our neighbors airing their books as well. When everything was spic and span and the books returned to their shelves, we sat down to eat our supper of browned-flour potato soup in a corner especially assigned for the last few *chametz* meals.

When the seder began, our poor home seemed luminous. My father sat like a king on his throne, leaning back against the pillows my stepmother had puffed up for him. We listened with intense curiosity as my father elaborated the Haggadah in Yiddish, every word clear and sonorous. Even the *oyrech*—the impoverished guest that my father brought along every year from synagogue—was spellbound. My father did not pronounce the Haggadah with precision and grace just for us. He wanted to make sure that Berel, the next-door neighbor who claimed he didn't know how to make a seder, could also hear the story of the exodus from Egypt.

The next morning, after my father left for shul, the neighborhood children emerged from their houses to show off their new clothes. Spring was in the air and I felt wonderful in my new dress, my patent-leather shoes, my new white socks. I wished Passover could go on forever.

I feel glad my mother had such memorable Passovers. Passover is the gathering of the clan, the time to see and appreciate the connections, not just to the Jews who escaped Egypt in the night but to those at the seder table and at seders of generations past. My brother, Josh, who has become the chief seder maker in our family, sings the *Kiddush* blessing over the wine in strong and crystalline fashion, a brazen show-off, but we love him for it because his voice, my mother testifies, resonates with the chords of our dead grandfather in Otwock. The dishes he and his wife, Fay, serve smell and taste of the Otwocks of Poland and Russia. There is a sense in the bright white tablecloths and sparkling dishware and ample piles of matzoh and brimming glasses of wine and all the children gathered around the table of having endured together for another year, just like the Jews of the Exodus, and, given my parents' history, this is not something we ever minimize. How much more so, given the squalor that so often blemished my mother's upbringing, did a luminous Passover mean to her.

"By the time you were a teenager, you spent a lot of your time watching over your smaller brothers and sisters," I say, resuming our interview.

"Yes, after Esther my stepmother gave birth to Chana Leah, and when I was twelve she had Shimon—Shimele. I loved these children and played with them constantly. My stepmother wanted me to help, and I did. But I had a new distraction. Girls my age were joining Zionist organizations like Chalutz and Trumpeldor. My neighbor Chana took me with her to Chalutz. I had a wonderful time dancing horas with the boys. I remember a fifteen-year-old boy looked straight into my eyes and I was attracted to him. When my father found out what I'm doing, he came to the hall. I remember he had his walking cane on one side and Yossel, my stepbrother, on the other and he shouted at me like he had never done before. I remember his fingers holding on to the cane like he was going to raise it against me. But he didn't. He was angry and I knew why. He was trying to keep me out of trouble with boys whose behavior was too free.

"It was around this time that my stepmother began spitting blood. She too had tuberculosis. Whenever she coughed, she had to lay on the bed and rest. I didn't know how to help her and was glad I could just watch the three small children and keep them away from her. Once, I bought her a wedge of watermelon from a pushcart. I remember her pale face as she sat up in bed and ate it with such hunger. 'You know, Rochele,' she told me, 'this is the only food I feel like having. It soothed my heart. Thank you very much.'

"I washed the floors every Friday for Shabbos. I ran all her errands around town. My stepmother seemed to stop her criticisms. She even complimented me for the way I sewed dresses for Esther and Chana Leah and the way I darned socks."

As she talks, I realize that though she is barely out of childhood, her days living at home are about to end. Her composition book describes that fateful moment when at fourteen years old she left home, a moment that would make her grow up long before she was ready and help cultivate the embattled and combative stance that would abide well into my childhood.

∽ In June of 1933, just before my fourteenth birthday, I graduated Public School Number 2 in Otwock. It was a joyous occasion. Many girls went no further than fifth grade and I had finished the seventh. My stepmother spoke with pride about me to her neighbors. The graduates collected money and arranged an evening of song, music, and dance in the school auditorium, complete with a torte from Cuciernia Lapaty, Otwock's most famous confectionery. The torte had sumptuous layers of chocolate, fruit, and marzipan and I never again ate anything as memorable.

But graduation meant I had to find a job to help the family put food on the table. My stepmother, who at eleven years old had worked as a maid, urged my father to send me off to Warsaw to earn a living. My younger brother, Yasha, was already out of the house. He was just twelve years old, but he was living in my grandmother's town of Parysow and learning the craft of shoemaking. It was my turn now, my grandmother said. Whatever my father's misgivings, a rare visit by his sisters, Deborah and Sarah, seemed to help make up his mind.

"Joshua, you won't have to worry about a dowry for her, that's for sure," Sarah told my father. "She's so pretty, knock on wood."

"Maybe I won't," said my father, "but right now I worry how to make a mensch of her so she can support herself and help me too at the same time."

My father let them know that his wife, Bluma, thought I ought to find a job as a maid. But his sisters would hear none of this, and argued loudly with him.

"Why are you sending her out to become a maid?" Deborah screamed.

"And such a nice girl," Sarah said.

Working as a maid was not something Golants did.

Sarah said she knew a man who owned a flour business who needed someone to pack bags. But Deborah, the older sister, thought that was too grimy a job for me and made an alternate suggestion. Sarah and her husband owned a small knitting business in Warsaw, and had over the years given jobs to Jews from the Golants' hometown of Mordy.

"Why can't you give her a chance to learn knitting just as you give to strangers?" Deborah said to Sarah. "You can afford to feed another mouth until she learns."

I could see Sarah had been put on the spot. Why would she want to take on the burden of a callow girl, one unacquainted with a big city? But she agreed to hire me. And so my father found a palatable way to succumb to his wife's wishes. He took me to Warsaw, we stayed the night at Sarah's house, and the next morning he asked me to accompany him to the bus depot, where he would catch a bus back to Otwock without me.

Tears streamed down my face as my father waited to board the bus. My father too seemed sad as he bent over to comfort me.

"*Far vos veynstu, Rochele?* Why are you crying so, Rochele?" he said tenderly. "Don't worry. I'm not leaving you with strangers. I'm leaving you with an aunt."

"I don't know why I'm crying," I said, brushing away tears with my forearm.

As he mounted the bus, my father gave me twenty zlotys and told me to buy a new coat. He didn't want to be embarrassed before his sister by his daughter's shabby clothes. ❧

As we sit in the quiet kitchen, our voices echoing faintly off the plaster walls, I find myself disturbed as I hear the story of my mother's parting with her father at the bus depot. With my modern sensibility, my grandfather's sending my mother off at fourteen to earn her own living seems to me like negligence, jars with almost everything else my mother has told me about my grandfather. I remember myself as a gawky adolescent. Yes, I was already traveling freely around New York on my own even if I felt wobbly, but at least I was confident that every night I would come home to a family that cared what I had done and where I had been. I want to understand this watershed episode of my mother's life, and so I ask her a simple question: "Why were you crying?"

"Crying? I didn't cry. I couldn't hold my tears. I didn't know nothing about Warsaw and I kind of had a feeling that Sarah didn't want me. I had experiences that people don't want me that much. My grandmother wasn't so happy when I came to her in Parysow because she couldn't deal with a small child. And when I came back my stepmother didn't want me. And here they were sending me to this aunt who didn't want me."

"Then why didn't you say something to your father when he asked why were you crying?" I persist, ignoring the agitated state these memories have put her in.

"I told my father, 'I don't know.' What am I going to tell him, that I don't like to go away from home? How could I tell him that? I wouldn't dare to tell that. I knew I had to leave home. Do they do that to children here? It never would happen. That's why I cried. But I couldn't tell him.

"My stepmother wanted me out of the house. You can't understand that. Of course, you can't understand that. Thank God, you can't understand that."

But she hasn't talked about her disappointment in her father. I suspect that he lacked a certain quantity of backbone, and I wonder if she realizes that.

"Yes," I say. "But why would your father have obeyed his wife?"

"My father insinuated to us that he cannot wait until we go to work and help support him," she replies, her voice softening with sadness. "You asked me a question, so I told you. When I was a kid he used to tell me, 'I can't wait until you grow up and give me a little help.' Just as I wanted you to go to college to prepare you for a living, that's the way they prepared us for a living. If I had a mother, she wouldn't have wanted me to go out on my own. A mother is something unique. You take it for granted, but that's the way mothers are.

"Besides, my father wanted to have a peaceful life with his wife. She didn't let herself be led. She had a voice and opened a mouth and complained to him. And, I wasn't hers. Stepmothers are a different ball game altogether. She didn't have enough food for her own children. Why should she give us food? That's the truth; OK, so I told you. Let's put it this way: She wasn't a witch. She wasn't the worst. After all, she took care of us. But she wasn't a good woman."

She pauses and looks down, maybe worried that she has violated some unspoken divine law.

"I don't want to talk critically," she says. "They all died, *nebech* [pity], from Hitler."

7

My first friends in this country were refugees, kids whose families, like ours, had ended up in apartments near the West Side hotels they had been settled in after they had arrived in New York. In the scruffy, low-rent neighborhood between Central Park West and Broadway that housed a hodgepodge of Irish, Italians, and Puerto Ricans, the refugee children found one another. Perhaps it was simply because we all spoke Yiddish. But there might have been something more. We knew one another, knew in our young bellies that our parents were the same dazed and damaged lot, had the same refugee awkwardness, the same whiff about them of marrow bones and carp. And we knew also that we had a splendid adventure in store for us: we had this rich American turf to explore.

On almost the first day, as I stepped out of my house onto my stoop, widening my eyes like new-foaled Adam to take in this untried world I had been plunked down in, I spied Maury and he noticed me. I did not rush out to make a friend. No, I was scared, wondering where I was and what I would be doing. Children flashed by looking easy and familiar with one another. How would I ever penetrate their circles? I found myself clinging to the balustrade at the top of the stoop, afraid to venture down. The sidewalk might as well have been paved with quicksand.

Maury was a tall, slender boy with shaggy, overgrown hair who at seven was already cursed with thick-lensed glasses. That first day he was wearing a pair of faded blue cowboy pants with mock chaps. The pants had clearly been worn first by someone else.

"Hey, look at me!" he shouted, breaking the silence.

He ran over to a parking sign, bounded off the pavement, and seized the midpoint of the steel pole, braiding his legs tightly around the pole as well. In five swift yanks, he hoisted himself to the top, where he slapped the sign with a loud *ping* that resonated off the tenements and brownstones flanking the street.

I wanted to climb the pole too, but it seemed fearfully high. What if I reached the top and fell to the ground and cracked my head open? I could see my mother's alarmed eyes, hear her screams resounding off the tenements. I grabbed the pole as high as I could, and tried to pull myself up, but the weight of my body seemed elephantine and my hands kept sliding down.

"You gotta grab the pole with your legs, dummy," Maury chortled.

He showed me how to grip the pole with my ankles, but my palms burned the higher I got and at one point I collapsed on top of him in a heap, the two of us breaking into laughter. Then Maury pushed me off him and again scooted to the top of the mast, jeering at me and laughing triumphantly. I had just come to this block and already everyone in these buildings on both sides of the street could see what an oaf I was.

In fact, closely observing the scene was Maury's four-year-old brother, Isaac. He was sitting on a window ledge of their second-floor apartment across the street, held from falling by his mother as she fed spoons of farina into his mouth. I could see he was grinning at the spectacle of ineptness below him. He soon appeared on the sidewalk and he too swiftly clambered up the pole. Then his brother joined him, and the two of them frolicked at the top like pirates in a crow's nest.

So I learned right away that friendship in New York City was cutthroat. One had to be on one's guard always, and keep a sharp knife poised. Once I learned that, though, I found that the streets were the best playground any child could want.

Our jumping-off point was the stoop. It was a stage on which a whole repertory of dramas was acted out day after day, night after night. For us, the stoop was a castle, complete with crenellated battlements, from which we would leap on top of our invaders, smiting them with swords made of balsa boards we pulled off old orange crates. Or it was the calvary's fort against the attacking Indians, whom we would shoot with our crate-board rifles.

On summer nights, our parents would take over the stoop and the dramas would become more adult. Men and women slouched on the steps, unwinding and gossiping and luxuriating in whatever breeze would come their way. Some of the men would drink cans of beer while others smoked cigarettes or cigars. Even the refugee Jews, too busy most of the time to indulge themselves, left their steaming apartments to taste the crisp night air. Everyone paused to take in the nightly battles between parents and children stirred up by the jingle-piping pizza or ice cream trucks. I would plead for one of the small pizzas but my mother would refuse, telling me not to eat *chazeray*, a word that literally means "pork" but, spoken with so contemptuous an intonation, can make any food seem like slop.

On the sultriest of nights, tension crackled in the air. We could hear men and women screaming at each other through open windows, and dogs barking in discomfort, and babies bawling, and the whole world seemed to feel a keen irritation at the strain of holding everything together. Sometimes the pent-up pressures would explode. On a distant stoop, two Puerto Rican women quarreling over a man would set upon each other, grabbing hanks of hair and ripping each other's clothing. Entangled in each other, they would come tumbling down the steps while some beer-drinking neighbors tried to break them apart and others roared with pleasure. Such incidents would bring the whole block together in wonder, and people would linger longer that night on the stoop, murmuring intimately as if they had together discovered some deep, shared mystery of the heart.

My parents and the other refugees, though, kept their distance. In their poverty, they knew they would not descend to such levels of vulgarity. These were the goyim—Polish or Puerto Rican or Italian, it did not matter. Their way of life, the beer and the fights and the indolence, would not be ours. It took a year or two until my parents figured out and transmitted their rules of the territory. There were no lectures, no philosophical discourses, but it was always understood by the refugee children that even if our parents never earned more money, never left this neighborhood, our way of life would remain rigorously apart.

Somehow, every group must have handed down a similar clannish outlook because even in our freewheeling neighborhood, where children played on the streets long after nightfall, Irish kids tended to play with other Irish kids, Puerto Ricans with Puerto Ricans, and refugee Jews with refugee Jews, mingling at the edges once in a while for a pickup game of Ringolivio or Johnny-on-the-pony or, on a raw winter's day, a slapdash fire in a corner trash can.

In that first year, I made an Irish friend named Eddie. For some irrecoverable reason, I followed him to tap dancing lessons in a dingy second-story hall above a row of Amsterdam Avenue storefronts, even taking two of the dime-a-lesson classes. But what most stands out in my memory is Eddie's scooter. His father must have built it, for it was made out of a milk carton nailed to a two-by-four that had been fitted at the bottom with wheels scavenged from an old pair of roller skates. It was makeshift, but it had royal trimmings. "EDDIE" was spelled out in shiny bottle caps nailed to the front of the carton. Inside the crate, there was a shelf where Eddie stashed his prize possessions—a baseball glove, a pack of baseball cards, a bag of marbles.

Mornings, Eddie would come racing down the block, pumping the asphalt with his right foot to pick up speed, then cruising toward me as smoothly and ostentatiously as if he were handling a Cadillac convertible. The wind swept back his hair, a cocky smile lit his face, and the very sun seemed to cooperate by glinting off the "EDDIE" bottle caps. I longed to be Eddie, to have his charm, command his attention. But could I ask my father to fashion me a scooter? Would he understand what a scooter was? Where would we get the roller skates and the milk carton? And would I have to show him how to spell out the letters for "JOEY"?

Eddie, though, vanished from my life. His parents must have moved and no one—not his parents, not mine—thought that some farewell ceremony might have been warranted.

There were other Jewish kids on the block, kids whose parents were not refugees, but in that first year or two there seemed to be a wall between us as well, a wall of class, income, piety, and language. So

I fell back on refugee kids like Maury. No one was around to organize activities for us or take us to museums, but we improvised our own adventures. We would find empty soda bottles along the curb and turn them in for the two-cent deposit at Mr. Zlatagorsky's candy store, enough sometimes to buy us each a Hershey bar and a piece or two of bubble gum. Maury told us there were also treasures to be found in the incinerator closets of the newer, fancier brick building catty-corner to mine. So we went from floor to floor searching the incinerator closets, and sure enough we picked up discarded games and a broken radio, whose innards we spent an hour investigating.

Maury taught me there was big money to be made by fishing in the gratings in front of the shops around the corner on Columbus Avenue. The gratings provided the air and light for the store basements and one outside the five-and-dime looked down on a broad ledge that collected a flotsam and jetsam of cigarette butts, candy wrappers, bottle caps, broken glass, keys, but also sometimes a coin that had fallen out of a passerby's pants or purse. Maury peered through the grating and if he spotted a dime or quarter glinting below, he took a length of string and a piece of bubble gum and chewed the gum until it was soft and moist, then lashed the string around the belly of the gum wad. On his hands and knees, he dropped the line through the grating and tried to swing it over the coin, a maneuver that took finesse and patience. With my face pressed against the grating, I saw Maury strike his quarry, let it rest there until the gum adhered to the coin, then gently pull on the line, landing the coin like a seasoned fisherman.

We would use the money to head once again to Mr. Zlatagorsky's candy store and this time buy a package of Topps cards with its powdery, cloyingly sweet-smelling gum and the prized picture of a baseball player—a Yankee, we always hoped. In the off-season, the bubble gum would come wrapped with a portrait of one of the American presidents, or, most exhilarating for me, Scoop cards. These cards, which were available for only a season or two in the early 1950s, were emblazoned with newspaper headlines and melodramatic photographs trumpeting such quirky events as Lindbergh's flight across the Atlantic, the explosion of the *Hindenburg* dirigible, the capture of John Dillinger. The cards may have been a huckster's gimmick, but they introduced me to the colorful parade of my new country's history, and probably gave me a taste of journalism's amphetamine rush.

No one had any toys worth a damn, so we jerry-rigged our own. There were street games like Skelly, where a bottle cap filled with wax or a banana peel as ballast was skimmed along a course of thirteen boxes chalked on the pavement while a "killer" cap was entitled to shoot the other players off the course. A beer can pounded into the pavement and wedged around a shoe made a wonderful racket when you clattered down the street. Two empty tin cans lashed together with a long strand of twine gave you a walkie-talkie. And that ersatz gizmo provided the occasion for another flash of my father's bravado.

There was a rumpled old Polish man who boarded in the apartment of our building's superintendent. With baggy pants, fraying suspenders, a wrinkled hat, and a wooden cane, he looked like the lovable 1950s television character Charlie Weaver. The Polish man, though, was embittered and grouchy. He didn't like our playing in front of the house, claiming we were too wild and noisy, and sometimes he would pop out of the alley alongside our building and run after us, waving his cane menacingly in the air until we scurried around the corner.

At dusk one summer day, we were talking through our tin cans, warning of a Japanese horde invading over a distant hill, when, with no forewarning, the old man bolted out of the alleyway and surprised us before we could run off. He pulled the walkie-talkie out of our hands with the hook of his cane, then pounded the cans into uselessness with his good leg. We watched in horror as our walkie-talkie was destroyed.

"You didn't have to do that, you old bum," Maury said.

This infuriated the old man and he raised his cane high in the air and, with his hobbling lope, took off after us. We dashed off and turned the corner, when suddenly I glimpsed my father striding swiftly toward us. He was returning from work and had seen the whole encounter. At first I thought he was angry at us, but he ran past us toward the old man and, with his arm stiffly outstretched, stopped him in his tracks. He grabbed the old man's cane and cracked it in two across his right knee.

"Don't you ever hit my children," my father said. "I'll kill you if you do that to my children."

The old man, shaken and ashamed, moved timidly away. My father was trembling, his chest heaving rapidly, spittle streaming from his lower lip. His fury, the inextinguishable mass of it, confused and frightened him also. This was not just an old man he was angry at. This was anger welling up at an entire civilization that had wronged him irreparably. Maury, Josh, and I were left dumbfounded.

With all this freedom—my mother was either at work or crazily distracted—one of us was bound to get into a serious scrape and I did. It was a bleak winter day, one of those gray days when the prettifying glaze of a fresh snowfall has begun to acquire an ashen veneer and the tenements have reemerged in their essential shabbiness. Two of the neighborhood boys had started a fire in a corner trash can, a large, roaring one whose flames thrashed wildly about the wire mesh of the can. The neighborhood kids ringed the can, not just for the warmth but to marvel at the power of what the boys had done.

As the flames consumed the garbage, the older boys ordered younger ones to ferret out more paper. I took off in a frenzy because I knew I could show these kids my stuff by coming through with a thick stack of newspapers. I didn't look at the traffic. No one had ever taught me how to cross the street; my mother had just warned me to watch out for cars. I didn't see the green Plymouth rolling down Manhattan Avenue until I heard a piercing screech and saw its front grille hurtling toward me. I bounced off the car and landed on my back, hitting my head on the asphalt and falling into a daze.

Maury, Josh, and the other boys and dozens of neighbors circled me as I lay on the ground. Mothers poked their heads out windows to see if it was their child. Mr. Zlatagorsky came running out of his candy store, and when he saw who it was lying on the asphalt in front of the Plymouth, he raced off to get my mother.

She was looking out the window too, drawn by the squeal of the brakes and the commotion of people running. She could see by the terror on Mr. Zlatagorsky's face that something dreadful had happened, and she ran out of the house.

"It's Joey," Mr. Zlatagorsky yelled at her. "Come. Your boy. He's been hit by a car."

It didn't matter what he had said. She knew everything and knew how dire it was, and she lashed out at him in an anguished madness, tearing at his cheeks and eyes with her fingernails.

"What did you do to my son?" she cried. "What did you do to my Joey?"

"I didn't do anything," he said, wrestling her off. "I just came to tell you. Come, you'll see him."

He took her forcefully by the elbow and led her through the crowd. I was tossing wildly, the way a baby sometimes does in the moments before waking. My mother crouched over me, brushing my hair, and sobbing and moaning with fright. Her child had been injured, damaged, maybe irreparably.

An ambulance pulled up. The attendants studied the situation, then lifted me on a stretcher and carried me into the back of the ambulance, with my mother walking alongside, smoothing my head and weeping. I woke up on the way to St. Luke's Hospital. My left hip and thigh were hurting badly and I was simpering.

"Joey, you're all right," my mother said. "I'm here with you. You're going to be all right."

She was laughing now amid her tears as she saw my eyes blinking open.

At the hospital, doctors poked at me and X-rayed me and told me that the car had sustained more damage than I had. I had a large purplish bruise on my thigh and an egg-sized lump on my forehead, but I was, in fact, fine. I reveled in the doctors' attention and wanted to stay, but they let my mother take me home that afternoon.

My mother put a freshly ironed sheet on my army cot, and a clean pillowcase on my pillow, and tucked me into bed and kissed my forehead. She cooked my favorite soup, mushroom sprinkled with fried flour. My father came home early from work, bringing a Nestle's Crunch bar and his own kiss on the forehead. Josh, who could not take his eyes off me, as if I were some object of fear or wonder, ran errands for my mother and brought me anything I asked for. Mr. and Mrs. Levy next door came by to see how I was, and so did Junior, a handsome, genial Puerto Rican teenager who had enlisted in the army and was home on leave. He let me try on his army parade cap, with its shiny leather brim, and that seemed better than the Nestle's Crunch and the mushroom soup. Mr. Zlatagorsky too came by after he closed his candy store. Mr. Levy asked him what had happened to his face, and he laughed a deep and mirthful laugh.

I was a boy who prized distinctions, and the accident remained a distinction for me for years afterward. It was my badge of courage. I had survived a calamity. But not until much later did I realize how unbearable it must have been for my mother, who had suffered so many losses already, even to have imagined that her son might not come out of the accident alive.

8

My father was raised as a farmer, but I never knew him as a farmer. I knew him as a man who worked with machinery, a man who twisted wrenches and screwdrivers, a man whose fingertips smelled of machine oil, whose clothes were stained with machine grease. There was, however, a farmer inside my father, and on occasion, he materialized.

When I was a young man, I rented a summer house in the Berkshire hills of Massachusetts that came with a vegetable garden already seeded by the owner. In early summer, my father came for a visit and we walked the grounds. To me, a city rat, the garden looked like an indistinguishable mass of amorphous green leaves pushing through the soil. My father made the distinctions right away.

"You have beets growing," he said, recognizing the subterranean plant by the shape of the leaf. "And carrots. And tomatoes."

To prove his point, he squatted down and plucked out a small beet. It was a beguiling act, but it also had a sad, wistful quality to it, like a baseball slugger clumsily swinging for a home run late in his life. The farmer raised in Polish Galicia had by then been all but extinguished by the demands of transplantation to urban America.

But back in our first years in America, my father's heart still resonated to the scrape of a plow and the whistle of a scythe. And it thumped with excitement when he learned that one of his kind, Yonah

Baranek, had been able to start an egg farm in the town of Lakewood in central New Jersey. Yonah, a Polish city boy whom he had met in the displaced persons camps, had gotten financing from one of the Jewish agencies and was making a go of it. Surely my father, a farmer by birth, could do as well. So when Yonah invited us down to take a look at his farm and those that had been started by other refugees, my father persuaded my mother to go.

We took our valise, filled with weekend clothes and sheets and pillowcases, down by subway to the Port Authority terminal and boarded one of the old Lincoln line buses to Lakewood. We had never been out of New York City, and, once we passed the Lincoln Tunnel and the long stretch of gasworks along the Jersey Turnpike, we were enchanted by the countryside rolling by. My mother opened a window and deeply breathed in the air, sweetened by freshly cut grass and spring wildflowers.

"The air," she said, "is like Otwock."

This was a refrain I was to hear throughout my youth. I thought she was simply bragging that the air of her hometown was the standard by which other airs were to be measured. Otwock's air, after all, drew Hasidic rebbes and tubercular patients alike from all corners of Poland. I realized later that such boasts were her way of reconnecting herself—and discreetly connecting us—to the town she had not seen since the Nazi invasion. The sweet air must have recalled walks with her father among the pines and chestnut trees; recalled the Hasidim, with their twitchy gait, hurrying to and from their rebbes' villas; recalled the tumbledown marketplace with its grizzled, loutish peddlers. This was a world that was swept away in the war, and she could not yet tell her children very much about it. But she could remember the air.

My father did not talk at all about his early life, and my picture of life on his family farm was about as vivid as that of Old McDonald's farm. I knew the family raised horses, cows, and chickens and grew several varieties of vegetables, and that was about it. Later, as an adult trying to wrestle from his stripped-down picture the texture and quirkiness of a lived life, I learned that his family's farm in the rugged Carpathian village of Borinya was part of a large tract of land that had been divided among several children, and my father was to receive a

portion of his father's tract when he married. There was a single synagogue and my father walked more than a mile to get to it. Life was
measured by Sabbaths, and each Sabbath was named after its Torah
portion—Shabbos Bereshis for the story of Creation, Shabbos Noach
for the story of Noah. Borinya had a courthouse but no school that
went beyond the fifth grade. There were hayrides for teenage boys and
girls. Jews and goyim did not mix, and the goyim were an abiding
menace, one that could strike at the flimsiest pretext.

Well into his seventies, he finally had the courage to tell me something else: that there were so many Berger cousins in Borinya that on
Simchath Torah, the celebration of another year's cycle of Torah readings, he and his father could walk from one Berger house to another
for a festive drink and not be done until midnight. In telling me this,
my father was giving me the barest glimpse of the scope of his loss.

These paltry details—about all I was able to squeeze out of my
father—were all to come. Now, though, my brother, Josh, and I were
sitting on a bus speeding us to what could be yet another new life, a life
something like the "Farmer in the Dell" that we sang about in kindergarten, a life of cows and horses, barns and corrals. Yes, it was going to
be new, but what would happen to the sturdy embrace of Manhattan
Day School and the homespun aroma of macaroni and cheese or fish-
cakes wafting up from the cafeteria? And what would happen to the
friends I was making on the jigsaw streets of my corner of Manhattan?

After two hours, the bus arrived in Lakewood and at the village
stop we saw Yonah standing beside his dusty brown station wagon, his
smile gilded by two or three gold teeth. He took our bags and placed
them in the back among the large egg cartons and empty mesh cages
and drove us to his home. Surrounded by feathers floating in the car's
air and the warm, gamy smell of chickens, we drove through bleak
fields set apart from their neighbors by thin stands of trees and bushes.
Each plot seemed to have two or three weatherbeaten shacks that
Yonah informed us were hen coops.

"This one is owned by a Jew, and this one is also a Jew's and this
farm belongs to a greener," Yonah happily told us as our eyes panned
across the passing fields.

I had never seen refugees in this setting before. To me, they were urban animals who rode subways and took strolls on Broadway in topcoats and fedoras. Their accents seemed out of place on a farm, on the lips of men in denim and workboots.

At Yonah's farmhouse, Mrs. Baranek, in a smudged and unpressed dress, and their two daughters came out to greet us. My mother hailed them boisterously, though I could tell immediately that she eyed the female attire and the farmhouse with a note of distaste. Yonah led us around his plot of five acres, almost all of it uncultivated. (The worthlessness of the soil for other types of agriculture was why this area of central New Jersey had become a lively enclave for chicken farming.) The hub was the two henhouses, long, squat wooden structures whose coat of gray paint was flaking in patches. Inside, it was dim and there was a rich sensation of heat, not from any radiators but from the bodies of the chickens themselves. The plump brown hens eyed us suspiciously, startling as we approached and backing off.

As he hurried from cage to cage to show us his handiwork and explain the details of his business, Yonah, who had been a shoemaker in Europe, was engagingly proud. His prominent Adam's apple rose and fell excitedly, like the necks of one of his chickens. He had cobbled this enterprise together without any farming know-how or a competent understanding of the costs involved. Yet somehow he was surviving. My mother, however, kept a reproachful eye on the whole business, and her scorn did not abate over lunch back at Yonah's house. I could see her taking in the worn and pitted kitchen linoleum, which also bore the strawy stamp of Yonah's boots, and the old-fashioned icebox and stove, older even than our own antiquated models.

We spent much of the rest of the day on a faded floral sofa and hard-backed chairs talking about the economics of farming, with occasional forays back to the coops. Yonah tried to explain to my father the elements of mortgages and interest payments, while my mother, whose grasp on finances was keener than his, seemed to squirm at the questions my father braved. A profit could be eked out of this business, Yonah insisted, if a man and his wife worked hard together and were willing to do so seven days a week. Chickens did not take weekends off from eating feed or laying eggs, and their caretakers could not take weekends off either.

It was this part that my mother found especially repulsive. She had no intention of spending a Saturday or Sunday rising early to spread chicken feed through a smelly coop or cleaning the bottoms of cages. She had grander, more cosmopolitan visions of what her life might amount to, visions that she had tasted in her teenaged years in Warsaw. She had belonged to a choir, met people who talked politics, went to Greta Garbo and Loretta Young movies, read Tolstoy's *Anna Karenina* and Adam Mickiewicz's poetry. The war had truncated that life, but she clearly had not consumed enough.

The final blow to any hopes of our having a pastoral future was our night sleeping over on the Baraneks' kitchen floor. For my parents, the Baraneks put down two old mattresses that they had stored in a coop, and for my brother and me they fashioned small mats out of their own quilts. The house turned chilly at night and was particularly cold at floor level. The air was dusty and feathery. None of us slept well. In the morning, we rose early to have breakfast and catch a return bus to New York.

"If you paid me a million dollars, I wouldn't spend even a day on a farm," my mother told my father as the bus huffed out of Lakewood.

It was an expression she must have picked up from the Americans working in her hat factory. But it was the final verdict on any thoughts we might have had of becoming American farmers.

To squeeze out the cash we needed to keep going from month to month, we took in boarders. That may seem like a punishing frugality in our indulgent age, but taking in boarders had long been an honorable business among the immigrants of the Lower East Side and the Bronx. Even if by the 1950s it was no longer commonplace, it hadn't quite disappeared either. Besides, my mother was accustomed to having them around. Her father had taken in boarders in Otwock.

My brother Josh and I detested them. We had three boarders during my years growing up, and each was a distinctive presence whom I despised in a distinctive way. If Miss Hennyhen received the full blast of my scorn, it was only because she was the first intruder into our family circle.

Miss Hennyhen's name was probably Hannahan, but since no one we knew spoke English well enough to correct us, we pronounced it "Hennyhen." She was a graying spinster with a dour temperament who spent much of her day knitting and scrutinizing us, an Irish Madame Defarge. For a change of pace, she might rearrange the knick-knacks that rested on fine lace doilies atop her dresser. If she went out, it was sometimes to the local pawnshop on Broadway—the "pony," she called it—with its classic sign of three brass balls, where she would trade some of her possessions for cash and buy back others. My parents gave her the room that conventionally should have been reserved for my brother and me, and so, in our eyes, she started out with two strikes against her.

Mornings, emerging from a haze of dreams, I would lie in bed and hear her pad in her slippers toward the bathroom and knew I would have to contain my bladder until she finished all her ablutions. I could tell what she was up to by slight variations in the sounds of running water, first a pebbly stream, then the howling cascade of the toilet bowl, then the brisk gush of the bathtub faucet. I was repelled.

In the evening, she would join us in the living room, sitting possessively in our one snug armchair in the corner, knitting her doilies and sweaters for her niece in Florida. Occasionally, she would look up with an expression that I was sure contained contempt for our raw immigrant ways. Indeed, I felt her eyes on every gesture I made and could not relax in her presence.

She even disturbed my first grapplings with sex. My first friend, Maury, had a sister, two years younger, named Sarah, a pretty girl with dark pageboy-cut hair and dark eyes. Sarah and I had already checked each other's secrets out in an alcove behind the radiator that heated the ground-floor hallway. But hers must have continued to tantalize because some weeks later, while playing in my parents' bedroom, I wanted to have another look. On who remembers what impulse, she, Maury, and I crouched down in the narrow alley between my parents' bed and the wall, with Sarah sandwiched between Maury and me. We wrestled our pants below our knees and gazed upon one another's jewels. The torrid scene soon spun out of control when my brother, Josh—he must have been barely five at the time—joined us. Never one to let a chance for attention pass, he stripped off not just his pants, but all his clothes, clambered on top of my parents' marriage bed, and began to leap acrobatically up and down as if it were a trampoline. He laughed wildly, madly, drunk with his newfound power to shock and entertain us.

Into this orgy walked Miss Hennyhen.

"What are you children doing?" she screamed. "Get your clothes back on."

My brother continued to giggle excitedly, but, full of shame, I fumbled to slip my pants on and close my zipper as Maury and Sarah scattered to the winds.

The incident clearly had a greater impression on me than it did on Miss Hennyhen. As far as I know, she never even mentioned it to my parents. But I never forgave her presence. That was it. It was not her, but the fact of her that chafed so. Why did I, alone among my classmates and friends, have to endure a stranger living in my home? Where was my family's pride?

My mother, a woman who twitched between choices as if they were the poles of a magnet, did not like the fact of Miss Hennyhen either, but she could not surrender this opportunity to make a little extra money. Her husband's bare-bones income was paying for food, clothes, and shelter, but not much more. Her own income during the hat season covered the cost of yeshiva and allowed her to squirrel away savings for the crises her life taught her were sure to come. Mostly though, a child's need for an individual room was something remote from her experience. She had never had a room of her own, sometimes not even a bed of her own. She had slept with her sister in a single bed that was put up at night in the kitchen, and in some years on two chairs squeezed together. Sometimes she even slept with a brother. The fourth room at 102nd Street was a luxury, she figured, and cots in the living room would suffice for her two sons.

But to me, with all the aches of deprivation, having a stranger padding around our house seemed the deepest, most humiliating wound, the most obvious testimony to our second-class citizenship. And we weren't even citizens.

9

My parents' friends were all refugees. My parents had latched on to them in the hurly-burly of the DP camps or in New York among the boatloads of recent Jewish arrivals, and because neither we nor they could claim more than a relative or two who survived the slaughter, scarcely any brothers, sisters, uncles, aunts, or cousins to speak of, we became each other's families. Certainly, my parents' friends had the blood mystique of relatives. Mordchale Weinberg was my merry dwarf of an uncle, full of jests and pranks and a yen for fun, and Moishe Granas was my shrewd uncle, the one who knew all the angles, smart deals, and profitable connections. Mrs. Herling, a soft, roundish woman, was my warmhearted, benevolent aunt, and Mrs. Cooperman the aunt whose unsparing eye kept me on guard.

My parents and their friends did not spend time with one another as friends usually do, leaving the children home and going out to the movies or for a stroll so they could converse freely on grown-up matters. No, they spent time together as relatives do, with the children always trooping along and milling about. They visited one another several times a year, taking subway trains to the bottom of Brooklyn or the flanks of the Bronx, always bringing the gift of a box of cake tidily bound in bakery cord. The cake was laid out, the coffee or tea prepared, and, usually, my father, or Mr. Granas, or Mr. Weinberg would pull out the family's one bottle of vodka from a hall closet and flaunt it over the table.

"Do you want a schnapps?" my father would propose with a devilish gleam, as if he were asking everyone to join in an illicit act.

The matter always seemed to be pondered gravely and with great reluctance.

"What for?" Mrs. Weinberg would protest. "Do you want to get me *shikker*—drunk?"

"I can't drink," my mother would say. "It goes right to my legs and then I can't stand up."

"One little glass," my father would urge.

"All right, just a bit," the women would consent.

Somehow, everyone joined in, and my father would pour each guest a shot glass. Noisy and boisterous in crowded apartments that looked out on grimy airshafts, they munched on sponge cake and told countless stories, stories about the pathos of their ragged homes in Poland or the stinginess of the Garment District bosses they worked for or the naivete of American Jews or their own flinty indomitability. Mr. Herling might recall how he managed to survive his concentration camp by cunningly giving the German commandant stylish haircuts. Or the crafty Mrs. Erlich would confide in whispered tones how she rescued her husband from a Russian jail, not by relying on principled legal arguments—which she scoffed at as silly in a degenerate country like the Soviet Union—but by baldly paying the prosecutor a thousand rubles to drop the case.

If the stories threatened to be humiliating in their self-exposure, they could be cloaked in the form of a revealing joke.

"A Yid, a hunchbacked Jew in Warsaw," began one of my mother's jokes about Poland, "climbed aboard a bus and dropped in his fare when he heard the bus driver scolding him: 'Jew, you have to pay two fares, one for you and one for your hump.'

"So the Jew reached into his pocket and put in another fare. When he took his seat, the Jew alongside whispered to him, 'How could you let him talk to you like that? Why didn't you refuse to pay the extra fare?'

" 'Shah! Don't worry,' the hunchback replied. 'I fooled him. I didn't tell him about my hernia.' "

These were stories about the wiles of survival. They weren't about pride or valor or prowess. In a corrupt and racist continent where the decks were stacked against them, the impoverished European Jews were always scraping by on a willingness to do what was necessary to survive, even if that meant surrendering pride or principle. In America, though, pride and principle seemed to be paramount, and as I eavesdropped on these stories from the periphery of the kitchen table, I learned subversive lessons that were out of step with the America I was absorbing. American history and culture were starting to teach me to stand up for myself and fight for what I believed was right, and my parents and their friends were teaching me to maneuver and outsmart and go at obstacles in roundabout fashion, and, at all costs, to keep myself intact. And since their lesson had proved right for them, had been tested in the cauldron of bitter experience, it was a hard lesson to shrug off.

As the evenings wore on and the food and drink loosened their guard, my parents and their friends could fall back on stories that were almost lyrical in their evocation of the homes that had overnight been snatched from them.

"In the summer," my mother would say, "they used to send me away to my grandmother's house in Parysow. They wanted to save a little on food. My grandmother was rich. She had a business making boots for the army. Rich? Hah. Here the people on welfare are richer than she was. But in Parysow, she was rich. She didn't want for food. I would go in a horse and carriage that belonged to a poor Jew who made the trip from Otwock to Parysow a few times a year and collected a few pennies from my family. Each year he stopped to rest his horse at the same spot. I remember there was a meadow surrounded by a forest, and the meadow had wildflowers, beautiful yellow and blue wildflowers. And I got out of the carriage and walked across the meadow and the wind was blowing a certain way that made me feel happy, deeply happy. And I was not that often happy. That picture in the meadow stays with me all these years. I was seven or eight, but I can never forget it."

If our families had a sense of shameful poverty or loneliness, it was not salient enough to crush them. There were gales of laughter as they remembered that poverty, how little they had to eat and how special the occasion had to be for an egg or chicken to materialize.

"In my home," Mrs. Herling would say, "we would eat an egg once a month."

"Ha!" my mother would parry. "We ate an egg once a year—on Passover."

If they did not boast about their deprivations, they would flaunt their paltry advantages. Mrs. Cooperman would say, to my mother's arched-eyebrow skepticism, that her education had advanced as far as gymnasium, as high school was known in Poland. My mother would counter that her father had been selected to be the cantor for the High Holidays at her town's most prestigious synagogue. Everyone in town, she said, raved about Joshua Golant's voice.

I tiptoed around the edge of these conversations and lapped up not only the theatrics but the salty Yiddish phrases they had smuggled in from Europe. Sure, I now was largely fluent in English and wanted my parents to speak it impeccably as well, but the rough-hewn expressions and the world they illuminated were hard to let go. *"Mit eyn tochos ken men nit af tsvey chasenes tantsn"* ("With one behind, you can't dance at two weddings") was an earthier way of saying you can't do two things at once. *"Lord Kochs fun de Gezovne,"* the made-up name of a pompous aristocrat, put a stiletto through an affectation; an *alte cavalier* cut an over-the-hill roué down to size. My mother remembered a bon mot uttered by the apprentice of the neighborhood shoemaker in Otwock. When she chatted a little too freely once, he warned her not to talk too much. Every person, he told her, is rationed a certain number of words and once he exhausts his portion, he dies. She took him very seriously.

The quality my parents and their friends valued most was generosity. Someone could be a ne'er-do-well, but if he lavished an extra quarter on a good coffee cake for his guests or an ice cream cone for his children's friends, he was a sport. When each dollar pinched, being a sport was just about the best thing you could be.

Mr. Weinberg was a sport. He was a bantam-sized tailor with a few wisps of hair on his pink scalp and a small face that had been warped in several places, with a nose leaning in one direction and a mouth tilted to the other. But he had a bountiful smile that declared his zest for living. My family would visit his apartment on the top floor of a ramshackle three-story wooden house on Gerard Avenue off 161st Street that, at certain times of the day, was literally in the shadow of Yankee Stadium. As we climbed the dim staircase, the stairs would buckle and the banister sway. We always knew when we reached Mr. Weinberg's floor by the fold-up bed and European trunk he stored in the third-floor hallway, so cramped was his apartment.

The times I remember most vividly in his tiny living room, over-whelmed by the few pieces of furniture, were the Passover seders. Both families gathered around the table, or actually a table joined with Mr. Weinberg's sewing machine console, so there would be room enough for everyone. Mr. Weinberg would pour the wine magnanimously, until it hovered balloonlike at the brim of each shot glass, and say a forceful blessing addressed personally to God as much as to the table. Mr. Weinberg really took charge of his seder, in a way that my father, who took his cues from my mother, did not. He directed us to wash our hands or take a bite of parsley or make a matzoh sandwich of horseradish and a paste made of wine-soaked chopped apples and wal-nuts. With an impish show of mischief, he would squirrel away the middle matzoh for the children to unearth with a great clamor later in the seder. And he coaxed everyone to sing, leading them by example. In that croaky voice of his, he sang from his depths, hauling up memories of Passover seders with his family in Poland, reimagining them for us in the confines of that Bronx apartment.

"*Chasal Sidoor Pesach Kehilchaso,*" he sang wearily toward the end of the Haggadah, his eyes shut tight with the exquisite intensity of recollection, his voice registering the right notes of plaintiveness and fatigue.

And I knew whereof he came. The way Mr. Weinberg closed his eyes and the quiver in his throat told me he came from some place down the road from my mother's home. I did not understand then that he was conjuring up a world that was no more. I knew his parents, like my mother's and father's parents, were dead, but I did not realize then that the Jewish ghettos and *shtetlach* in which he and my mother had grown up had also been snuffed out. Perhaps I did not realize this because that world was so vibrant in my mother and Mr. Weinberg, who I came to believe were messengers of a sort from that shattered world.

Every house we visited seemed to have the same smells of fatty chicken soup laced with dill and the same dim light. The three Herlings lived in a single room dominated by a double bed and their dining table, with a tiny archaic kitchenette on one wall. In that room their son, Simon, would drape a sheet over two chairs and the bedpost and he and my brother and I would sit underneath, three Indians in a tent, while our parents murmured in Yiddish at the table over their cups of tea and their pieces of sponge cake. Mr. Herling would examine my hair and tell my mother he could tell I was intelligent. I parted my hair on the right side rather than the left side, he pointed out. My mother beamed. She expected a barber to be an expert on such things.

On more than one visit, something would happen to make Mr. Herling remember his four-year-old daughter, who had perished in the war. He would tell us how he and his wife and their daughter were living with Mrs. Herling's mother. The Nazi tanks and trucks stormed into their town and, in stages, young men and women were deported to work camps. When their turn came to go, the Herlings thought their daughter could be safely left with Mrs. Herling's mother.

"She was such a beauty," Mr. Herling would say, his eyes moistening with tears. "She had blond hair and blue eyes and a pretty smile. You would have liked her, Mrs. Berger."

Mrs. Herling would lay her plump hand on her husband's arm and nudge him not to become too emotional, as if it were entirely his loss. I would stiffen in fright. I did not understand death. I had never seen it. I knew it was something incalculably convulsive. People seldom talked about it and when they did, it was like this, with an air of impending doom. Time seemed suspended in the Herlings' small room and almost anything seemed possible. But the quiet was sometimes broken by Simon, with some prank or stray remark that would anger Mr. Herling.

"Be quiet!" he would snap.

Simon seemed to bridle at signs of his parents' distraction from ongoing life, whatever the cause. For many of the refugees, the waves of melancholy over their lost ones distracted them from their living families, an added and enduring curse of the Holocaust. Their children, after all, demanded rapt attention like all children and may not have appreciated their parents' burdens.

Simon's birth in a concentration camp was a mystery to many in our circle because men and women were usually kept apart in adjoining camps. Moreover, any Jewish baby would have been a priority for extermination. I once asked Simon about this and he gave me a simple explanation. Mr. Herling was the camp barber. The German officers, appreciating his haircuts, permitted him first to visit his wife and later to keep his baby.

My father never spoke about what he had imagined had happened to his parents and brothers and sister, and my mother did only rarely. They could not say much because they did not know much, did not even know for sure in which extermination camps their kin were murdered. Yet my mother would let her feelings seep out in circuitous ways.

"I sometimes think of my father and what he suffered," she would say. "Not what he suffered in injuries from the Germans. But he loved his children. And to think of what he must have suffered just to know they were suffering."

I didn't want to think of my parents and their friends as sufferers. I wanted to see them as American Joes and Janes, and I would grasp at any sign of their normalness. That is probably why I cherish certain encounters between my parents and their friend Karol Strenger, screwball that he could be. Mr. Strenger would show up at our house several times a year unannounced. Months would go by and we wouldn't hear from him and then, while we were eating our Sunday breakfast, there would come a characteristic pounding at the door. The firm, hammerlike blows sounded like the Gestapo, but inevitably it was Mr. Strenger.

Tall, handsome, with curly black hair, broad shoulders, and the callused hands of a laborer, he would appear in his cracked brown leather motorcycle jacket, his young daughter, Tanya, in tow.

"Have you been a good boy, Joey?" he would say gruffly to me after I opened the door. His grin was big and toothy and had a vague air of menace.

Even if I said yes, I had been a good boy, he would take my arm, twist it behind my back in a hammerlock, and ask, "Are you sure?" tightening the lock with each answer I gave until I cried out in pain. My father would laugh along with this rough prank. Perhaps he thought such pranks were a rite of manly passage. Perhaps he did not want to embarrass Mr. Strenger by asking him to stop. Between cries and wishes that my father would rescue me, I giggled, and somehow I didn't really mind. I liked the attention, and even as a small boy, I understood that this was Mr. Strenger's grotesque way of showing affection. His next victim, after all, would be my brother, Josh.

After this flamboyant entrance, Mr. Strenger would get down on his haunches—the same peasant crouch my father used when polishing our shoes—and he would take off Tanya's lime-green snowsuit with an uncommon tenderness, as if he were slipping the packing off a fine figurine. That contrast of the gruff and the tender is one of the features that most stands out about this rough-hewn man.

Without waiting for an invitation, he made himself a place at the table, sitting half turned away as if he felt he were not quite welcome. He reached for a slice of rye bread, placed it flat on the palm of his left hand and slathered the butter on with his right, then speared a slice of herring out of a bowl of cream sauce and chewed it and the bread with great heartiness. My father would sit across from him chuckling with embarrassment at his complete disregard of even my parents' standards of etiquette.

What was one to make of Mr. Strenger, for so we called him? He was a survivor, though I doubt even my parents could spell out anything about his life before the war. When one friend has lived through the concentration camps, the details are memorable. When all the friends have, the details begin to mingle and blur. Mr. Strenger made his way to Palestine, met an American nurse and married her, and she brought him back with her to New York. They had a strained marriage and a chief cause was that the unskilled Mr. Strenger was unable to get a well-paying job, so Mrs. Strenger, with her nurse's salary, became the family's breadwinner. Mr. Strenger ended up spending his days taking care of Tanya, earning some money fixing the plumbing in the West Side rooming house they lived in, and sweeping the stoops of the other brownstones nearby. This rugged man spending his days as a baby-sitter was a paradox. In those preegalitarian years, only someone with his muscleman's build could have brought it off; a frailer man would have been scoffed at.

But what I most treasured about Mr. Strenger's visits were the times he and my father would leave my mother at home and take Tanya and us to Central Park. They were two regular guys out with the kids on a Sunday, just like a thousand other Manhattan fathers. One unforgettable time they meandered toward a clearing near Eighty-sixth Street that had a playground and two pieces of gym apparatus—a horizontal steel ladder and a horizontal steel bar.

"We had one of those in my school, Joey," my father said of the horizontal bar. So silent was he about his home life that this was the first time he had ever told me he had even been in school.

My father went over to the bar and dangled from it by his arms, then kicked his legs up and spun his body through his arms in a backward somersault. His feet and head almost glancing the ground, he hung there until his face reddened to crimson, then he spun his legs back through his arms until he was dangling upright once more. I watched with enchantment as he performed several more somersaults, backward and forward. I had never seen my father play before—just simply play. He never threw a baseball with us, never rode bicycles on weekends or kicked a soccer ball with friends. He was a man who worked for the necessity of it, deriving no pleasure and having no energy left over for pleasure. The impulse to express himself in any way, athletics included, had been, it seemed, extinguished by his brutal life. That day, I began to sense that there were reserves of agility and competence in my father that he was not revealing to us. An Olympian gymnast could not have delighted me more.

And my delight in that sunny Central Park meadow doubled when Mr. Strenger, taking off his leather jacket, took his turn on the horizontal bar and managed only a single clumsy somersault, his face reddening with exertion as he tried. He could not spin back to an upright position and collapsed on the ground. His muscular legs and body were too heavy. My father's thinness, which I had always been slightly ashamed of, proved a significant advantage. My father kidded Mr. Strenger, and Mr. Strenger gave him a playful punch in the arm. The sight of those two refugees, so carefree in that meadow on that spring day, gave the spot a lilt that it retains even when I walk in Central Park today.

Still, death and loss always kept rearing up at the most unexpected times, often the merriest ones.

I remember a birthday party in Motele Tropper's house about a year after we were in this country. Motele Tropper was a jeweler, a trade that left him a little better off than his friends, and he was able to afford a party for his one-year-old boy. The apartment in East New York in Brooklyn was full of people, more than I had ever seen at any of these refugee gatherings, and there was vodka and whisky, large helpings of corned beef, cole slaw, and herring, and a swirl of loud talk and laughter.

What lingers is leaving the building past midnight and stepping into the frosty air and coming across one of the guests, a large brawny man, sitting alone on the steps in the soft glow of a streetlamp. The man was very drunk and he howled and roared and shouted Yiddish curses I did not understand into the night and then abruptly cupped his hands over his eyes and began to sob. My parents and others tried to comfort him but he could not be consoled.

Who remembers now what was ailing him, but I can imagine what thoughts a simple birthday party, with its gathering of families and its outpouring of laughter and embraces, might have evoked in a refugee man who had no family to sustain him.

10

In her early years in this country, my mother was a restless and turbulent woman. Recalling her then, the sense I always get is of someone who had to rebuild the universe, but had only five days instead of the six God took for himself. She never rested, never stood still. She worked five days a week hunched over a machine that stitched fine straw hats, her right foot welded to the power pedal, her fingers deftly gliding around the treacherous, pummeling needle. On many nights, after she'd already spent the hours back home cooking and washing up, she could be glimpsed sitting stoop-necked on the edge of the sofa, moistening a tip of thread with her lips and straining with her tired, myopic eyes to slip the thread through the eye of the needle so she could restore a button on my or Josh's shirt.

She was always sprinting, like a long-distance runner who had stumbled and had to make up a hundred yards. All the survivors, most of them arriving in this country in their late twenties or early thirties, had to make up for lost time. The years that most people use to launch a career had been squandered in war and the limbo of the refugee camps. With no time for schooling or training, they had to take the low-skill, low-wage careers in dressmaking, upholstery, and shoe manufacturing, trails that American Jews had blazed a generation or two earlier. If they accumulated a small nest egg, they sometimes bought dusty candy stores and laundries, shabby tenements and dingy SRO hotels—damaged goods at fire-sale prices that Americans had too much dignity to touch.

With not much of a nest egg, no mercantile instincts, and a husband with a factory job, my mother saw her only chance for security in thrift and hard work. What's more, she had only one relative—her dead father's youngest brother, Yudel, who arrived in New York a few months before we did—and no experienced friends to guide her through the American maze. She had to make instinctive seat-of-the-pants judgments and so she sniffed the air for useful information. She tried to find her way through gleanings from the radio, and from my father's retellings of the Yiddish paper. But for her, every decision, every purchase, every commitment was redolent with consequence, and so filled with unbearable tension.

In the second grade, our class at Manhattan Day School was asked to put on a play to commemorate George Washington's birthday, a series of sketches about his life. The teacher, Mrs. Hansel, asked me to play young George in the legend of how he chopped down a cherry tree and confessed his crime to his father because he could not tell a lie. I was heady with excitement. My part was one of the livelier ones. I wanted to be sure to memorize my lines correctly. I also wanted to get the right costume. But what did George Washington look like? Where would my mother find the kind of outfit he would have worn? And how would she spare the money to buy it?

My mother was pleased that I was chosen for a starring role, but the thought of putting together a costume seemed to make her whole face quiver. It was yet one more thing in this country she had no idea how to do, and would surely be another encumbrance in her consuming days.

"What kind of costume?" she asked brusquely.

"A costume of Washington," I said.

"The one who was president?"

"Yes," I said. "He was a general. He led the American soldiers in the Revolutionary War."

"You want me to get a general's outfit? How am I going to make you look like a general? What does your teacher want from me?"

She went to the closet and scanned the clothes. Nothing was right, of course. There would have to be an expense and I could see that worried her. But she was also eager to come through for me. She took me to a dingy, narrow old-clothing shop on 104th Street near Columbus Avenue, where people were pawing at cartons of worn shirts and pants like bears going through garbage. Wedging her way to the front, she found a pipe rack of men's suits where she spotted a set of GI khakis left there, no doubt, by a veteran who had returned to Manhattan after the war. The uniform was half again as big as I was—the belt loops of the pants reached almost to my chest and the sleeves of the shirt ballooned against my arms—but it cost seventy-five cents and it would make do for an army general like Washington.

That night, after dinner, she sheared the strong seams of the pants with a razor blade and snipped away at the khaki cloth of the shirt, calling me in every few minutes to size up the swatches against my body. Hunched over her black-and-gold Singer sewing machine, she stitched the pieces into a pint-sized GI uniform fit for a midget soldier.

I tried it on and checked myself out in the mirror and, boy, was I in heaven. With my khaki shirt, khaki pants, and the brown shoes that my father had spit-polished for me, I was one smart-looking soldier. I could not wait to have my classmates and teacher see me, was sure they would recognize the costume's professional quality and be impressed. When he came home that night, my father took one look at his natty, uniformed son and roared with delight. He also suggested a fillip. He bounded up the stairs to an apartment on the fourth floor where Junior, our genial teenage Puerto Rican neighbor, had just returned from another tour at Fort Dix. He came back with Junior's black-brimmed parade hat, slipped it over my forehead, then showed me how to tilt it back on my head so it would stay put.

When I arrived at school in my military guise, Mrs. Hansel looked puzzled. I could see this was clearly not what she had in mind for young Washington, and my heart sank. My mother and I had done something inappropriate. Our refugee ignorance and clumsiness were showing again. But soon an affectionate smile crossed her face, embellished by what must have been a conspiratorial gleam in her eye. I say conspiratorial because she came up with her own clever flourish on young George as an ersatz general. She suggested that when I declare to the audience that I cannot tell a lie, I should accent the words with a crisp salute.

And so I played George Washington chopping down a papier-mâché cherry tree in a GI uniform. This was my immigrant mother's creation. My only regret was that my mother was working and could not see my performance. I wish she had because, when I gave that salute, I brought down the house.

From the time I was a small boy, I was charmed by maps. My guess is that having been tugged halfway across the world before the age of reason, I wanted to put my journey in some sort of frame, even wrap it in glory. Warsaw and Otwock, Berlin, Bremenhaven, and Landsberg, the Atlantic Ocean, and the Bug River were not mythical places for me. I had sailed the Atlantic through a storm. The Soviets choked off our DP camp in Berlin. My mother had clandestinely crossed the Bug at dawn. My parents' stories filled the places where they had been with romance, adventure, and the sticky glue of family love. Just to see Otwock on a map confirmed that this was not a place that my mother made up but a real town a few miles outside Warsaw, at a given point of latitude and longitude, with a population that had been calculated by a census. When my mother said she had to take a long trip by railroad and horsecart to spend the summer at her grandmother's home in Parysow, the map confirmed how long a journey this must have been, what rivers and other landscape she had to traverse.

My appetite for geography grew swiftly. I was enchanted that every country had a capital, the pulsing seat, as I saw it, of authority and decisions, its energy and dazzle highlighted on the map by a circled star. I soon memorized every capital. If you told me Afghanistan I would say Kabul. Ceylon was Colombo; New Zealand, Wellington. I liked knowing that the Caspian Sea was the world's largest lake, the Nile its longest river, Greenland its largest island. A map imposed a despotic order, one frozen in time and space, on a world that to me seemed mercurial and evanescent. Daily life could swirl chaotically, but in my explorer's world, every country had defined boundaries and a capital and a ranking in land size and population that I could lock in permanently with the simple act of memorization.

But I had only the sketchy maps of the tattered third-grade social studies book. So I asked my mother for a genuine atlas. To my surprise, she did not recoil. I remember her taking me down by subway to gritty Fourth Avenue just below Union Square and the bargain-bin emporium of S. Klein's, with its humble trademark of a measuring square. In those years, a center for used books was flourishing along Fourth Avenue. There were more than a half-dozen shops, with lopsided aisles of dark-stained wooden shelves crammed with moldering, fraying books. The shop ceilings were tall and tin-coated, and between the bookcases there was a diffusion of floating dust splintered here and there by the light that struggled through from the sidewalk windows.

In the shop we entered, the paunchy bookseller seemed to have yellowed like his books, his faded flannel shirt embedded with the fine residue of thousands of moldered pages. When we told him what we were after, he recommended a 1949 *Hammond's*. It had a solid red cover and was so tall and broad that when I held it to me, its top edge covered my face. It had large, colorful maps of what seemed to me every significant country. It had lists of the tallest mountains, the longest rivers, and the largest lakes.

All in all, this was what I had dreamed of, and the price—three dollars—did not unhinge my mother. Indeed, I sensed for a moment that she was tickled by this half-pint child who knew that Kabul was the capital of Afghanistan and Colombo of Ceylon. It was another confirmation that her father's Golant intelligence was being handed on, that even with the anarchy that had shattered her life, something of value was seeping down to her children. She handed the money over and the atlas was mine to keep.

I still have a distinct memory of being led by my mother across the traffic of Fourth Avenue—she was probably heading to Klein's to see if there was a slip worth plucking out of the clamorous, jostling discount bins—and feeling a lilt in my step as I hugged the atlas to my chest. I had made something that was important to me happen. I had gotten my mother to journey down to Fourth Avenue to buy me something I wanted. This was a new and intoxicating power.

*   *   *

We could not afford summer camp, but my mother found a way to do even that for me. She learned from someone that there was a summer camp in Rockland County called Loeb Home, a charitable institution that took in Christian and Jewish children convalescing from injuries or diseases like polio and offered them less rough-and-tumble programs than standard camps. With animal alertness, my mother made her way down to the organization's Midtown Manhattan office and informed an official there that I was recovering from tuberculosis.

It was not completely a lie. As an infant, I must have briefly been visited by the tubercle bacillus, probably while I was stricken with pneumonia. Whenever it happened, I proved forever positive on the skin tests for tuberculosis. I'm sure the knowledge that I had a run-in with tuberculosis must have been a terrifying experience for my mother, given how the disease had ravaged her family. Still, by the time I was seven there were certainly no lingering effects from the disease. Yet my mother easily persuaded the charity official that I could use a convalescence and he signed me up for a free three-week stay.

Did I protest as modern American children might have had they been sent off to an unfamiliar, forbidding destination? No. My life had been one unfamiliar journey after another and, given the urgency of so many of our decisions, it never occurred to me that I could draw a line. So on a warm July evening, after a meandering trip through what seemed like an unrelenting wilderness, a bus dropped me and my valise off in front of a cluster of squat brick buildings in the middle of the woods. The valise, the same one that had carried my family's possessions over from Germany, was almost as big as I was. (It was never a *suitcase*, always a *valise*, probably because the Yiddish word is also *valise*.) It had grown paunchy with the changes of clothes my mother had given me to protect me through not just a torrid summer but, it seemed, a bitter winter as well. An orderly hauled it for me into one of the buildings and up the stairs and dropped me and the valise off in a long room that looked like a hospital ward. Six beds were arrayed on one side of the room and six on the other. The children who filled those beds appeared, from the lively chatter, to be quite familiar with one another. I was the immigrant once more, and the children fixed their gaze on me.

At the head of this room behind a broad desk sat a beefy nurse with stiff, silver hair and a ruddy complexion. She hoisted the suitcase onto her desk as if it were no heavier than a dictionary, clicked open the latches, and rummaged through it, inspecting it, no doubt, for contraband. She turned to me with a pitiless glare.

"You have enough clothes here for four children," she said, with bone-dry irony. "Were you planning to stay for a year?"

The room exploded in laughter. I stood there and said nothing, feeling awkward and very alone. My parents had done something inept again and I was the victim. The nurse carried my valise over to my bed while I passed the gauntlet of scoffers. I pulled out a pair of pajamas and undressed, sure that the boys were scrutinizing every article of clothing, laughing at my ungainly body as well. I lay in bed trying to stop myself from crying. But my chest and throat kept tightening and heaving, and I muffled my sobs in the blanket.

I was in alien territory again, this time without my parents. So I kept my counsel and followed directions. In camp, that was enough to get you by. Every moment was plotted and I was able to make myself feel somewhat at home, even feel part of the group, just by going along. I initiated no conversations, made no particular friends, and wasn't even aware that I should. Besides, whatever my refugee peculiarities, I was not such a freak here. There were boys and girls on crutches, in wheelchairs, without hair. Not knowing what a convalescent home was, I must have thought these campers were a cross-section of America's children.

I played baseball. I splashed in the pool. I was inducted into the mysteries of lanyard making. I observed. Somehow, I ended up one Sunday morning attending worship in a spare blond-wood chapel and found myself gazing up at the forbidden image of Jesus. In yeshiva, we were not even permitted to utter the name of this gaunt figure with the drawn, plaintive face. He was "J.C." or "Jiminy Cricket" and there was sometimes a note of mockery in the utterance. Had it not been for such derision, I might have felt comfortable with Christ's image. After all, he had the hollow face of a refugee; my parents' friends' had faces like his. Instead, as a Jewish boy, there was for me something ominous about being in the chapel, as if I might be struck dead for lingering in

Christ's presence. I sat through the hymns, holding the prayer book to my chest, imitating the reverent looks of the children around me, but praying only for the service to be over.

It did not occur to me that I could protest to someone that I was not Christian. Surely the American authorities would not have made a mistake. There must have been some purpose in my assignment here. Besides, if I told a counselor, he might have scolded me for alerting him so late. I may also have thought no one else in the camp was Jewish. There were certainly no yarmulke wearers, and revealing you were Jewish, I had been tacitly taught, was not something you did casually. By the second Saturday, though, I learned that a few of the boys in our group would be breaking away after breakfast to attend a Jewish service. I realized that I must have misunderstood the first announcements of chapel services. But I summoned the courage to let someone know and they changed my schedule so that I did not attend Christian chapel again.

The second Sunday was visitors' day. A sleek bus rolled up on the sunny lawn that afternoon, its doors wheezed open, and out streamed the parents, my mother among them. She had not written me to say she was coming, so this was a surprise. She was wearing a light summer dress and she had put on fresh red lipstick. She looked, to my camp-famished soul, simply beautiful.

I took her by the hand and showed her around the grounds, showed her the buildings and the ball fields, showed her my room and even the chapel. A reservoir of stories and observations poured out of my heart. It was as if I had not spoken for weeks, and maybe I hadn't. Somehow, all the places and things that had caused me such misery seemed precious now because I could tell her about them. I did not weigh her down with misfortunes. I never did, and perhaps I did not admit them even to myself. I looked happy, and that made her happy. She told me that my father and brother couldn't come, but they both missed me terribly.

As we walked about, we crossed paths several times with the father of one of my bunkmates. He was paying close attention to her and I could tell by my mother's girlish laughs that she seemed to enjoy that attention. I was not jealous for my father's sake. I was pleased that an

American man was interested in her. It increased her stature in my eyes. I found myself talking with the man's son, whom I had never approached before. Soon, the man offered to take our photograph. We stood smiling in front of a thicket of bushes, my mother's hand resting on my shoulder, which at that point reached up to her waist. She breathed in deeply and, inevitably, compared the air of Rockland County with that of Otwock. The man snapped our picture and asked my mother for our address so he could send us the photograph.

We had gotten attention from a genuine-article American, and that gave me a little more confidence for the rest of my stay at Loeb Home, as if I had passed some threshold test. The camp lasted only one more week and I remember it as rather pleasant. I even got to attend the Jewish service, though it was not as memorable as the Christian one. With my repacked valise, I came home in fine spirits and my mother was convinced that camp was a place in which I thrived. She promised that next year she would send both my brother and me for a full summer.

Like most private schools, Manhattan Day School functioned on several planes, not all of them visible. On the surface, status within the school was determined rather impartially by how well a student performed in Hebrew and English studies. But in more subterranean and powerful ways, status hinged on a family's wealth and position. I might get A's in all my subjects while Joyce, whose parents' gifts subsidized scholarship students like me, might get B's. But when her mother visited she was treated like royalty and mine never seemed to garner more attention than a nanny might get, or so my newcomer's touchy bundle of sensitivities kept telling me.

Even if they could not articulate it, most of the students sensed this hierarchy, came to understand that there were layers of meaning and motive beneath the current of daily events.

One Rosetta stone that revealed the true gradations of status was the yearbook—not so much the articles but the advertisements printed at the back. There would be full-page ads, costing $100 when that was a considerable sum, by families like the Sterns honoring "Joyce and her classmates." Dickie Hochstein's family would place a full-page ad with a picture of a relaxed Bing Crosby smoking a pipe made by their company. The idea of my father getting Bing Crosby to do an advertisement for his ironing board cover company would have been too implausible even for a fairy tale. My father didn't even know who Bing Crosby was. Yonah Baranek, the owner of the chicken farm in Lakewood, was the kind of person he fraternized with.

Another tip-off was the deference that certain parents could command. Jonathan Green's mother, in coiffed hair and a silken cream blouse, could sail into class one day and take up an hour showing us slides of her trip to Egypt. There she was, standing poised and confident in front of Luxor or Abu Simbel or the Pyramids, the very ones we were reading about in our Hebrew classes on Exodus. It was not just her trip to Egypt that felt so beyond my reach, a voyage, after all, that was taken not for some crucial purpose, like visiting an ailing brother, but just for the fun of it. No, it was the fawning respect our teacher showed Mrs. Green, as if she were a statesman who had just come back from securing the Vatican's recognition of Israel. The teacher, I was certain, would never show my mother that kind of respect. I could only imagine how sturdy life must be with a mother like Mrs. Green. Yet I had to make do with my mother, and so I had to work hard to get her to come across so that no one would ever know that Luxor and Abu Simbel were places she had never even heard about.

In second grade, my Hebrew teacher was Mrs. Emma Gordon, a chipper but steel-willed, elf-sized woman with piercing blue eyes and a cauliflowerlike head of graying curls. Every Friday, just before lunch, she staged a Shabbos dinner so we could better understand the rituals of Sabbath, taste its sacred blend of cheer and peace. The low wooden tables we used for arts and crafts were joined together and covered with broad sheets of white pulp paper—our tablecloths—and students took turns chanting blessings over the candles, wine, and challah. The wine was grape juice, the challah Tam Tam crackers, but it was still a transforming moment at the end of our week, letting us know, as the eve of Shabbos itself was meant to do, that the week's cycle of toil was drawing to a close.

To lend these proceedings a maternal hand, a different mother was invited in every Friday to bring in the provisions. Inevitably, I knew, it would one Friday be my mother's turn. That was a prospect I dreaded.

She worked on Fridays. Would she be able to spare the day to come to school? Would she find my asking her to do so one more annoying pressure in her taut week? Would she know to bring the right foods? And what would my classmates make of my refugee mother with her mangled, Yiddish-accented English and her timorous disposition? Sure, she was a firebrand with family and friends, sometimes to the point of tactlessness, but I had seen that in crowds of more imposing people, she could linger at the margins and grow uncommonly bashful.

When I informed her some weeks ahead of time that it was her turn, she seemed to sulk. Looking back, I can imagine how hard it must have been for her to contemplate asking her boss for the day off, to weigh the possibility of forfeiting the extra pay she received for piecework.

"Tell your teacher your mother works and cannot come in," she said firmly. "I'll buy the food but you will have to bring it in yourself."

I was not going to let her get away with that. I was not going to be embarrassed in front of my class. I would pluck her guilt strings, since my mother was as vulnerable to the pressures of conformity as I was.

"But all the other kids' mothers came in for Shabbos," I whined. "They brought the grape juice and crackers themselves."

A few days before the Shabbos rite we snaked through the aisles of a supermarket on Columbus Avenue. I pointed out the kosher brand of grape juice that I had seen other mothers bring in and I located the Tam Tams. I could see her trying to calculate how many bottles of juice and boxes of Tam Tams to buy so that there would be enough for all but not so much that she would fritter her money away. As always, at the checkout she scrupulously monitored the cash register to make sure we were not overcharged. The expense had in fact been a burden, I could tell—almost a third of my ten-dollars-a-month tuition.

When the fated Friday came around I was still in suspense. As my mother rushed off to work, she told me she would try to show up, but added ominously that I should take the bag of Sabbath provisions with me in case she didn't.

In school, I handed Mrs. Gordon the bag of grape juice and crackers and spent the morning, lunch period, and the early afternoon in a state of agitation, fearing that my mother would not come and, at the same time, fearing just as much that she would. As Mrs. Gordon imparted her lesson—it might have been about Noah's beholding the rainbow after the flood—students' arms kept springing up to answer her questions and children pleaded and groaned to get her to call on them. I was usually one of the champion pleaders and groaners, but on this day I was distracted and slow to respond.

The hour for our Sabbath rite was drawing closer.

Then, I heard the door inch open and there, in the widening space, was my mother's shyly smiling face. She was wearing her most elegant clothes, a blue cloth coat, high heels, and, in the fashion of the day, diaphanous white gloves. She looked better than I had ever seen her, even radiant. Struggling to be unobtrusive, she slipped around the side of the room to find a seat in the back. I smiled quietly to myself. Out of the corner of my eye, I checked my neighbors to see if they were aware that this was my mother. I guess I had wanted her to show up more than I wanted her to stay away.

"Class, this is Mrs. Berger," Mrs. Gordon said genially. "Please welcome her."

"Shalom, Mrs. Berger," we responded in unison.

Though Mrs. Gordon had done pretty much the same with every child's mother, I could never have imagined that this big a fuss would be made over my mother. In my mind, she wasn't prominent enough for such a fuss. But Mrs. Gordon was not only a lucid teacher but, to her core, a decent and gracious woman who was not a pushover for any hierarchies the school administration maintained.

My mother sat patiently to the side gazing on as Mrs. Gordon brought her lesson to its finale. My arm shot up to answer Mrs. Gordon's every question, and when she called on me and I got the answer right, I turned a sidelong glance to make sure my mother had noticed. Then, Mrs. Gordon had us put away our books and marshaled several students to cover the tables with the paper cloth. On her own, my mother rose and began pouring out cups of juice and laying out paper plates of crackers. I could not understand how she had learned to do these things right, without my telling her, but sure enough she had. Still, with my classmates surrounding me, I did not quite acknowledge that she was there, as if she were someone else's mother.

Mrs. Gordon gathered us around the table. Ilana Langer said the blessings over the candles, closing her eyes and circling her hands in front of her face, though not with the mystery of anguish and rebirth that my mother brought to this incantation every Friday night. Then Mrs. Gordon picked me, as I knew she would, to say the *Kiddush,* the extended Sabbath blessing over the wine. I stood at the head of the table, chanting the words almost flawlessly, looking up every once in a while to glimpse both Mrs. Gordon and my mother smiling with pleasure. Dickie Hochstein made the blessing over the Tam Tam crackers and we launched into a round of a half-dozen Sabbath songs. By this time, I had relaxed enough to sing as exuberantly as my classmates, most of whom were simply glad that their Hebrew studies were finished for the week.

As the class broke up, Milton Moses came over and whispered to me, "Hey, Joe, you have a pretty mother!"

I blushed because while I did think my mother was pretty, I never suspected anyone else thought so. Still, I knew my mother had passed some test that I had set, had not only shown up but shown up splendidly. I did not even cringe when, as she left, she stroked my hair and said, "Joey, you did beautifully. The teacher likes you. She told me you're a wonderful student."

I wished I had told her then, "You did beautifully too, Mommy." But in the self-absorbed way of all children, I did not. She could have used that praise too.

11

Right away I felt that nobody there wants me," my mother tells me. I am in her kitchen with my reporter's notebook, and my gray-haired mother is continuing her reminiscences of her childhood, although that childhood ended at fourteen when her father sent her off to live with her aunt Sarah in Warsaw and make her way on her own.

"At home my stepmother didn't want me. And here my aunt Sarah didn't want me. She had a maid, Bayla, a Jewish girl from her home-town in Mordy. That first night she put me into bed with the maid. We slept one next to the other in a narrow bed. I cried all night. I didn't even know why. The next morning, my aunt Sarah was making break-fast for her daughter, Rachelke. My aunt went over to Rachelke and said, 'What kind of eggs do you want, fried or sunny-side up?' I was very hungry and in my home we had an egg maybe twice a year. So I waited for the eggs eagerly. But then she came over to the maid, took a loaf of bread and cut off two slices for her just like my stepmother used to do, and then she cut off two slices for me. She treated me the same as she treated the maid."

"No eggs," I say.

"Eggs? Forget about it. Joey, I have to tell you things, you're going to think I'm crazy. I had a life, a few lives, believe me."

Her aunt Sarah operated a small hat-knitting business right in her apartment. In one large room, girls who had come to Warsaw from the provinces sat around a long table fashioning knitted hats, gossiping, and singing merrily as they coiled and jabbed the needles. My mother tells me how she envied their self-reliance, while she felt herself to be a dependent burden. Those feelings intensified as she began fumbling every assignment her aunt gave her. Her aunt asked her to deliver a box of hat samples to a merchant and my mother lost her way in Warsaw's busy streets and secluded courtyards and never found the store. Her aunt tried to teach her to knit but she seemed unable to grasp the simplest technique.

"This is so unlike you, Ma," I say. "You always told me how quickly you learn such things."

"I was under stress," my mother replies. "Because I felt I wasn't wanted. That's when a child is in trouble. So I couldn't learn. To learn you have to feel wanted. Every day something didn't please my aunt and she screwed up her face in unhappiness. On Friday her husband arrived from a business trip. I think he was in wholesale fruits. So she started telling him all the troubles she's got with me. I listened through the wall. So what do you think I did. I went outside and bought a newspaper and looked for a job and I found a job. As a grocery clerk. The store even had a small bed that I could sleep on at night.

"My aunt and my uncle made a big *tsimmes* [fuss] when they heard I had a job. 'Did you hear, my husband, what Rochele accomplished today?' my aunt said to my uncle in a phony way. 'Imagine, just being one week in this city, and all on her own, without telling anybody, she bought a newspaper and found a job.' 'Well, I'm not surprised,' my uncle said. 'I knew all along she was a smart girl.' I sensed that he too, like my stepmother and aunt, was encouraging me to leave. It would be one less mouth for him to feed."

In recalculating the slights and neglects she suffered, she is no longer looking through the sentimental lens we use for those who have died in tragic fashion. She is registering the credits and debits more stringently.

"That first job lasted a month. But I had to leave after a few days. The *balbues* [the boss] was having a love affair with a girl who worked in that store. He got into such a fight with his wife that I got frightened and looked for another job. I lived from day to day not knowing where

I would sleep. I stayed at first with some relatives, but they were poor and had no place for me for very long. One time I knocked on the door of a man I didn't even know. He was a relative of my stepmother. He lived alone. That's how desperate I was. He gave me a suspicious look, but let me in. I slept there for two or three nights, then he told me that the superintendent did not let strangers stay overnight. Joey, I had no more self-respect. And I lost more each time I went begging for a place to sleep. One night I went to the Central Station of Warsaw—just like the homeless people today are sleeping in Grand Central Station. There were people waiting to travel all over Europe and I found a seat and spent the night sleeping off and on. Could you believe this about your mother?

"The one time I remember very clearly was finding a place to sleep with a woman, Noma, that my family knew, and her son, Motche. I wrote a story about it."

    ❧ Noma was the wife of my stepmother's brother. She had three sons and was as poor as a mouse. Cynics used to say that her husband managed to provide her with a third son just before he died of tuberculosis. The middle son was Mordechai, but everyone called him Motche, and that nickname better suited his impaired speech and his insignificance in the neighborhood. He stuttered severely and the words that came out were further hampered by a lisp from a protruding upper lip. When he finally stammered a word, he said it twice, as if to make sure his listener got it right. I had known him in Otwock when Noma would come and live near us so her baby Yankele, a frail child, could breathe fresher air. In Otwock, Motche was preyed on by the smaller children and made the victim of grown-up jests.

"How old are you, Motche?" people used to ask him, just for a laugh.

"Th-th-th-then. Th-then," he would answer, pleased that someone had paid him some attention.

Nobody cared where he went, not even his mother. He would often disappear for an entire day, roaming the streets and villas of

Otwock like a stray dog. He always found his way home and sometimes looked for me and gave me an apple or a pear, which he mag-
ically pulled from his torn pocket.

"Where did you get it, Motche?" I asked.

"I th-th-th-thook it, th-thook it," he replied.

"Where from?"

"The, the, the thores, the thores."

He gazed at me with large, tender eyes that craved my appreciation. I knew that he swiped fruits and candies from merchants. But
I was a kid too and, except for sharing his stolen apples, I didn't
bother about him enough to warn him not to steal.

When I arrived at number 63 Smocza Street looking for a place
to spend the night, I had to step down seven steps to an alley that
led to the backyard, and there a rear door led to Noma's one-room
basement apartment. I entered and saw Noma looking out the overhead window that was level with the sidewalk. Her face was as gray
as the damp walls surrounding her. As we talked, I learned that like
me, Motche, at fourteen, was already working a variety of odd jobs
to help out.

Motche soon appeared and it was apparent that he had acquired
the features of a young man, though he still bore his familiar downtrodden look. His speech had improved slightly. While he stuttered,
he no longer repeated each word. As Noma and I discussed where I
might sleep, he stood there with his hands in his pockets. Noma and
her children slept on fold-up cots and rows of chairs they put
together every night. There would not be room for me. But Noma
had an inspiration. One of Motche's jobs required him to sleep for a
few nights a week at a certain couple's apartment to keep it safe
from prowlers while they traveled on business. It had two comfortable beds.

After we ate a supper of potato soup, Motche and I left for the
apartment. The beds were indeed large and soft, but they were right
next to each other. Motche, understanding that I had to undress,
turned the other way, pretending to look at a book on a shelf. I got
in bed quickly, pulled the blanket over me, and fell asleep immediately.

It was no dream when I found myself in Motche's arms in the middle of the night. He pressed his chest against mine, delicately yet ardently. There was so much gentleness in his embrace. I wasn't afraid of Motche. His tender affection soothed away the struggle of my day and kindled some hope that I might survive Warsaw. ∿

"Ma, did your father know where you were, where you were spending your nights?"

"Oh, Joey," she replies, as if I asked a foolish question. "Who had a telephone? We didn't have electric lights even. Besides, they weren't so scared about what would happen to children the way we are today. You didn't hear of murders or kidnappings. They didn't molest children."

"But you were only fourteen years old, after all. Did he not want to know how you were surviving? Couldn't he write?"

"He didn't," she finally admits. "He didn't know where I was."

This is not a thought she wants to dwell on. She shifts the story and turns the focus on the second important male figure in her life, her half brother Simcha. Simcha was her mother's son by a previous marriage, and my mother had already told me of seeing Simcha at their mother's funeral when she was almost six and he was roughly fifteen. At seventeen or eighteen, he contracted tuberculosis and began hemorrhaging blood and so came to the Marpe sanitarium in Otwock for a temporary cure. My mother sneaked into the sanitarium and when she saw how ill he looked, she began crying. But he insisted on remaining cheerful. He reached into a drawer and pulled out two hard-boiled eggs wrapped in a napkin.

"I have no appetite, so enjoy them," he said. "Next time I'll save you something else."

As she tells me the story, my mother has tears in her eyes.

"He gave me a lot of love, a lot of love," she says. "When I was a little girl, he made a little money and he had a bicycle and he took me on the frame of the bicycle and he went around to people he knew and he showed me off. He would say, 'This is my sister,' and people would say, 'What a pretty girl!' I didn't care whether I was pretty or not. If you don't have enough to eat, what do you care if you're pretty or not. I didn't take care of myself. I didn't even look in the mirror."

By the time she was fourteen and working in Warsaw, Simcha was back in the Marpe sanitarium undergoing another cure. On my mother's first visit back to Otwock after leaving home, she visited him there, a visit she recorded in her composition book.

 Each patient had a round sputum pan on the floor next to his white metal bed and another on the night table and had to report any blood he saw in the sputum. The unremitting coughing and spitting made the room sound like a wood choppers' camp. When I walked in, his eyes opened wide and his smile was full of love. I wanted to hug him and pour out all that I had suffered in Warsaw. But I was afraid to draw very close.

"I could not find any more jobs in Warsaw," I confided with shame.

He looked at me with a tender smile, the smile of someone who understood the impossibility of being fourteen and on your own in Warsaw.

"Don't worry, Rochele," he said. "As soon as I get out of here I will find you a job."

He did not get out of the sanitarium that quickly, but on someone's recommendation I found a job in Otwock as a companion to the wife of the grand rabbi of the Ger Hasidim, a widely esteemed sage who was known as Sfas Emes [Language of Truth]. He would come to Otwock to spend the summer and was joined there by his followers. His wife, the *rebbetzin,* was in her late sixties and in delicate health and needed help with dressing and other personal tasks. I lived with them at their boardinghouse, the Pensionat Zolberga, and the three meals were so ample I found myself gaining weight.

On the weekend, the prosperous Hasidim in their shiny silk caftans streamed into Otwock to join their young wives and observe the Sabbath with their rebbe. On Friday night and after synagogue Saturday morning, the Hasidim sat in the pension's large dining room, the men in one section, the women and children in another, while eager waiters rushed about, fetching meals and clearing plates. In between courses, the men sang *zmires* that conveyed their joy in Sabbath and their deep love for the Maker of the Universe. As they sang or hummed along, their cheeks flushed crimson and their eyes glinted with mischief or sometimes with a plaintive sadness. Some of the young men, a few quite good-looking, threw shy glances my way, which I occasionally acknowledged with a smile.

The Hasidim complimented me on my chores for the *rebbetzin*. But Simcha, when he got better, talked me into leaving.

"This work is not for you," he said. "You're too intelligent. You won't get any further in the Hasidic world than baby-sitting."

I sensed that his objections were motivated by his own discomfort with Orthodox Judaism. But I was persuaded to quit and join him in Warsaw. My brother had already tried and failed at several kinds of business ventures, but by the time I returned to Warsaw, he was buying seconds—slightly damaged goods—from Bech and from Brown and Rowinski, Warsaw's two prominent manufacturers of women's lingerie, then selling them to peddlers and retail stores. He was anxious about how long he could continue to earn a living. Aggravation would make him spit blood and when things didn't work out, he got aggravated. He knew that his troubles weighed on me so he tried always to greet me with a cheerful face. Tall and dark with deep-set blue eyes, he would smile and call me "Ruchaye."

Although his health forced him to live most of the year in Otwock, he kept a tidy apartment in Warsaw for his two days a week of business dealings and he told me I could eat and sleep there until I found a job. In Simcha's apartment, I found some old rolls and jam in a cupboard and ate them while I read through the daily newspaper ads. A shop that sold chandeliers was seeking a saleswoman. The shop was on one of Warsaw's most fashionable streets and was itself quite elegant, with sumptuous creations of brass and crystal dangling from the ceiling. The owner asked me to start the next day. I sensed I was about to take a step up in the world, moving from a worker toiling in grimy back shops to the representative of a gracious showroom. But by daybreak I had convinced myself that I had neither the clothes nor the self-confidence to work in so refined an atmosphere. I never showed up for the job.

Ashamed at my own lack of self-respect, I did not tell my brother about how I had thrown away a promising opportunity. When he came home that evening. I was simply happy that we had each other and I tried to put my setback behind me. My brother was hungry and sent me down to a delicatessen on Krolewska Street to buy a half kilo of cold cuts and six rolls. We made sandwiches and ate them with hot tea. It seemed like one of the most delicious meals I had ever eaten. ∾

"Even today I still think why didn't I take that job," she tells me as I look up from the composition book. "I probably didn't think I'm good enough to get a job like that. I didn't have a home. And a job like that, I had to come dressed up nice. You had to be outspoken, self-assured, and I knew I didn't have that. Today I can talk to the president of the United States and feel I am on the same level. But when I was a girl, I was different. I didn't have the guts to take such an attractive job."

She looks at me, knowing she is talking about fundamental character, knowing I might be ashamed of having so self-deprecating a mother, and she says tenderly, "I'm sorry to upset you."

She goes on with the story of her teenage years, when her life seemed a succession of rough jobs and transient beds. One of the better jobs she had was delivering dresses for a high-fashion salon, and she enjoyed walking the streets of Warsaw and bringing dresses to actresses and senators' wives, and somehow feeling part of their world. She spent weekends roaming Warsaw's streets and avenues, gazing in shop windows and imagining new possibilities for her life. In the evenings, she often went to the movies and seemed spellbound by the elegance of Fred Astaire and Ginger Rogers, by Sonja Henie's grace on ice, and by the waltzing couples in a film about the life of Johann Strauss. Such films opened up a world of charm and graciousness she had never known in the provinciality of Otwock. With encouragement from her brother, she joined a choir, Orpheush, that performed in Nowosci Theater, the best theater in Warsaw for Yiddish plays.

∾ Members of the choir became my first genuine friends in Warsaw. I began to feel that life was finally bestowing some of its favors on me. I even felt bold enough to take a week's vacation, and in the peak of summer visited my family in Otwock. I put on a fetching blue-flowered dress that the fashion salon's owner, Helena, had given me as a gift and a pair of white sandals that I bought in a store on Marszalkowska Street and I caught the train to Otwock. As I stood leaning against the door of the bouncing railroad car, a young man kept gazing at me and when our eyes met he smiled and I smiled back. For the first time in many years, I was feeling good about how I looked and how I dressed, and I appreciated the young man's attention.

When I reached my home, my father looked me over and seemed to light up with pride at what had become of the daughter he sent out into the world at the age of fourteen. I gave my stepmother, Bluma, a hand-knitted blue beret and I gave my father thirty zlotys that I had saved up during the months of work. My greatest pleasure was seeing the three children when they arrived from a day camp. Esther was now eleven, with dark, inquisitive eyes. Chana, taller and more slender than when I last saw her, looked as angelic as ever. Shimele, who was entering first grade, was stubbornly masculine and would not even let me kiss him. He was the first one to notice the box of chocolate candies I had brought and he ate them hungrily. To show off, he climbed the tall cherry tree outside the house as swiftly as a red squirrel and shook down a drizzle of cherries, but he would not share them with me or his sisters, only with his friend Moishele. I laughed at his antics as I sat on the veranda with my two sisters, who were studying me with intense curiosity, admiring my dress and sandals and pocketbook.

On the Friday morning after I arrived, my father woke me violently and made me rush in my bewilderment down the rear steps and out of the house. The building was on fire. A kerosene lamp had exploded in the home of the dentist who owned the building and lived in the apartment below. Luckily, my father and Bluma had returned from their Friday-morning visit to the market in time to rouse the children. As I stood outside in my nightgown staring at the flames devouring our home, I glimpsed my father, his face in despair. In a lifetime of barely managing to scrape by, this fire was an affliction he did not need. Almost nothing survived, and my family's apartment was now unlivable.

I realized I would have to work harder to help get my father's family on its feet again. But soon after I returned to Warsaw, Helena revealed she was closing the fashion salon. She had been listening to Hitler barking his threats on the radio and was becoming increasingly anxious about plans to expel that country's Jews and the contagious spread of anti-Semitism throughout Poland. She decided to emigrate to Palestine. For her these distant events had historical momentousness; for me they meant the end of my glamorous career.

I had to swiftly find another job and knew I could not be choosy. My family could not live into winter in the remains of the dentist's spare room. So I took a job in a workshop that made slippers, colorfully embroidered ones known as Zakopane after the Polish ski resort that originated them. I easily learned the craft and soon started making more money than many of the other young men and women I knew in Warsaw.

The years 1938 and 1939 were some of the best years of my life. The owners of the slipper workshop were kind. The wife opened her heart to me on many occasions. The husband, who was almost stone deaf, greeted me every day with a hearty "Good morning." They treated me as one of their children, feeding me, advising me, praising me. I found a room to share with two pleasant girls. There was an indoor toilet though no bathtub. In order to wash, we stood in front of a basin and undressed down to our waist and washed our upper body, then we covered our chests and washed the areas below.

I read Tolstoy's *Anna Karenina* and found myself deeply moved by the intensity of Anna's love and the heartbreak of her dilemma. My uncle Yossel, my father's youngest brother but only six years older than me, let me join his circle of political and intellectual friends. Yossel was an accomplished tailor and a strikingly hand-some man who enjoyed an occasional evening out dancing, even if his partner was not his wife. He and his friends took me along to the theater to see the poignant *Yoshe Kalb* and to the movies, where we laughed ourselves to tears at Charlie Chaplin's *Modern Times*. If I had no place to go on a weekend, I could always look for Simcha. He was something of a Romeo and spent time with many girlfriends despite his doctor's warnings that his tuberculosis was contagious. But he sometimes took me along to a Jewish writers' club and to a Yiddish socialists' club. It seemed that everybody was a socialist or communist. Simcha and I never joined the Communist Party, but I must admit we were sympathetic to their ideas, as were most of the young people I knew.

I was beginning to meet young men. One night I had a date with my first cousin, Moishele Golant. He was a frisky, elfin man with a merry disposition and an impressive tenor voice. We went to the theater and spent the evening serenading each other with Polish and Yiddish songs, sometimes singing them together. The evening turned romantic as Moishele leaned over and kissed me, but I would not let it become serious. I liked him very much, but he was too poor for me and, at that time, I was strong enough to have higher ambitions.

My life was becoming orderly and predictable and, after the chaos and misery of the years that followed my leaving home, order and predictability were no small virtues. The summer of 1939 was a particularly happy time, so happy for me that I had not even an inkling that the life I was getting to know was about to come to a tumultuous end. ◞

12

What do you remember about September 1, 1939?" I ask my mother in perfect journalese. September 1, 1939, was the date of the German invasion of Poland, the start of World War II, and journalist that I am, I want to know names, dates, and places, even if this is my mother I am interviewing and what I am asking is about the carnage she saw.

"That day I remember very well," my mother replies. "I was sitting in a delicatessen in the Jewish quarter. I was eating a sweet roll stuffed with salami and I heard the *balbues* [the boss] saying on the telephone that a bomb fell at the same time in Otwock and in Silesia, near the German border. I remember because that was the only day they bombed Otwock. I was worrying terribly about my father and his three children but I could not go to Otwock to check on them. The bombing had cut off the railroad.

"Then they began bombing Warsaw. The first few days I stopped going to work. I don't know what I lived on. I came to my brother, and near him there was a market, a very famous one, not far from Saxony Garden. A nice neighborhood. He took me to the marketplace and he showed me dead people lying on the ground. He said, 'You've got to get used to them. There's going to be a lot of people dead.' I wasn't interested in seeing it. It was a horrible thing to see."

"Where did he have all this experience with war that he could talk with such assurance?" I ask.

"He was eight years older than me. He was a small boy during the first war. Maybe I figured he knew something about war. They kept on bombing Warsaw and then they stopped and then they started. People were running to shelters. He told me, don't do it. The worst thing to do is to go in the shelters. They drop a bomb and they destroy the whole building, the shelter with it. The best thing to do is to walk around. That was his opinion and I listened to him. Who else should I listen to? I didn't have nobody else to listen to."

She pauses, her face strained. "Here, it's better if you read what I wrote."

For several days we roamed the streets while German bombers flew overhead and dropped their bombs, turning the neighborhood around us into an inferno. The air we breathed was bitter with smoke and heat and the streets and sidewalks were covered with rubble and the shreds of tenants' belongings. Dead horses were still tethered to their overturned wagons. Here and there were the human dead, their faces torn, their limbs mangled or missing.

During a lull, we fled to the Zelaznej Bramy (the Iron Gate), Warsaw's largest market. The stalls and pushcarts, usually brimming with produce, were forsaken and the market's only goods seemed to be the scattered corpses. I shrieked in horror when I saw a dead woman stretched on the ground in what seemed like a position of desperate flight. Her dead child was next to her.

Next to a locked shop, Simcha noticed a bulging sack. He unfastened its cords and discovered that the sack was packed with plump, juicy prunes. Evidently, the shop's owner had run off before he could rescue all his merchandise.

"This will tide us through the next few days," Simcha said confidently. "Food will be scarce."

We loaded the sack on top of a pushcart and rolled the three-wheeled cart to Simcha's apartment. While I waited downstairs guarding the cart, Simcha brought down two valises of clothes and boxes of the lingerie he sold. He proposed we make our way across town to the home of my aunt Chana Leah at Franciskaner 26. It was near the Vistula River, and Simcha reckoned the river would be a source of water if Warsaw's water supply failed.

"The Germans haven't finished bombing us yet," he said. "This has just been a taste. But if the bombs kill us, at least we will die together."

We weaved through the rubble and debris choking Warsaw's streets. Along the way, an old man asked if he might walk with us and place his valise on our pushcart. We obliged, but after straining to keep up with us for a distance he seemed to grow paler and weaker and finally asked for his valise back. He said he did not have the strength to go on.

"I don't care what happens to me anymore," he said.

We left him sitting on a curb, and I never learned why he felt so despondent, whether, like so many others, he had lost family in the bombing.

We tramped on for some distance then rested on a broken bench on the outskirts of Krasinski Garden, one of Warsaw's finest parks and incongruously green and lush as the seasons paid no heed to the march of world events. The park now was littered with dead soldiers and dead horses, and soon, across the park, we could hear the thunder of bombs. The blitz had resumed. Solid, thick-stoned apartment buildings that looked unshakable in their elegance were toppling like toy blocks. Everywhere was the stench of dead bodies, human and animal.

"Let's cut off a piece of meat while the horses are still freshly killed," Simcha suggested.

"You cannot be serious," I cried.

"I am very serious!" he shouted back. "We can't be particular. In World War I people ate rats when there was no food."

"Please, Simcha," I cried. "Please. I've had enough."

At Franciskaner 26, the courtyard was crowded with dazed families sitting on their belongings. As bombs rumbled in the distance, men were praying in woolen prayer shawls while women were wringing their hands in despair and children were bawling in fright. Among this huddled throng, I recognized my sister, Freyde Leah, and my Bubbe, who sat in bewilderment on a mound of clothing and bedding, murmuring prayers to herself.

Freyde Leah informed me that her husband, Leo, had already left for the east toward the new Soviet-occupied territory of Poland.

"I'm waiting for a letter from him," she said. "As soon as I hear, I may join him. Maybe you too will be able to join us."

Just a few weeks before, Hitler's foreign minister, Ribbentrop, and Stalin's minister, Molotov, had signed a nonaggression pact. The Soviet Union pledged that if Hitler invaded Poland it would not retaliate. In exchange, the Soviet Union would get to keep the eastern third of Poland for itself. The Soviet Union exercised that bargain on September 7, and young men and women like Leo, who were enticed by a socialist future or feared the approach of the Nazis, hurried to the newly occupied territory.

As we settled ourselves in the courtyard, my usually level-headed brother confided how much he envied those making the journey. Simcha had often talked of the Soviet Union as the Promised Land of justice, fairness, and equity. He told me of the *Communist Manifesto* and other writings of Marx, Engels, Lenin, and Trotsky that he had read in Yiddish and of the virtues of the Soviet constitution. How eagerly would he join them, he said, were it not for his tuberculosis, which made travel risky.

"But you, Rochele, should consider going there," he urged.

For the next few days, I lived with Chana Leah. Whenever bombs rained down, we hurried outside to the courtyard and sat there on our bags or boxes until the bombing ceased. When there were lulls, we returned inside. There our relations were less than congenial. My aunt Chana Leah was something of a *shlekhte shtik,* a mean-spirited person. She had always been jealous of the attention I got from my grandfather on summer visits to Parysow. And now, even as Warsaw was being destroyed around us or maybe because Warsaw was being destroyed, that mean-spiritedness flared up. Her slights to me were painful. When I complained to my grandmother she responded helplessly, "What can you do?"

After a few days, I could endure Chana Leah no longer and thought I'd do better in Freyde's abandoned apartment. On my way there I saw something that I still cannot forget. At one of the wrecked houses, my attention was drawn by policemen searching through the debris. I approached and saw the bodies of several small children with their little shoes scattered alongside. Walking through the rubble were parents, sobbing and wailing. One of these was a mother who was wandering about incoherently. She had lost her entire family. ❧

I sit in this comfortable kitchen in the leafy Riverdale section of the Bronx and it is difficult for me to believe that the woman sitting across from me has been through such hell. I ask her about the incoherent mother she saw and she fills in more details. As she does, she begins crying freely, even sobbing.

"Why was this crazy woman screaming all over the street, Joey?" she asks me. "All over the street. That scene affected me for the whole of my life. You know I'm very attached to children. I raised my step-mother's children and I had such love for them. A mother's love. And here in the rubble, to see those little bodies and those little shoes . . ."

As she weeps, I wonder why she expends all her tears for children she does not know yet scarcely sheds a tear when she talks explicitly about her own murdered young brother and two sisters. I suspect that the mother she saw in the rubble crying for her dead children was a palpable figure of sorrow. Her own dead perished in ghettos and camps, but she does not know conclusively where or how, has no mental picture to attach to their deaths, indeed has no proof, like a grave or municipal document, that they are dead. Without such pictures and proofs, her grief cannot seem to break through. But she has an indelible picture of that woman crying in the rubble. I believe that in some way the woman screaming among the rubble is herself, Rachel, crying for the little brother and two sisters she left behind in Otwock, for all her lost children.

❧ On September 30, after a month's shelling, Poland capitulated. The Germans strutted down the main avenues of Warsaw in long columns of eight, slim and arrogant in their starched uniforms. Singing triumphantly, they were greeted with zeal by the Endekees, the organization of Polish students who revered Hitler. The Endekees knew how to please the Germans. A large throng of Endekees walking along Gesia Street began pointing out which stores the German soldiers should attack. In one store, the soldiers pulled out a slight Jewish man in worn gabardine and a yarmulke and *tsitsis* [prayer fringes] and kicked him repeatedly until he slumped to the ground. I couldn't bear to watch and ran away.

The conquering Germans stood on the back of open trucks hurling loaves of bread into the famished crowds. On Nalewki Street, a thoroughfare crowded with fabric shops owned by Jews, I managed to snatch one of the hurled loaves. The crowd around me consisted mostly of Poles, but there were many Jews as well, and the Poles, especially the younger ones, kept shouting *"Jude! Jude!"* pointing out Jewish men, women, and children and urging the Germans not to throw them the precious loaves. There was nothing I could do to help anyone and, grasping my loaf of bread tightly, I fled once again.

I was worried about my father and his family, whom I had not seen since the bombing began and for almost a year before that, and so the day after the Germans marched in I decided to return to Otwock. The suburban railroad had been bombed out of commission, so I hiked the entire twenty-eight kilometers, lugging what was left of my brother's sack of prunes and a small bag of flour as gifts to my family. It took me six hours of brisk walking, along roads that were strewn with animal carcasses and human corpses.

When my father saw me alive and sound, he broke down in tears.

"I was afraid you were killed," he said. "I was so sure I would never see you again."

I was happy to see him, but I was terribly distressed by what he soon told me. Otwock, he said, had largely been spared by the German planes. But there was little food to be had, and he found himself having to scrounge food from the fathers of the children he taught.

"I was forced to do some begging from my *balebatim*," he said, pale with embarrassment.

It pained me to see my proud father talk of having to beg for food. I tried to impress him and my stepmother, Bluma, by showing them the sack of prunes that Simcha had scavenged from the abandoned marketplace. But for Bluma it did not seem enough.

"I wish we could have some rice to cook the prunes with," she said meekly.

She and my father let me know that food could be had in the market for enough money, and I began to grasp what it was they were asking of me.

"I have some money," I told them, "but not very much."

The children looked skinnier than I remembered. Shimele, who was eight years old, came over and started yanking my hand, pulling me toward the door and outside.

"Where are you pulling me?" I asked.

"Come, I'll show you," he said.

He led me for several blocks to a Polish butcher shop where the window display was stocked with hams and sausages.

"Get me some of this sausage," he pleaded. "You have money. Please."

"Shimele, but this is all pork," I replied. "It's forbidden to eat."

"I don't care," he said. "Please. I'm so hungry."

His pleas tore at my heart. I was afraid if I bought him a few slices of sausage, my father might get angry with me or with Shimele. I told Shimele that I had to make my money last so we could eat a little each day. I told him this in different ways, but, ravenous as he was, he did not seem to understand and I finally crossed the street and left him standing in front of the store, gazing at the sausages hanging in the window. ❧

"I don't know why I refused," my mother tells me. "I can't remember whether I didn't want to spend the money or because I didn't want him to eat *trayf* [unkosher food]. I wasn't religious anymore. Maybe I didn't want him to stop being religious. But he was that desperate to eat. Can you imagine? All these children, and Shimele too. They didn't make it to the deportations. They died from hunger. That's what I go around thinking. I can't forgive myself that I didn't go into that store and buy Shimele the salami. This is the worst thing I ever did in my life."

❧ One morning over bread and tea sweetened with saccharin, my father unburdened his heart. He confided that he didn't know how he would be able to feed his wife and the three children after the money I gave him was exhausted.

"Nobody is sending their children to *cheder* anymore," he said. "I can't make any money."

I promised him that as soon as I recovered my energy I would return to Warsaw and try to find work. But I also let him know that people were advising me to travel east to Russian-occupied territory and register for work in the Soviet Union. From Simcha and his friends, I had been absorbing visions of a better life in the Soviet Union, a life that provided education and medical care to everyone equally, a life where hunger and want were unknown. Perhaps I too could try to make it to the Soviet Union and, once I got there, persuade my father and his family to join me. Simcha and Freyde might come as well.

My father did not know what to tell me. He seemed uncertain of what a German occupation would mean, but at the same time he feared the Russians.

"The Germans were our saviors in World War I," he said. "We Jews looked to them to protect us from the Russian pogroms. Now the Germans seem to be our persecutors."

My going to Russia would mean I could not immediately help feed the family, he said. On the other hand, Russia might save me from starvation and allow me to help support the family in the long run. Torn and unsure, he got up from his chair and paced around the apartment as if he were digesting a difficult page of Talmud.

"Who knows how to advise you," he said. "Who even knows whether we will see each other anymore."

The next day I learned that the *kolyeka*—the Otwock shuttle— had been repaired and I decided to return to Warsaw immediately.

As I left, my stepmother pleaded once again, "Rochele, please send us a little *gelt* so we can have something to live on."

Upon arrival in Warsaw, I went directly to my employers at the slipper factory and learned that there was not going to be much work. The stores that carried their slippers had been destroyed. That afternoon I also went to see my uncle Yossel's wife, Fredzia, who told me she had received a letter from Yossel that had been mailed from Soviet-occupied territory. His letter contained detailed instructions on how we might follow him by smuggling across the Bug River near my father's hometown of Mordy.

"Come with us," Fredzia said. "So many young people are escaping the Germans. I'm leaving too, tomorrow with my friend Fela."

I was standing at a fateful fork in a road. If I fled to Russia, I could save myself and secure what I believed would be a better life. But I also felt that choice would be selfish. How could I worry about myself when my family was desperately hungry? I needed someone's wisdom and searched for Simcha. When I found him, I argued that I ought to stay in Warsaw and support my father. But Simcha firmly disputed me.

"What are you talking about?" he said. "Your father will get his *talmidim* [students] back. Jews like your father lived through many wars and many pogroms, and they always kept teaching children the Torah and Talmud. But you, you'll be giving up an opportunity to live in a land where you'll have a chance at a better education, where you won't have to lose yourself in menial jobs like embroidering slippers."

Too timid to have confidence in my own judgment, I grasped my brother's advice. I packed everything I owned, then rode back to Otwock to say farewell to my father. I took along all the pretty sweaters and skirts that I had managed, as a hopeful young woman, to accumulate. I would give them to my father so he could sell them for food.

I recall that last encounter in Otwock now as the saddest moment of my life. My feeble stepmother embraced me with tears in her eyes.

"We will be suffering hard times ahead," she said. "Please, don't forget us, Rochele."

I embraced my father too for what turned out to be the last time. I remember his sad, dark eyes and weary face as he let me go. Before I walked out the door, he gave me a pair of earrings. They had belonged to my dead mother, he said. He sensed that I was not going to return so soon and wanted to give me a keepsake. But I found the earrings haunting. I had been having dreams about my dead mother in which she seemed to try to pull me into the grave with her. For a child, there is nothing worse than the death of a mother. I did not want to have those earrings, and I eventually lost them.

Fredzia, who was going to take me with her to Russia, had already left, so with a small bundle of clothes and a red kerchief tied around my head, I made my own way toward my father's hometown of Mordy, which was near the Bug River. I took a freight car occupied by a half-dozen young men and women with the same intentions as mine. After an hour of standing as the train rumbled east, my legs grew weak and I felt a gnawing pain on the left side of my abdomen. I figured it was diarrhea and blamed a salami sandwich I had eaten the day before. But the pain was so bad I was forced to lie down on the floor of the freight car.

In Siedlice, the nearest station to Mordy, there were no horse-drawn carriages to be had so I walked for three and a half hours, a distance of fifteen kilometers, all with stabbing pains in my abdomen, and made it to the house of my aunt Deborah, my father's sister. There I found Fredzia and her friend Fela, who was in her ninth month of pregnancy. I kept hoping my aunt Deborah would offer me a glass of tea that would somehow alleviate my pain, but instead I got a sermon from her husband, Shmuel.

"You should not have left your father and his family," he admonished me. "You should have stayed home and helped support them."

In the evening, we were taken to a peasant who lived on the shore of the Bug River and had been paid by my uncle Shmuel to smuggle us across by boat. The peasant's wife served us tasty boiled potatoes and let us spend the night sleeping in the hay of her barn. In the twilight before dawn, we were awakened, taken to a dock, and we crossed the choppy river in a shallow, tottering boat. None of us could swim and we were all terrified. But we made it to Soviet territory and hid in bushes until we made sure there were no Russian soldiers about.

One by one, we emerged from cover and walked the few kilometers into the town of Siemiatycze. How welcomed we felt by the smell of fresh bread and rolls and a market where we could buy as much food as we wanted. After six weeks of bombing and privation, this was an inspiring change of scene. Still, our goal was to register for work, and registration could only be done in designated cities like Brest Litovsk. In my weakened state, Yossel, who had rejoined us, and Fredzia dragged me by train first to Brest Litovsk, then farther south to the Ukrainian city of Lutsk, then back to Brest Litovsk, but no bureaucrat seemed able or willing to register us.

As we rambled about, the pains in my stomach became unbearable and at times I turned delirious. I remember pressing my fingers inside my ears thinking that it would end my suffering. Finally, in Brest Litovsk, Yossel and Fredzia took me to the office of a doctor. So scarce was a doctor in this part of Russia that I had to stand at the end of a long line of people. But when the doctor, a psychiatrist who was reduced to seeing patients for all manner of ailments, finally saw me, he ordered that I be taken immediately to the local hospital and placed in a quarantined ward. I had typhus, which he informed me is bred in filthy and crowded conditions like those I had experienced in besieged Warsaw.

At the hospital, they bathed me and placed me in a room with other typhus-afflicted women. My stomach was swollen, protruding like that of a pregnant woman. For days, I lay in bed drifting in and out of consciousness. The women around me were as delirious as I was, raving wildly at times, then falling silent into comas. In the mornings, a nurse in a starched white uniform covered those who had died during the night and the orderlies carried the bodies out of the ward. It became clear that the doctors had given up on me. They had even stopped bringing me food.

"Am I dying here?" I pleaded with a nurse.

"No," she said. "We're doing what we can."

One day, nurses brought in a child of seven or eight with doleful eyes. She told me that she too had typhus and that her intestines had slipped outside her body and could not be restored by the doctors. She could no longer eat. Over the next few days, I watched this girl fade away into death.

Alone, demented, and in unspeakable pain, I too wanted to die. I prayed for days that the end would come soon. Then, one morning, I looked up and saw the soft, round face and tender smile of my younger brother Yasha.

"Are you hungry?" was the first question he asked me.

He produced some bread and lard and made me eat it in his presence.

"This will make you feel well again," he said.

Just seeing him made me feel hopeful. In the midst of all my adversities, someone with genuine love for me had appeared. He stayed at my side throughout the day. If a nurse chased him out, he found his way back again. He cheered me up and I began to feel better. He visited me day after day and each time brought some bread and lard. Who cared that the lard was not kosher? It was something I could eat.

Yankel, for that's what I called him, told me that he would soon be shipped to a job in Sverdlovsk, deep in the Russian interior in the Ural Mountains.

"Don't worry," he said. "Simcha arrived here yesterday and will be here soon to see you."

That news lifted my spirits even higher. Simcha, my protector when I was all alone in a friendless city, was nearby. By the time he visited, my fever was gone and I had acquired enough energy to walk around the ward, even though my stomach was still swollen.

"What happened to you, Ruchaye?" Simcha said, shaken by the haggard sight of me.

He reached into his knapsack and pulled out a package of cookies, a bag of dried fruits, and a brightly colored box of candies. He also brought along a thick winter coat and a hat that I could wear when the hospital released me.

"When you get out, try to find a way to get to Lvov," he said.

"I'll be there and wait for you. Then we will both register for work in the Urals."

I was delighted that Simcha would be making the journey through Russia with me. I stayed in the hospital for several more weeks—I had been there for three months in all—then joined Simcha in Lvov and registered with him for work. In two weeks we were aboard another freight train headed for a long ride into the unknown. This train stretched for half a mile and carried hundreds of refugees from Nazi-occupied Poland toward jobs in the coal mines and factories of the Urals. The journey of almost 1,600 miles would take us farther away from any possibility we had of returning and helping our relatives.

For the benefit of the new recruits to the Soviet cause, soldiers of the Red Army accompanied our departure with merry songs like *"Kalinka, Malinka, Moya."* The loudspeakers played patriotic anthems and marches. I felt the train jolt forward and a loud cheer went up among the passengers. Soon, we adventurers were facing one another across opposite sides of our bunks, our legs swinging in lively fashion, and we started getting acquainted. It was early in 1940 and a new chapter in my life was beginning. ❧

As I listen to my mother tell her story, I am struck by the bittersweet jokes history plays, how it mocks our most symmetrical logic. Her brother's advice to head for the Russian Promised Land was so patently wrongheaded. There was no Promised Land to be found in Russia, not then, not ever. Yet that misguided advice turned out to be precisely the correct one because she was able to escape the Nazi death maw. Yes, her Otwock family perished, but had she stayed with her family and helped support them, she almost certainly would have perished with them.

13

My father worked on Saturdays—the Jewish Sabbath—and that became my shameful family secret. Had he worked on that day in a neighborhood of secular Jews, I would not have cared. But we were living in a neighborhood with a dozen Orthodox synagogues where the parade of dark-suited men briskly striding toward synagogue with their children in tow seemed to define Saturday mornings. What's more, my brother and I were attending a yeshiva and no commandment seemed stronger, no observance more definably Jewish than keeping the Sabbath holy. Even more than maintaining a kosher home, sanctifying the Sabbath was the dividing line between the pious and the ungodly. By the time I was in third grade, most of my classmates would take for granted that Saturday mornings were spent at synagogue with their parents, or at least with their fathers, on whom the obligation largely fell. It was what you did on Saturdays, just as going to school was what you did on Monday mornings. But I could not take going to synagogue with my father for granted. With my father working, I had to go to synagogue on my own, and doing so was fraught with such uneasiness that I preferred to stay at home.

To be sure, I wanted to be in synagogue. Whenever I went to Ohab Zedek, the stately house of worship on Ninety-fifth Street that drew Austrian and other Jews of *Mitteleuropa* and the bulk of my classmates, I felt a deep sense of sacred mystery. From my seat toward the rear of the men's section, I would gaze across the rows of mahogany benches cushioned in ruby plush toward the spotlit Holy Ark, where the Torahs, the holy scrolls of our people, were hidden behind embroidered curtains, and I would anticipate the possibility of something wondrous and magical occurring. And it did. In that theatrical moment when the curtains were drawn open and the scrolls, sheathed in white satin, were lifted out of the ark, the great vaulted space between the balconies radiated with sunbursts of chandelier light and swelled with impassioned and melodious Hebrew voices. Who could doubt that some divine being permeated that chandelier light and was responding to that heartfelt consensual plea?

But too often the pageantry seemed to leave me feeling chilled and alone. For across those velvet-covered benches fathers were protectively enfolding their sons with their broad-backed bodies. As the spirit of God sheltered the congregation, these fathers sheltered their sons. But where was my father? He had forsaken me to fend for myself. And his absence forced me to reply to suspicions I was sure were being directed at me. If my father was not in synagogue, where else could he be but at work? On Shabbos? A disgrace.

Sometimes I tried lying. "My father davens at another shul where his friends go," I would tell my school friends in a preemptive strike, forestalling any questions before they arose. Or I would pressure my mother to take me to synagogue. Since there was no great tradition in her Polish town of synagogue attendance by women, it was not something she felt impelled to do. When she did come, she sat in the women's section and my brother, Josh, and I in the men's, and so I was still vulnerable to questions. "My father davens in another shul where his friends go" became doubly suspect. I figured that people would now surmise that my parents were on the verge of divorce, maybe even a greater disgrace than violating the Sabbath.

It was hopeless. At bottom I felt that, once more, my family was somehow out of sync with the symmetrical lives of other families in this synagogue, in my school, in Manhattan, in the world. Other Jewish families could arrange to be together on the Sabbath, to pass their day in the timeless fashion of Jews: a sober yet convivial morning in the synagogue, a satisfying and congenial lunch, the week's reward of an afternoon nap, a cheerful stroll along Broadway to catch up on gossip with other strolling families, a brief return to synagogue for evening prayers before a reluctant farewell to the Day of Rest with a poignant ceremony of braided candle and aromatic spice box. There was a sensible and harmonious pattern to such Sabbath days that I was sure was reflected in the way these families would spend the rest of their week. But this was not my family's pattern. My Sabbath, my week, my life seemed amorphous by comparison, ragged and adrift.

It was not just Sabbath, of course. The simple act of a weekend stroll on Broadway with my family began to grow uncomfortable for me the longer I stayed in yeshiva. That raffish boulevard displayed an assortment of degeneracies far worse than anything for which my family could be reproached. But I feared we would run into another yeshiva family who could see that my father was hatless and so were my brother and I, another mark of our halfhearted faith. Still, Sabbath remained the most raw and tender of days.

Needless to say, I was too young to understand matters from my father's point of view. After years of rousting about in Russian labor camps and DP camps, he finally had a reliable job. Besides, in the turmoil of war and its helter-skelter aftermath, he had lost the habit of Sabbath observance, and it truly was a habit. Surely, if he believed in God—and that had become a big *if*—then the ritual-destroying tumult of the war had been God's plan, and his Sabbath-defying job at General Textile must be God's plan too. And who was this God that my father owed him such obeisance, a God that had killed his six sisters; a God that had killed his peasant parents, who had done nothing but diligently work their farm and honor Him their entire lives; a God that had looked away as barbarians shot down harmless Carpathian Jews in their thatched-roof farmhouses? No, working Saturdays did not strain my father's conscience excessively.

And if he did go to synagogue, what would he have in common with these burghers from Vienna, Frankfurt, Brussels, and Amsterdam, who sneered at even prosperous Eastern European Jews as *poyers*— peasants—let alone a genuine peasant kid like himself? As someone who had been reared in the tumbledown synagogue of Borinya, he would feel as uncomfortable in this bastion of bourgeois Orthodoxy as an Irish rustic might feel in a High Episcopalian service on Park Avenue.

Of course, a day did come when my father was able to go to synagogue with me. There was some rare alignment of the stars. Maybe July 4 or Christmas holidays, which even General Textile honored, came out that year on a Saturday. I woke excitedly. My father was squatting in his underwear in the hallway, burnishing his shoes and Josh's and mine with the cheerfulness of a man who knew that for the first time in months, he would have two full days in a row of leisure. We gathered around the enameled metal table and my mother spooned out three cups of instant coffee and buttered three slices of rye bread, which my father embellished with sliced radishes. While we ate, she ironed matching charcoal-gray pants for Josh and me and two white shirts. She checked that every button was buttoned and the collars were straight. My father, stooping to our height, coiled our ties into Windsor knots.

In a suit, my father did not look like a greenhorn. With his broad shoulders and slender waist, suits always looked like they had been poured on him, and with the gleaming black shoe tips and rakishly angled gray fedora, he cut quite a dapper figure on the sunny sidewalks we traversed on our way to synagogue. Josh and I capered alongside, two sailboats proud to be accompanying his grander yacht.

Whatever grace he had accrued seemed to unravel somewhat when we entered the synagogue's great arched portal. In the vestibule, my father searched haphazardly for prayer books and prayer shawls for us and there was a sense of discomfort about him, as if someone were watching him and chuckling. Finally, we stepped inside the great velvety space and took seats near the rear. In the anonymity of the crowd my father seemed to relax. He took the time to find the right page in the prayer book first for me, then for Josh, and only lastly for himself. That too was typical of my generous-hearted father. Soon, he was deep into the collective murmur of prayer, rocking back and forth or swaying side to side with the other Jews. I followed his lead, standing when he stood, rocking when he rocked, trying to imitate the unfamiliar tunes, although I was conscious that my word-by-word reading of Hebrew could not keep pace with his rapid scan, sharpened as it was by thirty years of seasoning.

As I sat close to him on his right, there was something about the yellowed woolen prayer shawl draping his shoulders that made me feel he was wrapped in a divine embrace, and that the embrace extended to me as well, almost as if God occupied the seat right next to us and was stretching his broad arms around the back of the bench. Surely, with that shawl around him, my father was the equal of any of those Jewish Babbitts—the diamond traders, the export-importers, the small-time manufacturers, the dry goods merchants. For a moment, I could believe that this lovely morning would be repeated every Saturday from now on, that maybe my father would change jobs or his boss would find religion, that just by the simple act of my attending synagogue this day, God in his clever benevolence would gratify my wish and make my family just as respectable, as normal as everyone else's.

Of course, the hierarchy within the synagogue quickly asserted itself. After the Torah was withdrawn from the Holy Ark and paraded around the central *bima* and unscrolled and the reader began the ancient, lilting singsong, I could not help being aware of the succession of seven men called up to bless the Torah. Each one smiled humbly at the announcement of his Hebrew name and patronymic and, after intoning the blessings before and after the recited passage, each exchanged pleasantries with the rabbi. Wouldn't it be nice, I thought, for my father one day to be called for an *aliyah*? I knew these honors were extended mostly to the upright worthies who contributed money for the synagogue's upkeep and had the time to manage its affairs. Still, I was happy my father was at least in synagogue, and I wanted to make sure that his attendance was recorded by my classmates, that they knew I had a father just as they did.

I especially wanted Dickie Hochstein to know that my father was here. Dickie was the kid I, and many others in my class, envied and even deferred to. Strange as it may seem, at eight and later at ten and thirteen, he was poised, well-grounded, self-confident as if he firmly knew what he was about and was pleased with the lot destiny had laid out for him. Teacher after teacher admired the nuanced or insightful answers Dickie would give to their Torah questions. In one class, the teacher was trying to get us to define the Hebrew word *Yir-uh* as the attitude that Jews should feel toward God. It wasn't precisely fear, the teacher said, since we fear bullies and tyrants. It was a subtler quality, one that went beyond reverence. Dickie's hand jerked up and I knew he would be right, and of course he was.

"Awe!" Dickie said, his smile conveying his confidence and pleasure in the rightness of his answer.

After all these years, I still remember that answer. For awe was something I must have felt toward Dickie. It stemmed from small things like the medicine bottle of chocolate syrup he would bring in his lunch box to flavor the school's milk. Not only was I jealous of his mother's indulgences, but of the regal way Dickie would pour the syrup into the milk without spilling a drop. During recess, while I craved simply to be chosen for the punchball games, Dickie, with an air of nonchalance, was among the first players picked. Dickie, slim, wiry, with an angular eagle's face and bright brown eyes, wasn't the most powerful punchball player, but powerful enough and crafty, versed in the basics, and thus a valuable player. Friendship he could take or leave, so, of course, classmates sought him out. In synagogue, Dickie would pray like a miniature rabbi, a blanket-sized adult's tallis, or prayer shawl, folded smartly over his shoulders—he already knew how to don such a tallis—rather than the slender, childish stole that I wore. He would stand ramrod straight, his legs together at attention, then rock metronomically at the waist, totally absorbed in prayer. No other child seemed as ardent or mature about our faith.

And parents noticed him too. Whenever I would come home with a test that bore a 92 or 94 in the teacher's red pencil, my mother would say, "Wonderful, Joey," pause pensively, and then add, "And what did Dickie Hochstein get?"

Dickie was the gold standard. I was one of the three or four students to get honor certificates almost every year in school, but so was Dickie, and there was a general understanding in the class that Dickie's was a distinctive cut above. I knew this almost from my first day in first grade and had to endure it for another eight years.

On my father's visit to synagogue, I spotted Dickie sitting toward the front next to his father, a sturdily built manufacturer of smoking pipes who sported a thin, debonair Errol Flynn mustache. Dickie's father was one of the synagogue nobles, who regularly received *aliyahs*,

and whenever he returned up the aisle to his seat, friends and colleagues would nod respectfully at him or stretch out their hands to
shake his. With the Torah reading winding up and the rabbi's sermon
about to begin, I noticed Dickie getting out of his seat and heading
toward the back. Synagogue protocol allowed, even encouraged, children to leave the service during the sermon and caper in the vestibule
or on the Ninety-fifth Street sidewalk outside. I trailed Dickie and
caught up and we made some small talk, though I determined to bring
the conversation around to the subject of my father's presence in the
synagogue.

"My father came here today instead of the shul he usually goes to,"
I said.

"Oh," he said thoughtfully. "And where's your father?"

That was easy to answer since we were sitting near the rear. I
pointed him out and Dickie looked briefly at the slender, awkward
man sitting with my towheaded brother.

"So that's your father?" he said. "Good. So why don't you go and
be with him?"

And he took off impatiently and disappeared into the mysterious
back warrens of the synagogue. I didn't know and, recollecting, still do
not know what he meant by that enigmatic remark. Perhaps he was in
a hurry to go somewhere and didn't want me along. Perhaps he was
planning to hook up with his own father. He was nine or ten, after all.
But thin-skinned as I was, I took it as dismissive, as if he could tell my
father was a raw factory worker, no more impressive than any of the
factory workers his father hired and fired every day. I was wounded,
deeply so. And when I returned to my father's side and the Torah made
its circuitous journey back to the ark and the congregation finished off
the remaining Sabbath morning prayers, I decided that, from then on,
I would perpetuate the lie of my father's belonging to another synagogue and stop pressuring him to come to synagogue with me. His
joining me had not yielded any great premiums. He could continue
working on Shabbos for all I cared.

Sol Cooperman was the first kid in our crowd of refugees to have a
television set, and, oh, how envious I was.

To watch Milton Berle or Molly Goldberg or the *Colgate Comedy Hour,* I had to climb three flights of stairs and sit in front of his boxy Dumont. On the rotating weeks of the *Colgate Comedy Hour,* I loved Jerry Lewis's spastic antics, and Jimmy Durante's sawmill voice, and Ben Blue's sullen tramp, and Eddie Cantor's cow-eyed silliness. But I'd sit in the back of the Coopermans' living room and I'd be slightly on edge. I didn't know whether I could lie on the floor or sprawl across the couch. I fretted that laughing too loudly would irritate someone. If I was hungry I had to keep quiet about it. If I was sleepy I had to get up, walk down four flights, and cross the street to my house. I pined for a set of my own, one in my own living room, where I could do as I wished, even change channels to another program if that's what I wanted to do.

"I want a television set, Daddy," I nagged my father.

He smiled apologetically, but my mother filled in what lay behind his smile.

"We can't afford a television set right now," she said. "Daddy doesn't make enough money to buy television sets."

"Everybody's got a television set," I argued. "Even Sol has one."

"Joey, you're going to have to wait," she shot back.

My parents were right. We had just come to America three years before. My father was earning fifty dollars a week and my mother about as much, though she only worked during the half year of the hat season. We were living in a tenement with threadbare furniture. We didn't even own a sofa. How could I demand a TV set? It was becoming clear: I would have to swallow my disappointment and subsist on the Coopermans' set.

But then something happened that rekindled my pestering. I had been looking forward to catching Bob Hope's turn on the *Colgate Comedy Hour* but then was crestfallen to learn moments before the show was to start that the Coopermans were not home that night. They had gone to visit relatives in Connecticut.

"How am I going to watch Bob Hope tonight?" I said to my father.

"So you won't watch it," he said. "You'll watch it next time."

"But I'll miss the jokes he makes this time. That's why I want a TV set. I want to be able to watch television even if Sol's not home."

"So you'll miss one show."

"But, Daddy, everybody's got a TV set. Why don't we have one?"

"Don't bother me, Joey," he finally snapped.

I had bumped up against the place where he would not bend, and so I stopped imploring. But I would exact my revenge. I rushed outside and slammed the door so the thud would resound in my father's heart like the closing of a coffin lid. I sat on the stoop and brooded, hoping that my theatrics would draw some response. I gazed glumly at the building across the street. From the windows on the top floor to the plate-glass window of the Irish bar tucked into the building's basement, silvery screens shimmered everywhere like sequins on a gown. The roof itself had a half-dozen protruding aerials, evidence that television was taking over the building. On the building's brick facade, flat antenna wires snapped whiplike with every gust. Everybody, indeed, had a TV set, and tonight they all would be watching Bob Hope, even the drunks in the bar.

I sat there lamenting my impoverished lot, when I felt a strong right arm pick me up from behind and swoop me off the cold stone steps.

"You want to watch the television," my father said with a gruff chuckle. "I'll take you to a television."

I didn't let my guard down. My father had a way of turning many things that were important to me into a joke and this, I was sure, was going to be laughed off also. But I let him lead me into the Irish bar across the street whose TV set I had just been contemplating. It was a dingy place, smelling of sour beer, bad plumbing, and basement mildew. A half-dozen men perched on stools, some sitting morosely silent, some gabbing away with relish, some looking up at the flickering TV set mounted high in the bar's rear corner. Whatever cheer the place had came from the neon beer logos and the whisky bottles lined up along the back mirror.

This was not a place my father had ever been to before. The East European refugees didn't go to bars. They disdained the *shikere laydik-gayers*—the drunken idlers—who hung out there. But my father found two empty stools and propped me down on the one next to his. The top of the bar came up to my chest, and behind it stood a ruddy, wheat-haired bartender with a white apron across his ample belly. I had seen his beefy figure once or twice before when shouts in the night would wake me and I would look out the window and see him shoving a troublesome drunk up the stairs and onto the sidewalk.

"What can I get you?" he said, swabbing the counter in front of us.

"Two beers, mister, please," my father replied stiffly.

With the imposing bartender staring skeptically at him, my father must have figured that he should not be occupying two stools without ordering two beers. But his order did not blot out the bartender's dubious glance. He clearly didn't like men bringing their small children into bars. Nonetheless, he gave my father the benefit of the doubt, and two mugs of beer, golden and foamy, appeared in front of us. My father cupped the mug with both of his callused, broad-fingered hands, holding it the way a child might an unfamiliar ice cream soda, and tipped the beer into his mouth, the foam clinging to his lips. Drinking beer was not something he was accustomed to.

"Ah, that's good," he said.

Then he turned and brought the mug over to my lip.

"Take a small drink," he said.

I slurped the foam off the beer and tasted the amber liquid. It was icy and cold. Once more, I was being initiated into the world of hardworking men. My friends would envy me this adventure. Sol and Simon and Maury had never been in this bar.

And then a familiar melody jingled from the television, sprightly as always, followed by the emcee's chirpy words: "Ladies and gentlemen . . . Once again, it's time for the the *Colgate Comedy Hour,* with this week's guest host, B-a-a-ab Hope."

I had made it. There was Bob Hope backing into his monologue. I was not going to miss the show after all. There was a big grin on my father's face as well. Looking back, I'm sure it had nothing to do with Bob Hope or the show. Two or three years into America, he could barely understand most of the jokes. No, it was a smile that must have mingled relief and a little pride. He had come through for me. He had acknowledged that for whatever reasons he had been helpless to mend, he had been letting his small son down and he went out of his way to find a way to make it up to him.

14

Manhattan. What grandeur and polish was in that name for me, what power and swank. Soaring spires splitting the heavens. The wordless promise of ocean liners berthed on the Hudson. The frenzied hum of the Garment District. The rush of weaving, undulating crowds. The city beckoned to me, whispering of mystery, derring-do, enchantment.

I was as susceptible to these sensations as any other kid growing up in New York, but to me they had an extra lilt. I was exploring the city freestyle. My immigrant parents were as new to it as I was, and I had to be my own guide. While that might have seemed scary, it was also intoxicating. I was Balboa awestruck by the Pacific, Magellan daring the straits of Tierra del Fuego. I felt stronger, more reckless than I should have. Manhattan was not some place I took for granted the way a native might have. I was brought here from abroad. There was an unspoken purpose to my coming here. I had only to discover it. My parents could not help me much. They visited Manhattan's downtown in utilitarian fashion, to shop or attend to some practical refugee matter. Through them, my experience of the city was as fractured as that of the blind men with the elephant. I was sensing only a landmark here, an enclave there, missing the full sweep. I needed to swallow Manhattan in one bite, take its measure whole.

What stirred my yearning was a guidebook on the sights of New

York distributed by my school, a promotional pamphlet put out by what I remember as a life insurance company that we were supposed to take home to our parents. I studied the booklet's map, with Manhattan's landmarks indicated in red squares, and a plan dawned on me. Maury, Josh, and I would traverse the spine of the island, from my house to City Hall then back, a trip of maybe ten miles. I was fired up by the elegance of the route I traced, one that took us economically from point to point to distant point, one that might allow us to sniff in unanticipated corners. We would stop at the Museum of Natural History, Columbus Circle, Times Square, the Garment District, Macy's, the Empire State Building, the Little Church Around the Corner, Union Square, Greenwich Village, Chinatown, and City Hall, then on the way back we would wind our way east to the United Nations and return home. I didn't fully understand what distinguished these places, but if the guidebook certified them as the pick of Manhattan, they must be magical.

At the beginning of spring vacation, I grabbed my chance. I rose early, dressed quickly, hurried outside, and, in Romeo fashion, stood below Maury's second-story window.

"Maury! Maury!" I shouted. "Let's go!"

I was eight years old. When my daughter, Annie, was that age, I did not let her go down to the corner by herself. But Maury, Josh, and I were already roaming Central Park and venturing a half mile away to the seedy Park West movie theater, to see Bowery Boys and Abbott and Costello movies, laughing with delight even as we inhaled the fragrance of urine from the corroded bathrooms. With Maury at my side—he was all of nine—I would be safe. My mother, with her frenetic schedule, had given up watching us. Like many other mothers in that low-crime world of the early 1950s, she must have assumed we would end up all right. As someone who went to work at the age of fourteen, she did not see children as the vulnerable creatures of today's world. And the perils of Manhattan's streets must have seemed a rather tame contrast to what she had been exposed to as a young woman.

I only remember I called to her and she jutted her head and shoulders out our first-floor window. Over the chasm of the building's coal trough, I let her know of my plan to tour Manhattan and she listened with her customarily frantic distraction. Perhaps she didn't believe us.

Or like many parents, she may not have paid close attention to what her children were saying, sifting out a particularly clever or disquieting remark, and shrugging off the rest as charming blather. I figured that she might at least have been impressed with the precociousness of my conception to trek the island. But all she did was throw us a quarter for spending money.

We took off down Central Park West, which in my Dead End quarter of the West Side was a scruffy stretch of sooty, bulky apartment houses. Below Ninety-sixth Street, the buildings grew taller, plumper, more magisterial, and the trees and meadows of the park seemed to blossom into a gracious garden. The buildings acquired opulent names like the Eldorado and the Beresford, drab brickwork was replaced by marble and limestone, and the dreary uptown entrances became great billowing awnings shored up by glinting brass rods. We peeked inside the ground-floor and second-story windows and spied wooden replicas of clipper ships, gilt-framed paintings, indoor balconies, entire trees. How far this world seemed from our uptown dwellings. The starched and braided doormen were like palace guards, the residents their royalty. Today, the occupants might emerge in jeans and Birkenstocks, but in those more formal days, in my immigrant child's simplistic impressions, they seemed to step out in stylish suits and dresses, hailing cabs as if they were their own stabled carriages, dispensing tips, basking in attentive service.

We passed the museum but did not go inside. That was one place we had been to many times before. Sure, it was a repository of stuffed hides in dusty glass cases, but it left room for the imagination to soar, and so the locales it intimated seemed far more fantastic than any images that television was beginning to offer up. I remember looking up at the equestrian statue of Theodore Roosevelt, Soldier, Statesman, Naturalist, President. How many fields had he conquered? I probably didn't make the contrast then, but someone like Teddy Roosevelt must have had an inspirational appeal to an eight-year-old whose father slaved as a foreman at General Textile Corporation and came home too fatigued to carve out or even conceive of anything much better. Even if my father was consigned to a life of ignoble toil, maybe I, like Teddy Roosevelt, would one day ride my horse to glory.

A mile farther down, we sighted Columbus Circle, with the Italian mariner standing tall and bold atop a Greek column. Here was where Central Park West linked up with Broadway, a pivotal junction of world commerce, it seemed to me, the flurry of coiling traffic confirming that we had broken through to important new terrain. Like Christopher Columbus, I was charting my own route to a New World, even if it was a slanting passage from the Upper West Side south to midtown.

Maury, meanwhile, was busy with his own fevered imaginings, transfixed by the businesslike skyscraper that was then known as the General Motors Building. Several years later, Maury and I were to sit on a stone bench near the Battleship *Maine* monument, smoking cigarettes and gabbing, when Maury would look up at the GM Building and proclaim, "One day, Joey, I'm going to have an office in the top floor of that building." My first impulse was to laugh, since at that time Maury, a habitual truant, was barely staying afloat in school, had poor college prospects, and, with a mother on welfare, no money to launch himself toward anything much better. But Maury was a child of uncommon intuition who, given the lack of discipline in his home, could pursue his own fancies and cravings, so anything was possible. Besides, with his background, Maury could be forgiven the dream of a quick killing.

Like a favorable gust, the heady rush along Broadway swept us speedily forward. The way Broadway slanted across the boxy grid of Manhattan gave it great power and panache. It was a street that did things its own way. There were car showrooms with the Buicks and Cadillacs our parents seemed unlikely ever to own and blazing marquees for theaters to which our parents would never take us. There were sharpies and hipsters, willowy ladies and flamboyant rogues, types we rarely saw along our workaday uptown blocks.

After a mile, we came upon the glorious canyon of Times Square, the darting and flashing theater lights, the radiant Pepsi-Cola waterfall, the perfect smoke rings from the puffing Camels billboard, the flocks of pigeons tracing parabolas across the quicksilver sky. All seemed to celebrate our arrival. We had made it into the great throbbing heart of Manhattan, conquered this New World for our king and queen, whoever they were. I was discovering America, no matter what the historians insisted. And so to reward ourselves we spent a nickel on a Hershey's chocolate bar. That would have to do for our lunch. I figured that Josh and I ought to save the two leftover dimes in case our energy flagged and we needed to splurge on a bus back to our home. Maury, with his own nickel, bought a Hershey bar too and we split the provisions three ways.

We took off once more and headed into the roiling seas of the Garment District. Grubby men wheeled racks of dresses and handcarts piled with bolts of fabric through the narrow, jostling streets. The air seemed permeated with a powder of cloth particles and the acrid stink of motors. As I passed the hulking loft buildings with their tall, grime-encrusted windows, it occurred to me that during the hat season my mother worked here. She had never taken me to her workplace. But now seeing these buildings for myself, I realized she spent her day in an airless dungeon. As at home, she must have sat hunched over her machine in fierce concentration, squeezing down on the foot pedal, pushing the fabric through the machine while keeping her eye peeled on the driving needle, pausing only to bite off thread. Her only respite was a daily lunchtime release into the streets' human traffic to view—and only seldom savor—the delicacies in the shops along Seventh Avenue. Her annual bonus was a turkey her gruff boss, Leo, gave her at Thanksgiving. My father's Jersey factory, which I had never seen, was probably no better a workplace. No, my parents and their refugee friends were not to be confused with the businessmen and professionals I had seen along Central Park West. The refugees worked in the bowels. Now, when my parents returned from work smelling of a day's labor, I would know the kind of place they had been in all day.

I was only just beginning to form a consciousness of my family as occupying a particular stratum of society. I had not yet learned that the Garment District was historically peopled by immigrants, that the Holocaust refugees were working there now just as the East European Jews of the early twentieth century had done and the Puerto Ricans and Latin Americans would do a few years hence and the Asians a few decades beyond that. I only understood, standing there amid the garment factories, that where my mother—and my father—worked were dreadful places. That they permitted themselves to be treated like this made me more than a little sad. Unlike the Jewish tailors and cutters of earlier eras, the refugees were not romantic socialists who leavened their misery by agitating for a more just world. The refugees to me seemed more like docile serfs condemned to their bondage with no hope of release. Many of those who had been in concentration camps or survived by the wiles of hiding had not yet thrown off their frightened, compliant mentalities. Displaying the maddening stoicism of Bonscha Schweig in the Sholem Aleichem tale, they were grateful merely not to be working under a death threat. They could not imagine an alternative to bruising toil.

But more than all this, I simply hated that my mother worked, and seeing the Garment District for the first time only underscored this repulsion. Her working meant I had to come home during the season to an empty apartment. I had to keep an eye on my brother so he would not get hurt or sick. If my mother was late, I had to wonder if she was all right. Maybe she had gotten trapped in a smoky underground fire, or slipped on the stairs and gashed her head. That had happened once. None of my classmates, it seemed to me, had to worry about such things. Their mothers were home.

These thoughts did not linger because soon we were surrounded by the great retailing hub of Thirty-fourth Street, passing Gimbel's, Orbach's, and Macy's—where a sign told us the store had everything. Everything? A car? A house? An airplane? I had not yet developed an ear for American humbug, so it felt comforting to know that one day, when I had the money, there would be a store I could walk into and buy anything I wanted.

On Twenty-third Street, the Gilbert building—home of the toy company that made model trains and Erector sets—had two floors of sumptuously detailed trains coasting along a rolling terrain of hills and meadows and the gossamer Currier and Ives villages that I imagined existed beyond the city. Just off one stretch of track was a mailman who snatched a sack of mail out of a speeding train. One car had miniature logs that could be rolled right onto a flatbed and another siphoned a whitish liquid that looked like milk into a tanker truck. At the Edwardian station, an old-fashioned roadster with a handsome woman in a stole and netted hat waited to pick up a passenger. In the real life of this Gilbert exhibition hall, there were scenes that seemed to come out of Currier and Ives as well. Fathers were showing off the trains to their small sons. Why could my father not rearrange his life to work closer to home so he could take the day off and show his sons the marvels of a model-train layout? My father never took the initiative unless I begged. He was a man who from my childish perspective was blown about like a dry autumn leaf, at the mercy of forces he could not control. Did I consider how his survival in Russia had been a tale of incredible resourcefulness? No, I was too busy pondering what a true find this building was and how I would be able to boast about it to Simon and Sol. With no toys, no grand apartments, no charismatic parents, our pride had to be patched together from our exploits.

As we moved down Broadway and skirted Washington Square, the bohemian scene of Greenwich Village crept up on us. Even had we been older, we would not have been ready to feel its seditious tug. America was still enchantingly fresh for us and we were tickled to have been admitted as members of this envied club. Unlike the bohemians, we were not about to snub our nose at its shortcomings. We mirrored our parents' outlook. They made sure we understood how fortunate we had been to wind up in the United States. Whatever America's failings, we would never know systemic corruption and police-state terror. My parents' rugged experience—in Europe and Russia—was the one currency they had a wealth of and could hand to us as prosperous parents hand out an allowance.

Along Lafayette Street, we passed the headquarters of HIAS, a mammoth fortress that had once been the Astor Library but now had been taken over by the Hebrew Immigrant Aid Society both as its offices and as a dormitory for newly arrived refugees. Its large vaulted reading rooms had been cut up into cubicles to lodge families until a hotel or actual apartment could be arranged. I had visited the Granas family in this building just two or three years before. Moishe Granas was a slender, canny tailor who had befriended my father in the DP camps. He had an earthy wife and two children—Clara, who was two years older than me, and Jackie, who was two years younger. I remember, as a six-year-old, realizing how squeezed together they were in their cubicle and that the walls of their home—situated on a balcony circling the former library's main reading room—did not reach the ceiling. The clamor of scores of voices resonating off the domed ceiling made it difficult for our families to talk. Passing HIAS now with Maury and Josh, and realizing this was how a refugee family had been treated, I did not want to linger. (In a decade or two, the HIAS building—no longer needed for European refugees—would be taken over by a onetime refugee, Joseph Papp, and turned into the Public Theater.)

A dozen industrial blocks took us to City Hall. Here, at this dainty, colonnaded palace in a park, was the heart of the city's power, the place where commands were issued and the city jumped. I had just seen the new mayor, Robert F. Wagner, as my parents and hundreds of other immigrants gathered in the Mall near Central Park's Bethesda Fountain for I Am an American Day. There may have been a few refugees who imagined dire consequences should they not show up, but most were eager to join this patently political ceremony to express their loyalty in an era of loyalty tests. The short, plump Wagner passed close enough to where my family was standing behind a police sawhorse that I could see the pinstripes on his suit. I wondered what talents this man had that could carry him to the zenith of this city, put battalions of aides and fleets of limousines at his dispatch.

The sun was now slanting precipitously in the sky, and it was time for us to head back. Returning uptown, we took an easterly route so we could glimpse the United Nations. It was a trek of another three or four miles, and hot as our feet were feeling, tired and famished as we were, we hiked it briskly.

Looking back on this escapade many years later, I realized we were not just touring Manhattan. We were putting ourselves into the context of America. Until then we had been without a context, had just an academic idea of how we might fit in. But on our trek we had seen businesses we might work in, positions we might aspire to. There seemed so much there for the grabbing. If only we could unhitch ourselves of the millstone of our hapless parents, there was no limit to what riches we might snatch in America. And yet even as we felt this toward our parents, we also wanted to take them along with us. At this tender age, we knew they were not going to take us anyplace we wanted to get to. At most they could nurture us, in the most fundamental ways, as we hacked a path for ourselves.

There was not much to see of the United Nations in the darkened sky, except for an incandescent upright box, and besides, it was time to go home. I fished out the two dimes I had prudently put away and, on Forty-second Street and First Avenue, looked for a bus that was going to take us to the West Side. It was the number 104 and within an hour, an hour in which we slowly felt the blood return to our lifeless feet, we were dropped at Broadway and 102nd Street for the short walk to our homes.

When we saw her looking out the window, we could tell my mother was crazy with panic. She had already gone to the local police precinct to see if any children had been kidnapped or murdered. We managed to calm her down and soon she seemed mightily impressed by our odyssey, even if she did not quite believe it. We had walked from 102nd Street to City Hall and halfway back, taken in the best of Manhattan and survived. She had survived her savage journeys, but we, I felt, were starting to get a taste of survival as well.

15

Sunday was our splurge day, the one day when we could let go of our straitened weekday sensibilities, even become a little reckless. On other days, my mother rousted me out of bed with a great clamor. On Sundays, though, I could linger in the cocoon of my quilt, listen dreamily to the jazzy percussion of my father buffing the family's shoes on a spread of Yiddish newspapers in the hallway. He was home, and for one day we would be a family.

"Joey," he would say, when he finally heard me stirring. "Get up and go to the bakery. Get some fresh milk, Danishes, and a round rye bread without seeds, sliced."

I was eager to do so, to supply our Sunday-morning banquet, our chance to enjoy the bounty that my parents struggled for all week. As I ambled by the tenements lining 102nd Street, across the wide corridors of Columbus and Amsterdam avenues, I turned the bread order into a nervous mantra: "A round rye bread without seeds, sliced. A round rye bread without seeds, sliced."

I mumbled that order to myself all the way to the Cake Masters bakery on Broadway and 101st Street, where I paused at the window and stared at the display case filled with opulent confections: Viennese mocha cakes, stout seven-layers, shortcakes with glistening red strawberries as plump as if they were pregnant. Inside, I waited in the crowd of restless customers for the clerks—all women—to call my number.

Some of the clerks were unfailingly cheerful. Others seemed to have a dour edge of suffering, no matter what pleasantries they spoke. I could tell by their European accents that they were refugees like my parents. One of the women peeled back the metal tag with my number and I recited my mantra, remembering, yes, that I also had to get a container of milk. She gazed at me for an instant, amused by the little boy standing there with his complicated order. She had swollen, roughened hands that dexterously knotted the string around the box of Danishes with a few swift turns and twists. I watched those hands and noticed that on one forearm there was a long, faded, spidery number tattooed into the skin. Those were the numbers my parents spoke about when they would say of someone, "He has a number on his arm."

At that age, I did not appreciate what concentration camps were, couldn't figure out what it was about concentration that required a camp and produced so much death and sorrow. Friends of my parents had been in concentration camps and some, like Mrs. Salzburg, had numbers on their arms. I sensed in every smile or laugh of theirs an undercoating not just of pain, but of shame at what they had been through. I knew I wasn't supposed to stare at those numbers. But there was something about them that unnerved and fascinated me at the same time, as if the brand indicated membership in a secret, diabolical society. My mother had yet to tell me that my grandparents and uncles and aunts had in all likelihood been slaughtered in Treblinka. Yet I had an innate sense that there was something about the camps that was inextricably entangled with my family, even if I wasn't supposed to ask too many questions. In any case I could not take my eyes off the bakery clerk's tattooed forearm as it rocked convulsively while pressing down the blades on the bread-slicing machine. And I could not take my eyes off her arm as she smoothly slipped the sliced loaf of rye into a wax-paper bag, crumpling the edge of the bag into a handle and handing it to me. There was enormous dignity and even grace in all her motions, even as she brought the transaction to a halt.

"Enjoy the bread," she said, and then raised her voice toward the famished herd behind me. "Next!" she said.

By the time I returned home the metal-topped table was set for a small feast. The round rye bread I had brought was squeezed into the tableau and we took our places, arms quickly pronging at the food and smearing the slices of bread with butter. The sandwiches we assembled were ones we believed were original to our family. Between two slices of buttered bread we would put a sliver of herring, slices of egg, and pieces of cucumber, radish, tomato, and onion. The blandness of the bread and eggs offset the tartness of the herring, radish, and onion in a delectable combination. Although my parents had originated this concoction, my brother and I christened it, calling it the Deluxe Sandwich. We did not know what *deluxe* actually meant, but our dip into American hucksterism told us it conveyed elegance. Eating it was luxurious.

Somehow, as they devoured their sandwiches and gulped their instant coffee, my parents seemed friendlier to each other, funnier, their ribbing less biting. My brother and I would duel wits too and our parents enjoyed our cleverness even more than the sandwiches themselves. Sometimes the abundance of food made them recall the poverty of their upbringing. If my father would intrude with some recollection of his home, my mother would raise her eyebrows. Growing up on a farm, she would say, what could he know of the hunger she lived with routinely? Still, on Sunday morning the edge was off, and we could have been the most content of families.

If it was balmy outside, we might follow breakfast with a *shpatzir* along Broadway, where we knew we would run into other refugee friends who were spending their days in the same low-cost fashion. In summers, there was sometimes a picnic in Central Park, on a plateau on its northern frontier that featured a large biking oval and a narrow court where Irishmen hurled horseshoes. My parents and the Herlings spread blankets under a broad shade tree, swapped sandwiches of salami or chicken, and lay back to revel in the sunshine and the sight of Simon, Josh, and me wheeling our bicycles around the large oval. Every few minutes the serenity was broken by the *ping* or clatter of a plummeting horseshoe.

In winter, we often followed our breakfast with a trip to the Wollman ice skating rink in the southern end of Central Park. In those days, Wollman—we called it "Wollman's," as if belonged to some rumpled Jewish shopkeeper—might as well have been an Alpine resort. A dominant proportion of the Sunday-morning skaters were Europeans, comfortable Germans, Swiss, Dutch, French, and Austrians in vividly designed sweaters and tight stretch pants who were drawn to Central Park by the familiar pleasures of skating across a span of sun-washed ice surrounded by bare trees and tall, stately buildings and the calliope strains of Strauss waltzes. Several of the women, taking a break from skating, would sun themselves with three-sided reflectors propped under their chins like veterans of St. Moritz and Chamonix. Even in February, their faces were tanned a lustrous gold. These were the perquisites of wealth, I thought, and wished my parents not only indulged but knew how to indulge. In my bottomless envy, I didn't bother to consider that many of these Europeans, maybe most of them, were themselves prewar or wartime immigrants recovering from midnight escapes across nebulous borders or ocean passages to incongruous sanctuaries like Cuba and Brazil. What they had that my family didn't was a few years head start.

Wollman, though, was democratic. For ten cents, a child like myself could cavort among this haut monde and begin to feel a part. And, boy, did I cavort. Ice skating seemed to come naturally to me and by the second outing, I was circling along to the waltzes, slipping between tightly grouped skaters, jerking to a stop to head off a collision, gliding on triumphantly once more. Josh was often catching up behind me, and sometimes I raced to give him the slip. Through all this, out of the corner of my eye, I made sure to glimpse my parents, who were standing on the brick rampart overlooking the rink and smiling with pleasure.

Here were two refugees who had grown up in primitive Polish poverty where fun had to be contrived out of air. The only entertainment my father ever mentioned was a hayride he took with his sisters and cousins. My mother had fond memories of amusing herself by pretending to wash clothes by the river with her grandmother. Now my father and mother were watching their sons sporting among the prosperous, sharing their privileges. Whatever they had not accomplished in their translation to these shores, they had achieved this, and all for a dime entrance fee. This was the glory of America, and my cynical parents never belittled that. What may have made the experience bittersweet, gave the cheery calliope waltzes an undertone of sadness for my parents as well as many of the European skaters, was the knowledge of brothers and sisters who were never able to experience such moments of delight before their lives were cut short. But I was too young to appreciate this undertone.

One of the draws of Wollman was the presence of many of my Manhattan Day School classmates. There was my classmate Joyce, in a colorful skating tutu and sheer stockings over her long, well-turned legs, spinning twirls and slicing figure eights in the center of the rink under the tutelage of her private instructor. Most of the rest of us could not spend money on lessons, so we taught one another the basics. I taught Dickie Hochstein to skate. It was one arena in which I had the edge. Not only my brother but my friend Simon, Marvin Schenker, Howard Moses, Jay Zimmern, and others in my class soon flocked to Wollman, so that it became a kind of Sunday-morning club for yeshiva boys, a club where I was something of a luminary. By seventh grade I even organized a gang called the Mountaineers, whose mission it was to climb the rocky outcroppings—to us they felt like Himalayas—around Wollman. Yes, on Sunday mornings at Wollman, I was in my element.

It was not all champagne, however. Seeing the Europeans glide fluidly around the ice made me yearn for my parents to do so as well. So I implored them, promising I'd teach them to skate. They succumbed just once. My mother, who could be lilting on a dance floor, made some fleeting stabs at the ice that carried her once around the rink until she was exhausted. With some hours of practice, she probably would have become a skater. But my father, ungainly on the dance floor, was a specimen of clumsiness on the ice as well. Clinging with one hand to the railing as if it were the side of a lifeboat and clinging with the other hand to his pint-sized son, he clomped and wobbled and skidded but never achieved what might remotely be called skating. I could feel the terror in his grip. He barely made it once around the rink before giving up in defeat. I was embarrassed, a childish cruelty. After all, there had been no ice rink in his village of Borinya and his parents did not own ice skates. My father never articulated his handicaps and, in my eagerness for accomplished parents, I never gave him the benefit of the doubt.

But that day was an exception. Wollman was almost always a delight, and on one extravagant Sunday, we followed up the rink with a movie at Radio City Music Hall. What indulgence there was in that great entertainment cathedral—the soaring staircase, the sleek sculptures, the sheer immensity of the theater itself, with its colossal screen and tall burgundy velvet curtains. And of course there was the razzle-dazzle of the Rockettes' flawlessly symmetrical footwork. When we left, brimming with contentment as any American family might feel on a Sunday jaunt, my parents went one better and treated us to a meal at the Horn & Hardart Automat across Sixth Avenue. We never ate in restaurants. Never. A hot dog ordered at a delicatessen counter was as spendthrift as we went. So Horn & Hardart truly was a treat. The brass lions spouting coffee. The columns of metal-framed glass cells, each window springing open at the trigger of a few coins and dispensing its ceramic bowl of baked beans, or slice of fruit pie, or kaiser roll. I settled on the huckleberry pie my mother was urging on me. She had once tried a slice at lunch with a Garment District colleague. I plopped in my handful of nickels and watched with wonder as the glass window popped open to release a moist piece of pie. What a delicacy it seemed, and washed down with an excellent cup of coffee, it turned into an epicurean's delight. Life could not be finer. We left the place feeling flush, and spent the rest of that day feeling flush, as if we had just spent money we'd gotten from a well-earned bonus.

Looking back, that day seems a well-rounded coda to the first period of our immigration. It was obvious from the carefree ease that we had moved beyond the desperation of poverty and landlessness. Yes, we were not yet Americans, comfortable in our American skins. There were still about us the habits of foreigners pressing our faces against the glass of the candy store. But the sense of emergency was passing. And it seems fitting that a few short months after I devoured that slice of huckleberry pie in the Automat we moved on—literally—to the next stage of our lives, an apartment in the Bronx. Whether it was a move up was something that remained a subject of internal family debate for a few years to come.

It was Robert Moses, the Power Broker, the originator of the city's great highways, parks, and housing projects, who forced us to move. He doomed our building on the corner of 102nd Street and Manhattan Avenue so he could put up a checkerboard of low-income-housing projects that would run from 100th to 104th streets. Maury's mangier side of the street would somehow escape untouched, but our building, which had contained so much commotion and vitality, had three months left to stand. My mother had to hunt for an apartment all over again. She liked a place she saw on Riverside Drive. It was more than twice the rent we were paying, but she was willing to gamble we could afford it. My father, though, had heard from his friend the tailor, Moshe Granas, of new frontiers in the Bronx and a vacant apartment to boot. My rustic father never felt comfortable with the graces of Manhattan life, even in the rougher warrens of the West Side. The world of doormen and taxis, of bohemians and fashion plates, perplexed him. He was drawn by the blue-collar plainness of the Bronx.

When we saw the building that Granas had recommended it was obvious that it was among the Concourse's humblest, an unadorned six-story pile of weathered brown bricks braided by fire escapes at the end of a row of such buildings squeezed together flank to flank between 167th Street and 168th Street. Yet it was on the Grand Concourse, the Champs Élysées of the Bronx, with a broad avenue for traffic cut by tree-lined islands and dozens of cream-colored Art Deco palaces, one of which sat on the corner alongside our building. That was enough to offset my mother's misgivings and nudge her to consent. She decided to trust my father's instincts, as if they contained some divine message. Perhaps God looked out for men of simple needs like him.

And so we packed up our belongings in cardboard boxes scrounged from the neighborhood stores. A truck showed up, and with my father helping the brawny movers to save the cost—the moving company charged by the hour—and my mother scrutinizing the handling of our gimcracky furniture to ward off any scratch, we emptied our entire world at 102nd Street. Just before we left, I went back for one last look at our home and saw how vacant and bare it had become, when just a few hours before it had contained practically all the life that I could remember. I felt like weeping.

At some point, Maury and his younger brother, Isaac, came out to watch the bedlam of the move. I had no idea that our leaving for the Bronx would probably mean I would now see Maury only on rare occasions—our parents were not friends, after all—so I did not have the foresight to be heartbroken. Josh, who was now eight years old, and I, who was ten, squeezed into the back of the open truck, behind a protective metal flap that kept us from falling out, while my parents sat in the front alongside the driver. Maury, his black hair tousled, his shirt and pants unpressed, stood in the middle of the dreary street of low buildings with Isaac at his side. As the truck took off, he waved good-bye to Josh and me, shouting with a friendly laugh, "Have a good life, you finks!"

Waving back from the truck's hollow, I should have sensed how upset Maury really was.

16

From the day we moved in, my mother was offended by 1230 Grand Concourse. On Manhattan's West Side, she could stroll along Broadway among prospering and cultivated European immigrants and believe at moments that she too was prospering and cultivated. But 1230 Grand Concourse, with what she saw as its rabble of wage earners and storekeepers, offended her. Yes, they were American-born families, but as green as she was, she could tell they were common, small-time people.

After all, she was a woman of taste who, without much education, could still prize the great authors and composers. "Tol*stoy*" and "Cho*pin*," she would say energetically, accenting the last syllables as if fervor alone could express the refined sentiments she could not articulate. And she was attractive and stylish. In her late thirties, her wavy dark hair had not one gray strand in it. Her cheeks still had a youthful flush. Men, even fine men, still looked at her. She was meant for higher things.

"So what am I doing with a slob like Arnold Grubber living right underneath me," she would shout at my father.

"Shhh," he would say. "The neighbors will hear."

"I don't give, excuse me, a shit about what the neighbors think," she said.

I too felt the move had been something of a comedown. Where in the Bronx was there a street to match Broadway for vigor, style, and outlandishness? Where were the intriguing shops, the broad-shouldered buildings overflowing with polyglot humanity, the bustle of the furiously ambitious? Although I often felt deluged by my mother's opinions and energy, I nonetheless respected her, sensed that despite her coarse edges there was distinction to her. If she said Tolstoy was great, than he probably was great. Without articulating it, I too quickly agreed that we didn't belong at 1230 Grand Concourse, that we were meant for a nobler destiny.

The destiny of most of our neighbors, it seemed to me, was to spend the rest of their days watching life pass them by—quite literally. For on almost any sunny day, winter or summer, or any mild evening, a large slice of the building's residents—sometimes a dozen people—could be seen sitting in their collapsible aluminum chairs along the edge of the sidewalk facing the building's entrance. It was as if the sidewalk was their beach and the Concourse's noisy traffic behind them the background of roaring waves. They arrayed themselves in a colorful line against the parked cars, their eyes with a prime view of the comings and goings of 1230. Every once in a while they would lift their heads to the sun, surrendering to the warmth. But these respites were brief, for I felt their observation of the building's doorway was relentless. No quirk in clothing, no turn in mood, no shift in fortune seemed to escape their rigorous scrutiny. Every pretension, no matter how heartfelt, any groping for something distinctive would be appraised with the exacting eye of a jeweler and judged as flawed or synthetic, meant for some lower shelf.

The sidewalk regulars included Mr. Herbert Meltzer, a paunchy Hungarian who had come over many years before the war. Almost entirely bald, with a few wisps of white hair, he had a meat-red face with a cigar perpetually sticking out of it and a snarling accent, qualities that darkened the power of his cutting sense of humor. His wife, Dora, conspicuous in a woolly head of sulfur-and-gray hair, was also of Hungarian stock and also lusty tempered. But she was born here, an advantage she constantly bludgeoned her husband with. They were the Fred and Ethel Mertz of our block and liked to entertain their neighbors with their marital bickerings. When Mrs. Meltzer was not scolding him, she sparred with Mrs. Shreiner, squabbling over such great issues as which bakery on 167th Street, Sheridan or Sherbloom's, had the better rye bread. People said they were the best of friends, but few friendships were as durable as their rivalry.

My favorite among the sidewalk regulars was Mr. Waxroth, a stout, fortyish locksmith. An intelligent man, he regretted that having to work during the Depression had kept him out of college. But he possessed a *World Almanac* store of information and often needed to let people know about it. It seemed to me that Mr. Waxroth could identify the five Great Lakes, the original thirteen colonies, the twelve sons of Jacob, and the eight horses that had won the Triple Crown. The great ache of his life was that he and his wife, a spare, nervous woman, were childless, the result of some accident or violent attack whose details they shrouded in mystery.

I was now taking the subway to and from Manhattan Day School. Whenever I walked the twenty yards from the subway station at 167th Street to my building, lugging my satchel swollen with Hebrew and English books, I would spot the neighbors seated outside the building and feel as if I were about to walk through a gauntlet poised to pummel me. One cold stare from Mr. Meltzer would quicken my steps into the building. Who knew what he and the others were thinking? They were almost always civil, after all. But whatever deficiencies I felt my family suffered I could detect in the merciless eyes of those neighbors. In truth, even from my parents' narrow view, these neighbors were a step up in class from the transient pack that inhabited our building at 102nd Street. For the most part, these old Bronx hands were settled in for the long haul, with steady jobs and long leases. Sure, we had a sense—exaggerated as it may have been—of European advantage, but our neighbors, as a community of like-minded souls, had the collective power to even the score.

Then there was Arnold Grubber. For my mother, he epitomized everything that was coarse and vulgar about the building. Grubber was also a sidewalk regular, but he did not sit with the others. He posted himself across the pavement on the building doorway's stone steps. He spent most of his evenings and weekends sitting on the top step smoking a nasty-smelling White Owl, his thick, short thighs spread apart so that his big belly could lodge comfortably, his genital bulge contoured on one thigh. He would flip through the *Daily Mirror,* pausing now and then to wipe the sweat off his face with a swipe of his hairy forearm, or else he would gaze out resentfully at people walking by. Every once in a while he would clear his throat with a gruff gargle and spit into the mangy hedgerows fringing the building. Often he would hit the building. Cranky and sullen, he gradually stopped speaking to all his neighbors.

But he did occasionally speak with me. He would invite me to play hit-the-penny. We would put a coin down on the shallow groove between two large squares of pavement and stand on opposite ends trying to strike the coin. We would bounce the ball back and forth and announce the new score with every strike. A close game would draw the attention of the spectators in the beach chairs. Grubber would smile his rare smile whenever he scored a few hits in a row. A victory would make him feel particularly expansive, and he would start talking baseball with me. Grubber had actually seen Babe Ruth, Lou Gehrig, and Joe DiMaggio play, and I would feast on his tales of their heroics and his inside knowledge of the game. Now, though, he had come to hate the Yankees, whose home was six blocks down the Concourse. Their general manager, George Weiss, was an anti-Semite, he said. Had the Yankees ever had a Jewish player, he would ask to prove his point. I never bothered to check, but over the years I heard him lodge the accusation of anti-Semitism against Franklin D. Roosevelt, John Foster Dulles, Henry Luce, Ernest Hemingway, Charles Lindbergh, Charlie Chaplin, Ben Hogan, the French, and *The New York Times* (which he said explained why he never read the paper). I guessed he was probably right on some, but I figured that his aim when it came to anti-Semites was about as good as when he spat.

Despite my mother's disdain for Grubber and some of the other people in the building, the irony was that in the hierarchy prevailing at 1230, we were near the bottom of the heap. I learned that one day from a sixtyish woman, Mrs. Lefcourt, who lived on the ground floor. I was playing punchball with Josh, who was then nine, in the alley separating our building from the grander one next door. Every time I got ready to hit the ball, I broadcast an exuberant play-by-play in a folksy

Mel Allen twang: "Well, here we are, the bases are loaded, it's two out
in the bottom of the ninth, and it's Mickey Mantle's turn at the plate."
Or some such folderol.

As I hit the ball over my brother's head, I shouted, Mel Allen style
again, that the ball was "Going, going—it is *gone*," and triumphantly
rounded the building corners and other markers we used for bases.
The noise of these hijinks must have hit a particularly irritating level
because I was soon startled by a glimpse of Mrs. Lefcourt glowering at
us through the pearly reflection of her first-floor window, followed
swiftly by the bolt-action ascent of the window sash.

"I thought I told you kids I don't want you playing in the alley," she
barked.

I shut up, but Josh giggled nervously, and that enraged Mrs. Lefcourt.

"You better show some respect, you little mockies, or I'll call the
police," she said.

She pulled down the bottom sash as an exclamation point. We saun-
tered off in defeat, but the word *mockie* kept reverberating in my brain.
I wasn't sure what it meant. At first I thought it had something to do
with my being Jewish, but then I understood that it was aimed at me as
being a particular kind of Jew—a recent immigrant. Her insult had
included my parents. Despite all our pretensions, this was what these
Jews in the building thought of us. I never told my parents about the
incident.

But I didn't have to. My parents knew they were not fully accepted.
They were greenhorns. With few exceptions the people in the building
had been born in America or had come there as children. They devoted
their energies to spurning the queer habits of their own parents, the
whining accents and grating consonants, the smells of boiling chicken
and marinated herring, the trembling hesitation with every dollar
spent. They moved away from that world when they fled the tenements of the Lower East Side. They didn't want it following them. But
we carried with us all that musty Old World baggage. My mother
spoke with a rasping, guttural accent. Her vocabulary, by this time,
was large enough to manage daily commerce, but it was not always
swiftly accessible, so that she often struggled to retrieve a word and

reddened with frustration as she did. She still observed some of the Orthodox Jewish rituals that on the Concourse were becoming out-moded. Besides, who was she with her airs of refinement? She was no professor who had lost her station in the Nazi rise to power. She was a hatmaker on Seventh Avenue, a member of Alex Rose's union. Her husband was a mechanic in a New Jersey factory that made ironing board covers. In Poland he had been a farmer.

My mother seemed confident that people in the building would eventually discern her charm and intelligence. In fact, she was able to make friends with two women, Sylvia Goldstein, an effervescent lady almost ten years older with a teenage son and daughter, and Gloria Schwartz, a comely younger woman with two small girls who had a natural verve that 1230 could not contain. But whatever connections my mother would make, she felt her husband would eventually sabotage them. Five years in this country and he still could read only the Yiddish papers. He didn't follow baseball or football or politics—except the news about Israel—couldn't play poker or drive a car or tell a joke or stay awake through a good movie.

My mother, however, was determined that my father's lack of panache would not hold her back. The war and marriage may have robbed her of a grander fate than 1230, but she would show these people who she really was. On the High Holidays she seemed to try especially hard to make her point. Rosh Hashanah and Yom Kippur provided the chance for the Jews of the Bronx to parade along the Concourse, and she could show off her sons in all their Gimbel's finery to other families who were doing the same. She would take my father's arm and lock it around hers. She puffed out her chest, straightened her neck proudly, and, with a discreet yet assured smile, walked down the boulevard in almost swaggering fashion. My father, in a pinstriped navy blue suit that my mother had picked out, looked trim and dapper, a far cry from the rumpled man smelling of sweat and stale breath whom I saw at the end of every workday. Broad-shouldered, handsome, with his thick black hair and gentle smile, he looked impressive, and my mother showed him off too. I loved the warm, secure feel of his thick, callused hand, and when he looked as natty as he did on those days, I proudly held on to that hand on our stroll back from synagogue.

As we approached the 1230 gauntlet, my mother acted even more edgy than usual. A half block away, she inspected her brood, shouting off a necessary adjustment in a shoelace or button. I could feel her tension in the sharp tugs with which she straightened my burgundy bow tie as we neared the sidewalk gallery. She might say, "I don't give, excuse me, a shit about what the neighbors think," but even at eleven years old I sensed that what the neighbors thought mattered crucially.

My father offered the first greeting, extending his hand toward Mr. Waxroth at the end chair.

"*Gut Yontiv,*" he said. "*Gut Yontiv.*"

"Happy New Year," Mr. Waxroth replied.

Then my father shook hands down the line of beach chairs, parroting in a still-uncomfortable English a "Happy New Year" to each occupant and smiling an ingratiating smile. I watched this scene from behind, feeling spiffy in my pepper-gray worsted suit but irked that my father was lavishing himself so freely on these people.

"So where did you pray this morning?" Mr. Waxroth asked him.

"Rabbi Brodsky's shul," my father replied. "You know, the small shul around the corner from the big temple—down the hill."

Mr. Waxroth had bought tickets to the big temple, Adath Israel, the conservative synagogue right on the Concourse, which had a stately pillared entrance resembling that of an actual Greek temple. He mulled my father's information over, stroking his thick black mustache.

"Yeh, I know it, right around the corner from where I go," he said. "You know, I used to go to an Orthodox synagogue. But I need air-conditioning. It's hot. People's breath stinks. I get sick. I know what you're not supposed to do on Yom Kippur, but at least at Adath Israel people brush their teeth. So if you swallow a little water, it's no big sin."

My father chortled, though I wasn't sure who he was laughing at or what about.

Mrs. Shreiner looked my brother and me over and smiled.

"Ooh, Rachel," she bubbled to my mother. "You dress your children so nice. I can't even get Elliott to put on a suit. He's in the park playing ball, the big shot."

Behind her chiding I sensed a real admiration for Elliott's independence. He was the tough kid and Josh and I were Mama's boys dressing up to please our parents.

"You fasting this year?" Mrs. Shreiner said to Mrs. Meltzer.

"Fasting?" Mrs. Meltzer replied. "Sure. I'm cutting out ham with my eggs for breakfast."

A raucous laugh exploded along the entire line of beach chairs. My parents joined in too. Only Grubber, who was sitting across the sidewalk on the stone steps in a baggy brown suit, his collar open and tie loosened, did not seem amused. He looked up from his *Daily Mirror*, glowering, then spat into the hedges.

The probability was that our neighbors were reconciled to their modest lives at 1230 and resented us for scraping for something better, even something more authentically Jewish. The crisp press of the clothes we wore, the book bags bulging with yeshiva schoolbooks, the piano teachers traveling up from Manhattan, the sleep-away summer camps—all that effort galled them. Experience had taught them how futile it all was. Here we were worried about concealing our blemishes while they were snickering at our virtues.

17

The late 1950s were years of arrivals and additions. First my sister was born and then my uncle Yasha—the only other survivor in my mother's large family—turned up from Australia. My American family was becoming denser, but more perplexing as well.

The first hint that something was in the works came in the summer of 1956. My mother decided to keep us close to home, enrolling us at a low-cost YMHA day camp on 165th Street. She might have sent me back to the sleep-away camp I had gone to in the summer of 1955—Cejwin Camps in Port Jervis—where I had mostly thrived and even survived the double whammy of Hurricanes Connie and Diane, which had forced us to evacuate our flooded bunks. But that had been a difficult summer for her, and not because of the hurricanes. Josh, prone to weepy bouts of homesickness, had stayed behind in the city and been miserable. She did not want him to be miserable in the summer of 1956 because she had a new concern: she was going to have a baby. How was she going to work at the hat factory, clean and cook, mind her health, and keep my prickly brother, Josh, happy? No, she would leave him with me in day camp and he would be happy. In the Old Country it was axiomatic that brothers stayed together. I probably would have liked to return to Cejwin for a summer of old friends and fresh adventures, of crisp air and a bunk filled with the sweet fragrance of unfamiliar toothpastes, of splashing in a lake and the intimacy of campfires. But all that would have to be sacrificed.

I started to get to know the new Bronx neighborhood, catch as catch can. Home from the routines of a bland day at day camp, we played punchball in the paved yard behind our apartment house or in the narrower alley alongside, and sometimes we got chosen to play by the ragamuffins on the next block east, Sheridan Avenue, a more feral lot than the studious Concourse types. I was a fairly good punchball player. Josh at nine was still bumbling. Yet feeling my omniscient mother's penetrating gaze on the alley from our apartment, I had to make sure he found a place in the game. The Sheridan gang's star was a gawky tomboy named Shelly who could loft a Spalding from home plate over the wire fence at the end of the alley. I wasn't anywhere as good as she was, but neither were the other boys, so we accepted her as an unnatural phenomenon and made no efforts to belittle one another for being outclassed by a girl. Every now and then a neighborhood woman threw a pot of hot water down at us to drive us out. More worrisome was Henry, the superintendent of the building across the alley from ours. A short, squat black man, he was cursed with a hernia that gave him a prominent bulge just above his crotch. But his sprint, when he periodically rousted us out of the alley, was fast and churning, like a desert roadrunner's. It made the bulge of his hernia appear like his 300-horsepower motor. We dreaded ever being caught.

Occasionally, a red-haired, freckle-faced Sheridan roughneck named Michael would make an appearance. He was younger than me but a ferocious fighter. Once, for no legitimate reason, he punched my brother in the face, shoved him to the ground, then pummeled away some more. I stood there distressed but did nothing to stop it. I had gotten the tacit message from my parents that fighting could be lethal. The important thing was to avoid getting hurt, even if my brother wound up with an unavenged bloody nose. We sulked away, my brother sobbing and I leading him out of the alley before Michael decided to turn on me. I had let my brother down. But Josh was devoted to me, and he always seemed to sidle back.

Gradually we played more often with the kids in the Grand Concourse building next door to ours with whom we shared a side alley:

Charlie, a red-haired only child who had the magnetism to become our leader, and his tall, lanky friend Richie. We always figured they came from wealthy homes because their building was made of white, not red, bricks, had a doorman and an elevator, and apartments with two steps leading down to the living room. In fact, Charlie and Richie's families were just one or two rungs above us on the economic ladder. Maybe their fathers managed the factory rather than labored in it and earned fifty dollars a week more. Such distinctions, though, could be crucial.

All in all, we were shoehorning our way into American life. These weren't refugee kids we were playing with. They weren't all Jewish. They weren't all poor. We were finding a place of sorts in the neighborhood, awkward as it still felt. The American urban Mixmaster was doing its timeless job, introducing us to its motley cast of characters, teaching us the mores and lingo of the street, smoothing our coarse edges and coarsening some that were too dainty for the rigors of the Bronx.

By the time school resumed, it became obvious that my mother had grown rounder. Every day, she rose early, boiled us a pot of Wheatena or Cream of Wheat, hustled us off to the subway toward school, and waddled out of our apartment herself to take the subway to work. Manhattan Day School let out at 5:00 P.M., and we were usually home by six, but she was never there. She was working overtime, trimming as many hats as she could to multiply her piecework earnings before the income drought that would follow the baby's birth. Into her eighth month of pregnancy she worked until seven o'clock at night and sometimes came home after eight. I would look out our fifth-floor window to see if I could spot her walk—no longer as staccato as it had been—in the swarms emerging from the corner subway entrance. When the crowd thinned to a straggler or two, it sank in that she had not been on that particular train. I would look again in another ten minutes, in the meantime closing my eyes and praying that nothing bad had happened to her.

One rainy day she came home later than usual, heated up something for supper, sat down to eat, and started to cry.

"I fell on the subway," she finally confided. "I was rushing to get home and I slipped on a wet step. I hope it didn't hurt the baby. Don't worry, Joey. Everything feels like it's fine. I'm just worried."

I worried too. I had heard how treacherous pregnancy could be. A single fall could mean I would have a retarded or crippled sibling. How insidious that would be, subverting what I was coming to see as our family's fluid and uneventful journey through the cycle of years.

"Please, God, make sure the baby comes out normal," I murmured in the prayers I said to myself every night before going to sleep.

In late January of 1957, deep into her ninth month, my mother quit work. She was too tired to keep lugging herself downtown and back by subway and afraid that she would give birth on a factory floor littered with scraps of thread and straw. But once home she did not relax. She did all the chores she had not been able to do while working. She filled the freezer compartment with meat she knew she would not be able to shop for once the baby was born. She sent a package off to her aunt in Warsaw and a money order to her brother in Australia. She deposited the cash she had been squirreling away from the buff pay envelopes she brought home weekly.

While she was on a bus returning from the bank, she felt the pains of labor, sharper than she remembered them ten and twelve years before. Knowing my father was in New Jersey, she rushed on her own to a hospital. It was Lincoln's Birthday and Josh and I were off from school. When my mother did not show up after a few hours, I fretted that something terrible had happened, that perhaps she had slipped again, only this time it had been fatal. But then the phone rang. It was my father calling from Jersey.

"Mommy's in the hospital, she's going to have the baby soon," he said, in a voice both giddy and fearful. "I'm going to the hospital to stay with her. Make yourself something to eat for dinner and I'll be home later."

I didn't know or care about cooking, but Josh, more earthbound than I was, had been studying my mother at the stove. He fried us scrambled eggs with onions and we had it with slices of buttered rye bread. Then we waited for further news of this upheaval in our lives.

When my father came home toward midnight, the grin on his face was larger and his eyes had a glint of wonder in them.

"Everybody's healthy," he said. "Thank God."

"The baby's OK?" I asked. "It's a normal baby?"

"Yes, Joey, it's a healthy baby. That's what the doctor said. A healthy baby."

"Is it a girl or a boy?" my brother asked.

"It's a girl," my father said. "A girl."

He chuckled to himself, and there was something altogether inscrutable about the laugh. This man who had been brought up as the only boy among six sisters, six sisters who had been swallowed up by the war, was now going to be raising his own little girl.

The next evening my father came home early from work and took us to see my mother and new sister at Dr. Leff's Lying-in Hospital. I quickly realized that my immigrant mother was thriving. She was in a spacious, brightly lit room with two American women in beds next to hers and they were all gabbing genially like army buddies home from a war they had won. And there sucking on her breast was a small, doughy clump of quickening flesh with two scarcely open eyes. This was my sister. My father was fluttering around my mother and the baby, then looking over at us inquisitively, like an insecure chef eager to learn our reaction to his soufflé.

"It's got all its toes and all its fingers," he said, repeating an American expression he must have picked up from his coworkers. "It's a healthy baby."

We had to decide what to call the new baby, and my parents, aware of their own ignorance of American idiom, brought Josh and me into the consultation right at the hospital bed. There were only two choices. The baby had to be named after one of my parents' dead mothers.

"My mother was named Peseh Tutel," my mother informed us with a shy laugh.

That was the first time I had heard my grandmother's actual name. Yes, my mother had told us the story of how her mother had died of tuberculosis, but she had never uttered her mother's name. Perhaps she did not want to deepen some sadness she imagined we might feel by giving her mother the actuality of a name. In any case, I had never bothered to ask the name. Now when Josh and I heard it, we looked at each other and snickered.

"Peseh Tutel Berger?" I said. "That'll be a hit with the kids in the alley."

"Yeah," said a giggling Josh. "Hey, Peseh Tutel! Wanna go out and play punchball? Chips on the ball, Peseh Tutel."

My parents laughed right along with us, as if we were joking about a distant ancestor. They had been in America long enough to be amused by the quaint ways of their Polish shtetls, and they indulged us our insensitivity. They understood that the imported names of the shtetl's denizens would sound odd on the Grand Concourse. Peseh Tutel sounded odd even in Poland. Yet here it could reasonably be changed to Phyllis or Patricia. I said I didn't like the name Phyllis and that seemed to put an end to that. And Patricia, we sensed, wasn't Jewish. (When we immigrated here in 1950, my brother's Yiddish name had been anglicized to James, until friends told us James was not a Jewish name and Joshua—his real name—was in fact both Jewish and American.)

"How about Paulette?" my mother asked. "Like the girl in the building."

But thirteen-year-old Paulette in our building was gawky and freckled and not my idea of a beauty, and she could be acerbic to boot, so I exercised my veto again. When we ran out of the *P*'s, we turned to the name of my father's mother—Chava. Chava was a perfectly popular name in Yiddish culture, but its English equivalent—Eve—had acquired the gloss of a scheming, two-timing film noir vixen. I was taken by a variation on that name—Evelyn. The name belonged to the perky younger sister of a classmate. Since I had become the family authority on things American, and my father was silent and my mother indecisive, Evelyn Berger it became.

And there she was, wrapped in a blanket and suckling at her mother's breast as her father and brothers circled the bed. By whimsy and silence, we were making momentous decisions about her life, like the name she would carry forever, yet there was a sense of contentment in that hospital room. Our refugee family had enlarged itself in the New World to five with our first genuine American, born in the Bronx, New York, in the United States of America. It promptly crossed my mind that my new sister could become president of the United States, something Josh and I never could.

To celebrate, my father took Josh and me to a delicatessen on 170th Street. Instead of just hot dogs, he ordered a pastrami sandwich for himself and one for Josh and me to split. We had deliciously oily french fries—an indulgence my mother would have forbidden—and cole slaw and pickles and a piece of stuffed derma and we washed it down with Dr. Brown's Black Cherry Soda.

"So how do you like having a sister?" my father asked.

It was a simple but striking question because my father never asked us philosophical questions like this.

"She's a pretty baby," I said.

"She's a pretty baby," Josh agreed.

And she was. With a great clamor from the outdoor congregation of neighbors at 1230, who left their aluminum chairs to marvel at what was inside the pink bundle my mother hugged close to her, we brought the baby home. For the next month of Sundays, my mother's uncle Yudel and his family, and Mr. and Mrs. Lessen and the Weinbergs and the Coopermans and the Erlichs and the Herlings took turns visiting us to gawk at this new refugee offshoot while filling themselves on my parents' spreads of egg salad, whitefish, and herring, and squares of apple and sponge cake. My mother sat in our living room, with the baby nursing, chatting with the visitors as if she were a queen entertaining her court. Not everyone's delight was unalloyed.

"Why didn't you tell me you were going to have a baby?" Mrs. Cooperman said, with a pointed laugh. "I would have tried for one myself."

My mother chuckled, knowing there was a barb hidden in the question. My mother was secretive about her life's decisions, a habit no doubt picked up from the war or from the embarrassments of poverty. But she shrugged off such jabs. That was the way these small-town greeners thought.

With Evelyn's arrival, strolling on the Concourse assumed a nobler dimension. Josh and I took turns pushing the navy blue pram my father had bought so we could show off the baby as if it were ours. The baby's presence hastened our absorption into the sidewalk gallery of lawn chair sitters, who, after all, could not resist a baby. Indeed, when the weather turned warm, my mother and the baby were often invited to sit in an empty lawn chair. My mother would sing a Yiddish jingle and the baby, springing up and down on its chubby drumstick legs, danced on her lap as the neighbors gaped in wonder.

The new baby was a dark-eyed meddler, a wild card in a family that had settled into a predictable routine. With my mother soon working again, we hired a neighborhood woman, Molly, to tend to the baby during the hours Josh and I were in school. Molly left when we came home, and we had to learn to feed the baby, diaper her, and put her to sleep. Sometimes it seemed a chore, but more often I felt that my life had undergone a spirited transformation—making me feel happier and more at ease. I liked best sitting at the side of the crib, free now to open my voice in full-throated song, crooning the American standards I had grown to love, by Gershwin and Rodgers and Hart, like "Someone to Watch Over Me," and "My Funny Valentine," and "Love Walked Right In." And there was a theme song from a popular Gary Cooper movie that year, *Friendly Persuasion,* the story of a pacifist Quaker father trying to keep his family out of the Civil War, that seemed to linger as a song in my heart. "Thee I love" it began, and spoke of green medows and buds on a May Apple tree. Saccharine and 1950s square as the lyrics might seem today, I did feel love flowing to this baby, and looking back now I think it was something deeper and different than the love a much older brother might feel toward his baby sister. This baby had been a kind of reparation, making a small amends for all my parents had been through, rekindling life after so much death. She had glued the gimcrack pieces of our family together again, declaring by her birth that the Berger family had moved beyond the stagnation of mere survival and was venturing forth along fresh paths that would take them away from the ravages of the past. Besides, she had been born in safety, in the bourgeois ordinariness of the Grand Concourse, with my parents earning enough to pay the hospital bill and buy her a crib. There were friends, plenty of them, who were delighted by her arrival and wanted to take part in our pleasure, and we could afford to feed them. As our first native American, the baby had anchored us in the landscape. Our isolation in America was diminishing.

18

At my father's bar mitzvah in the rustic village of Borinya, he was called up to the front of the shul and given a chance to say short blessings before and after the Torah reading. Afterward the men drank shots of fiery whisky, tempering it with morsels of sponge cake and handfuls of chickpeas, and went home for their afternoon meal and nap. In that pious but unadorned world, that was all there was to a bar mitzvah. In America now, I had no great yearning for anything much grander, but my mother worried that her sons not be denied the conventions of the world in which we moved. One by one all the boys in my eighth-grade yeshiva class were having parties in cavernous catering halls with rowdy bands, cornucopian smorgasbords, and waiters in faded red uniforms heaving ponderous platters of prime ribs of beef. If that was what the other boys in the class were having, I would have no less, my mother determined. Where she and my father would get the money for such a splashy production, I did not bother to ask. But I could only imagine that all the movies, restaurants, lunches, vacations, newspapers, and taxis they had denied themselves must have amounted to something.

For me, a wearying stretch of toil lay ahead. The stalwart yeshiva boys didn't just chant the haftarah—the supplement to the weekly Torah portion selected from Kings or Judges or one of the Prophets. That sufficed for public school kids who went grudgingly to afternoon

Hebrew school. No, yeshiva boys were intellectual Samsons and read the entire Torah portion itself, with the haftarah as a mere encore. That meant I would have to memorize the singsong cantillation accompanying each of roughly two thousand words since the musical notes were not inscribed in the actual Torah scroll. It was like having to sing the libretto of an opera without the music in front of me.

Eight months before the big day, we retained a tutor. Rabbi Zion was the spiritual leader of the *shtibl* in which my parents' friend Mr. Weinberg worshiped, a roomlike synagogue one flight above a dry cleaner's shop. By the looks of the place, you could be sure that his congregants did not worship there for the grandeur. They liked Rabbi Zion, and I did too. Every week I would go to his apartment on Gerard Avenue off 161st, which was one floor below Mr. Weinberg's in the same tumbledown wood-shingled house. Rabbi Zion was Orthodox in the fervent European way but he had slowly adopted modern appearances. He was pleasantly stout, blondish, clean-shaven, and his English had the slightly rasping accent of someone who had immigrated as a teenager. We would work together in a musty, cluttered study where there was a bookcase of well-thumbed volumes of Talmud, a desk, a single bed, and a low armchair in which he leaned back while I sat upright on a hard wooden chair. I struggled not just to decode, but simply to hold up my burgundy-covered *tikkun,* a tome that contained the whole Torah in two versions. Running down one half of each page was the modern Hebrew typography with the vowels punctuated and the musical symbols denoted. Running down the other half was the more ancient cursive of the Torah, stark naked except for thin, ornamental fringes over some letters. The spare, sacred calligraphy made me feel as if I were reading the very handwriting of God.

"*Va-yomer Adonay el Mosheh boh el Par-oh* [And the Lord said unto Moses, 'Go in unto Pharoah']," Rabbi Zion sang, raising and lowering the pitch in a timeless undulation.

I would try to mimic his example. When I blundered, he would sometimes go back to basics, reviewing the do-re-mi of Torah reading, the *trup*.

"*Mahpach pashta moonach, zakef-katon, zakef-gadol,*" Rabbi Zion would chant, demonstrating where I had missed a rise or dip in the melody or a tremolo or two. *"Munach zarcah, munach segol, mer-chah tipchah, merchah sof pasuch."*

As the lessons progressed and I chanted more fluidly, Rabbi Zion began to relax, and more than once I saw him pick up the Yiddish paper and scan the headlines, even hiding his face so it was difficult to be sure whether he approved of what I was singing or not. He some-how kept an alert ear for any mistake, for if I mispronounced a word or botched a note, he would correct me from behind the Yiddish paper. When he wasn't reading, he would sometimes close his eyes in dreamy fashion. I would think he was asleep, but since he again detected every error, his thoughts must have run off somewhere, as if he were listen-ing not to me but to a swaying old man wrapped in a yellowed prayer shawl chanting the hoary melodies in the ramshackle house of prayer of his Polish boyhood. Without his confiding the reverie, I was sure it was the same kind of synagogue the grandfathers I never knew had worshiped in.

As the bar mitzvah day grew closer, we picked a catering hall, a band, and a photographer, and then we trekked down to the Lower East Side, to Louis Kaplan, a master tailor, and had him measure my father, my brother, and me for custom suits. This time even Gimbel's wouldn't do. Louis Kaplan was a whirlwind who told you what to wear and brooked no arguments, not even from my mother. He was short with a leathered face and there was always a cigarette dangling from his mouth, responsible, no doubt, for the coarseness in his voice and his occasional coughing fits. He ran his hands over my shoulders, legs, and thighs as if they were extensions of his body, with no respect for private feelings. But he wielded his chalk and measuring tape with confident precision and a sculptor's gift for molding fabrics to the con-tours of a body. The shop, despite its cut-rate Lower East Side con-struction, bespoke elegance. The fabrics were deep and supple and flowed off their bolts like water. The shirts in the glass cases were all French-cuffed and white on white. The bow ties were silk and in such rich shades as burgundy. The photographs of himself and his wife and sons on a boat in Sheepshead Bay confirmed that he had a thriving business and I felt privileged to have him chalk the large patches of navy blue fabric to match the outlines of my body.

We had to go back for two fittings, and when the finished suit was draped over my body I looked in the triptych mirrors and realized he had turned a refugee frog into a prince. And Josh, now starting to outgrow me, made a handsome consort in his matching suit. Kaplan picked out burgundy bow ties and cuffed shirts and then came forward with the coup de grâce: a pair of gold-and-black cuff links. It was the first time I had ever worn cuff links, and the gold twinkling out from below the sleeve of my suit jacket, the solid heft of the links against my wrist, gave my body a transforming dignity I had never felt before. More than my mastery of the Torah cantillation, these cuff links made me feel that, yes, today, I was a man.

We had to buy an evening gown for my mother, so we walked a few blocks to Division Street, where Levine and Smith sold coats and dresses fit for the carriage trade at straphanger prices. My mother—flushed and brunet—whirled around their velvet-draped shop in a ballooning royal-blue satin number like Loretta Young. I could see by her incandescent smile that she too felt she had been transformed.

"How do you think I look, Joey?" she asked me, as if I was the arbiter of good taste in our house.

Of course, I thought she looked fine, and after she specified a few alterations, it was done. We went home weary from shopping but weary also from the unshakable suspicion—a suspicion that by osmosis had now permeated down to Josh and me—that all the money we were spending would deplete our safety net for the crises that life had taught my parents would surely come.

Then came the morning of the big day. I slipped the white-on-white shirt out of its plastic sleeve, inhaling its camphory new-shirt fragrance and gliding my hand over its silky white cloth. I pulled the pins out as if I were disassembling a hand grenade, making sure to avoid any rips, and carefully unfurled the shirt and put it on. The shirt molded to my shoulders and the French cuffs felt crisp against my wrists. Louis Kaplan's suit felt tender and caressing. And my black Florsheim loafers gleamed up at me as emphatically as exclamation points. I looked at Josh, who was relishing his identical outfit in the mirror.

"Spiffy!" I said.

"You too," he replied.

Here was this younger brother of mine, lanky and already two inches taller than me, reveling in my day of confirmation as if it were his own. He had been so enamored of my learning to chant the Torah that he tagged along to some of my lessons at Rabbi Zion's. At home, when I practiced the uncantillated version of my Torah portion—my *parshah*—he willingly sat with a Hebrew Bible and checked my accuracy. As a result, he learned most of my *parshah* as well as I did. He loved me, even though, in my worries over whether an immature younger brother might diminish me, I too often found ways of dodging and snubbing him. But here he was, excited for me as if I had been nothing but a saint to him. How could I explain such indiscriminate potato love?

On a gray January day, the four of us strode rapidly along the wide Concourse to the synagogue, pushing my sister in a carriage. Everyone knew the synagogue, Tifereth Beth Jacob, as Rabbi Brodsky's shul. It was a modest house of worship, a one-story bunker sandwiched between two ornate temples, one conservative, the other Sephardic, and together, the three synagogues were powerful testimony to the flourishing Jewish community of the Bronx of those days. Inside Tifereth, a narrow vestibule led to the modest prayer hall, where rows of blond-wood benches ended at a small stage with the ruby-curtained Holy Ark. There was no balcony or vaulted ceiling to lend any splendor. And the congregation was modest as well, mostly immigrant Jews from the scrappy side streets of the Bronx. It was a Yiddish-speaking crowd and Rabbi Brodsky gave his sermons in Yiddish, which is why my father felt comfortable there. The regulars struggled along from year to year to pay the rabbi's salary and heat the synagogue in winter. During the Yom Kippur appeal, the congregation's officers would roam through the packed crowd and worshipers would whisper what they planned to give. The information was passed on to the president, sitting behind the altar, who would announce the amount publicly in his gravelly voice, as if we were at an auction.

"From Mees-ter and Mee-sus Ketz, eighteen dollars for *Chai*," the president would say, mentioning a number the congregation knew was the numeric equivalent of the Hebrew word for "life."

It was crass, but it got the job done, feeding vanities and spurring rivalries and ratcheting up the amounts that were donated. Occasionally, they even auctioned off the *aliyahs*.

"*Finif dul-lar far Cay-en,*" the president shouted, letting everyone know that the bid for the first *aliyah,* which went to a descendant of the *Cohanim,* or Israelite priests, was five dollars. Could anyone top that? was the implied question. Twenty-five usually took home the bacon.

The prayers, though, were always passionately fervent, particularly on Yom Kippur, when the white-robed cantor prostrated himself on the dusty floor and moaned and sobbed as he beseeched God for mercy for his congregation of guileless, unembellished Jews facing another year of turmoil and peril.

The role model for all of us was our beloved rabbi, Samson Brodsky, a slight, unaffected man who never seemed to need the congregation's adoration and saw his job as providing spiritual and moral direction—not opinions on Israeli and American politics. Every so often, with quick, businesslike steps on the way to and from synagogue, he would pass my house on a Sabbath and spy me playing punchball. I had no yarmulke on my scalp and my casual clothes testified that I had no intention of sanctifying the day. But he pretended not to see me, apparently sensing that an acknowledgment would embarrass both of us. I would get to where I would need to be in my own good time, he seemed to think.

When we arrived at Rabbi Brodsky's shul on my bar mitzvah day, the *Shacharith,* the long morning prayer, had already started even though there were just a few Jews scattered around the benches. But there in the front row was my friend Simon, more than punctual as always, and his father, with his impish, mustachioed smile. Simon too was excited for me—the first of his friends to brave this ritual.

"Hey, Joe," he whispered, "I don't want to make you nervous, but your fly's open."

He got me to look, and of course it wasn't open, so I laughed. That was Simon. But concerned about propriety, I quickly tempered my face to one of earnestness. I put on the silk prayer shawl my father had bought me and began to pray as if I were the rabbi's eldest son. Every

My mother in Lys'va in
the Soviet Urals, c. 1941.

Rachel and Marcus, in their
civil marriage photograph,
on December 5, 1943, in
Lys'va.

With my mother in Lys'va, c. 1946.

My mother taking a stroll on the Kurfurstendamm in the American-occupied zone of Berlin, c. 1947, after the war.

My father and my uncle, Yasha Golant (my mother's brother), in front of a barracks at the Schlachtensee DP Camp in Berlin, c. 1947.

At two and a half, then known as Srulek, I'm surrounded by other refugee children in the Schlactensee DP Camp. I am in a white shirt and dark shorts second from the right in the second row.

With Josh (on back of the tricycle) and a stray dog at the Landsberg DP Camp, where we were transferred during the Berlin blockade of 1948.

At a refugee birthday party in Schlactensee DP Camp shortly before the camp was evacuated in 1948. Josh, putting food in his mouth, and I are at bottom right.

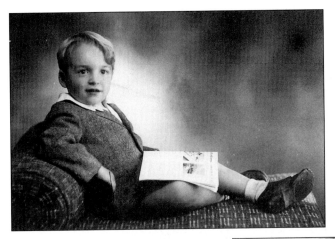

Posing for a professional photographer
in Landsberg-am-Lech, Germany,
c. 1949.

With Josh, left, in Manhattan's
Riverside Park in the mid-1950s
shortly before we left for the Bronx.

Evelyn capering in a Bronx park in 1958 with Daddy, in his
characteristic crouch, reveling in the sight.

The West Side gang in Central Park.
From left: Josh, Simon, me, and Maury.

My family at my bar mitzvah, 1958.

My mother and father in front of our apartment house on the Grand Concourse.

With Josh and Evelyn in the Catskills during our last summer at the bungalow colonies.

With Simon Herling and Clyde Haberman and my first car, a gas-guzzling Buick Electra convertible, c. 1967.

My mother graduating from Hunter College in June 1987 with
(left to right) her daughter-in-law, Brenda, son-in-law, Jimmy Hartman,
grandson, Jakey, husband, Marcus, and daughter, Evelyn Hartman.
"That day, we felt something noble had happened to us."

With Brenda and Annie at Annie's bat mitzvah, April 2000.

few minutes another of our guests would arrive, and nervous delight would flare inside me as I realized all that I had set off, how my birthday had brought all these people out of the warrens of Brooklyn and the Bronx: my mother's uncle, Yudel; Mr. Weinberg and his son, David; Mr. Cooperman with his sons, Sol and Charlie; Mr. Lessen; Mr. Salzburg; Mr. Granas; and Sammy and Leon, two men who worked with my father at General Textile. Their wives or mothers, I knew, were somewhere behind the curtained partition that concealed the allure of the feminine from our straying eyes.

With every psalm and prayer, we drew ineluctably nearer to the moment when I would have to stand up before the entire congregation and show what I was made of.

"*Va-y-hi bin-soa ha-aron, va-yomer Mosheh,*" the prayer leader boomed out, with the congregation replying: "*Kuma Adonay ve-yafutzu oy-vecha, ve-ya-nu-su me-sa-necha, me-pa-necha.*" (And it came to pass, when the ark set forward, that Moses said, Rise up, O Lord, and Thine enemies shall be scattered, and they that hate Thee shall flee before Thee.)

I knew it was time. I accompanied the Torah on its journey from the ark to the altar, where it would be read as wizened Jewish men approached from all sides and touched the silk sleeve of the scroll with the fringes of their prayer shawls, kissing the fringes afterward with almost sensual delight. On the altar, I joined the reverent cocoon of grown men protectively encircling the Torah. As my family's éminence grise, my uncle Yudel, the only sibling of my mother's father to survive the war, had the first *aliyah*. He stood next to me, tall and lordly, with a slightly mischievous Vladimir Horowitz smile, and quickly murmured the blessing. And then all eyes were on me. I approached the parchment, sallow and callused like the skin of a Patriarch, looked at the solemn, sable-black lettering, and began to attach the melody that I had drunk into my being.

"*Vayomer Adonay el Mosheh bo el Paroh,*" I earnestly began in my high-pitched alto.

And I was off. Rabbi Zion had taught me well and I was strutting my stuff. With no more than a stumble or two, I sailed through the first passage and when I was done Uncle Yudel gave me his smiling seal of approval and a pat on the back. He was followed to the altar by Mr. Lessen, my uncle Yasha, Mr. Herling, Mr. Cooperman, Mr. Weinberg, and finally my father. I would chant a section and after saying his blessing, each man shook my hand with a distinctly different vigor, a handshake with another man rather than a boy, or so it felt in my dizzily abstracted state. They were sealing my entry into the noble brotherhood of conscientious Jewish men.

I said the haftarah well also and then came time for a speech I had concocted with Rabbi Zion. As the platitudes turned into some stabs at interpretation, I looked down at my crowd of refugees squeezed together like pigeons in the first five rows. They were in my corner, exulting in my success because it was their success too, testimony to their having painstakingly glued together the shards of a broken Jewish world. Through the small curtain at the top of the partition, I even glimpsed my mother, surrounded by a cluster of refugee women, holding my little sister on her lap, and gazing up at me with glowing eyes. What must have gone through her mind at that moment? Perhaps she thought of how much promise her son held of becoming a Torah scholar like her dead brother Yosef, a Golant twig worthy of descent from her father, Joshua Golant, and his father, Binyamin Golant. Or maybe she was transported back to the jostling Jews of Otwock—fourteen thousand of them—who observed screwball ceremonies like bar mitzvahs and *mikvah* immersions and circumcisions and then were herded together in a ghetto and sent off to the slaughter of Treblinka. Or it might just have been pleasure in how I looked in the tailored suit and burgundy tie she had managed to piece together with the help of Louis Kaplan.

That evening, there was a release of long-subdued exuberance. The photographer put the two prettiest girls I knew, Betty Weinberg and Yudel's daughter, Barbara, on either side of me and had them each kiss me on the cheek. Friends from Manhattan Day School—everyone from Dickie Hochstein to Marvin Shenker to Howard Moses—sat beside me on the dais and enjoyed great gobs of prime ribs and baked Alaska and pounded me on the back in congratulations. There were a few American-born cousins we had unearthed—distant ones, but cousins nonetheless—and my father's colleagues from General Textile, and my mother's coworkers from her Astor Place hat factory, and Charlie Bleiberg and Richie Dickstein from the alley, and Sylvia Goldstein and Gloria Schwartz from the building, and Mr. and Mrs. Lessen and their teenaged daughter, Carol, who drove their Mercury from the innards of Brooklyn, and, of course, a smorgasbord of greeners.

The high point came when the band's lusty, raven-haired songbird belted out a version of the comic Yiddish classic "Romania," drenched in Old World nostalgia and brio, that had everyone clapping and stamping the floor. My father took my sister, not yet a year old but beginning to feel her walking legs, and placed her on an empty stretch of dance floor. Giddy with the attention, she rocked up and down to the music on those pudgy legs, smiling in astonished conquest while my father laughed his wet gurgling laugh and everyone gathered round to gaze in enchantment.

My mother danced the night away with Mr. Weinberg and the other Fred Astaires of the greener world. The band leader arranged for her to dance one waltz with me, and whirling her around the floor, I felt a new sense of mastery.

"The vodka goes straight to my legs," she giggled as I led her back to a chair.

There were horas galore and in one of them my father, Josh, Simon, Sol, and Yonah the egg man lifted me up in a chair and spun me around the room like a conquering hero.

It was hard to believe, but these people had not lost the capacity for merriment. These baggy-pants Jews tore open long-straitened hearts and gloried in this achievement, this triumph. Hitler was long buried in Berlin and we were dancing and singing and gorging ourselves to celebrate the arrival at thirteen of one child who, fortunate to have parents whose flailing choices turned out to be the right ones, managed to be born far from the gas chambers.

Although we came to America knowing no one, we had in eight years cultivated a world of our own, a world of survivors like us, and some new American allies as well—from work and school and the alley. By hard work and thrift, we had gathered the resources to throw a splashy party like this. We had established new lives, new identities, even, and chiseled out a foothold after many nomadic years. Were we really refugees any longer? Did refugees throw parties like this or have a suit tailored by Louis Kaplan of Division Street? Maybe it was time to move beyond the old self-imagery, shuck off our congenital trepidation and take on some new perspectives, approach the world with some deserved confidence.

19

For years, my mother pleaded with her brother, Yasha, to immigrate from Australia to America. They were the only survivors of their Otwock family, so why should they live on opposite ends of the globe? she argued. Yasha had married as a displaced person in Germany and, too impatient to wait for an American visa, shipped off with his family to Australia, a land he knew nothing about and where he had no one. Such was the desperation of many of the DPs to resume normal lives.

By the late 1950s, he and his wife, Ann, had given birth to three children. The oldest, Benny, was just a year younger than Josh; the middle son, Joey, was three years younger; and their youngest, Esther, was only a few years older than Evelyn. Cousins, my mother argued in her letters to Yasha, should grow up together. Yasha might also feel less lonesome in New York, which had a far larger colony of greenhorns than Melbourne. Besides, Yasha was not finding any great fortune in Australia. He had done dirty jobs like picking sugarcane and oranges in the blazing tropical sun. Now he was working in a shoe factory. He could work in a shoe factory in New York.

These points my mother made in the letters she periodically sent off to Australia, occasionally with some cash, and every few months she would open the flap of our mailbox in the vestibule of 1230 Grand Concourse and there would be a thin blue air-mail envelope with stamps bearing Queen Elizabeth's portrait or a kangaroo and a Melbourne address in my uncle's spidery, slanting hand that so resembled my mother's. In those letters he related the news of his sputtering progress, but always with the disappointing conclusion that they were going to try to make a go of it in Australia.

I too missed Yasha, though I no longer recalled much about him except fat chipmunk cheeks smiling down on me under a dark sweep of hair and eyes that radiated his merriness of spirit. Yet even with my vaporous memories, my mother was able to bring Yasha alive for us with legends of his generosity: how he had saved her life with bread and lard when she lay sick with typhus, how a month would not go by in the DP camps when he did not buy us a toy or two. With great peals of laughter, she recounted how Yasha bought me a train set followed soon after by a tool set and how I had taken my new hammer and smashed the trains. She also boasted how nimble and resourceful he was. Every time my father got us lost or stumbled over a subway map, she would tell us how this would not have happened to Yasha.

"In one day here, he would find his way around New York City like it was the back of his hand," she would say.

Then something must have changed for the worse in Australia, for a letter came indicating that my uncle had succumbed. He would make the journey, he wrote, if my mother could help arrange his immigration papers. The letter left her exuberant, but fretful about how she could possibly set up a new life that would satisfy him and his family and keep them close at hand. When his visa came through, she went about preparing for his arrival with her usual frenzy. She scoured the blocks off the Concourse for an apartment and found one just two blocks away on Sherman Avenue. (For some arcane reason the streets east of the Concourse were named for victorious Civil War generals like Sheridan, Sherman, and Grant.) She paid the apartment's rent for six months before my uncle came just to hold on to it in a tight market. She subwayed down to Sloane's on Fifth Avenue and bought Yasha's family a sofa, then crossed over to Macy's and purchased beds with Sealy Posturepedic mattresses and box springs, a sleek chrome-and-Formica dinette set, and, as her special treat, an RCA Victor TV in a mahogany console. She did not scrimp on quality and plundered much of our savings.

As I looked around their apartment, waiting only for its occupants, I couldn't help but remember that it took us five years in this country to live as well as Yasha's family would live the moment they walked through the door. Somewhere in my resentful heart, angry at the squalor my family had endured, I begrudged them this bounty. But my mother wanted her adored brother to start life in this country in comfort. She did not want any regrets to lure him back to Australia.

Then one wintry Sunday morning, eager to hold on to just a few more minutes of sleep against the clamor of my early-rising parents, I felt an apparition hovering over me. There overhead were the bulging cheeks of my uncle Yasha, framing his fat-lipped smile and bright dark eyes and doughy face.

"Joey," he said, "it's your uncle Yasha come all the way from Austraal-ya."

His English immediately struck me as of a wondrously strange variety: broad Cockney-flavored vowels with the jagged edges of an East European refugee. I leaped out of bed and he gave me a bearish embrace and a too-wet kiss on the side of my head. He grinned at everyone and guffawed and told my parents how much I and my brother looked like this or that dead relative. Tears twinkled in the corners of his eyes, but I could tell he was ecstatic to be back with his kinfolk. My mother stood nearby, alternating between tears and laughter also as she looked at Yasha.

"Every time I look at him I feel like crying," my mother said, chuckling and sobbing all at the same time. "I don't know why."

What must it have been like for her—after eight years of being utterly alone in the part of her being that her husband and children could never know, the part that was intimate with Otwock's piney air and its hodgepodge of ragged, pious Jews and the sainted figure of her father—to be finally together in the same room with someone from that home? With Yasha, she could laughingly remember the bed they had slept in crosswise with other siblings, their stepmother's canny ways with stretching a chicken among seven mouths, their grandfather's weakness for a shot of spirits and a wedge of herring. At the same time, Yasha's dark-eyed potato face rekindled the faces of the brothers and sisters she had lost and would never have near her again. Any laughter must have been laced with heartache.

Yasha showed off his three children, each of whom seemed bashful and excessively cordial, although behind their diffident masks lay my uncle's clever, darting eyes. My aunt Anne, a cheerful, plumpish woman with ash-blond hair and bottle-thick glasses, fussed about our house, dropping bromides about how badly her luggage had been handled and New York's perplexing helter-skelter. My mother's way with her was tolerant and purposefully polite, and it began to dawn on me that my aunt's giddy manner and small talk were not rooted in the earthy world of the greeners I knew. Indeed, my mother confided to me a few days after the arrival that Anne was not really a greener.

Anne was not born Jewish. She was a German woman whom Yasha had met as a DP in Berlin. Whatever loathing the Jewish men may have felt toward Germans, some did not mind romancing the fräuleins, and once that barrier was cracked the standard palette of human emotions took over. Most of these men had for years been deprived of a woman's tender body and sprightly company. My mother speculated that Yasha did not brave the surviving Jewish girls because the poverty of his Otwock home had stripped him of his self-assurance. But what, after all, was so alluring about the emaciated and feral Jewish girls who survived the war? And why should anyone remain loyal to his faith after a war that, in some eyes, saw God abandon his own chosen people? Anne was a decent, responsible woman who came from a family that, my mother told us, had not gotten caught up in the Nazi mythology and had tried to go about its own business before and during the war. Yasha, my mother believed (not giving any credence to the possibility that Yasha and Anne just might have been in love), had been swept up by the headiness of a new infatuation and of a kindly family that pampered him with food and the comforts of a home he had long been without. When the sparks of fresh romance had worn off, he did not, as other Jewish young men did their fräuleins, forsake Anne. He married her and had her convert to Judaism.

Her three children seemed overwhelmed, shy beyond American norms, standing quietly and awkwardly and following their parents' directions to the letter. Did I even begin to understand that they had just been wrenched from a world they had barely grown accustomed to and now had to make sense of an America I was still struggling to comprehend? Did I remember what it was like arriving in New York seven years before? I gave them no slack.

Just before we had breakfast, my uncle and aunt hauled out the trinkets they had brought from Australia and from the island of Fiji, where they had stopped on the way to America. With an energetic fanfare, my uncle, impresario of this gift-giving ceremony, produced a stuffed kangaroo and a feathered native Fijian doll, which he turned over to my deeply delighted sister.

"This is from Fay-jay," my uncle told my mother. "And the women really dress like this, Rachela."

There was a conspiratorial twinkle in his eye, no doubt a reference to the modestly racy youth of him and my mother and their friends in Warsaw or Russia.

For my parents, Yasha pulled out a gaily colored blanket, and my mother overexulted, doing her best to hide her misgivings about her brother's squandering of money. Josh and I got boomerangs, the genuine articles, maybe the only authentic ones in the Bronx. Mine was of a honey-colored wood, heavily shellacked, with paintings of naked native hunters on its rounded side. My uncle, in his quirky English, showed us how to angle it so when we hurled it into the sky, it would return.

"Hoist it up this way," he said with an eager smile.

How absurd it must have seemed to my mother that this man who grew up studying Talmud in Otwock was now teaching a scrappy Bronx kid who was born in Russia how to throw a weapon created by primeval aborigines in Australia. Me, I could not wait to get out into the park and try it out.

All in all, it was mostly a heart-stirring day of immersion in the unfamiliar vat of clannish glue. But the euphoria began to crumble in the weeks that followed as my uncle could not find a job. And during that time, my mother's edgy concern for her brother sometimes made it seem like she was adding their lives to the list of those she ran. While my uncle could shrug his older sister's intrusions off with a joke or a laugh, my aunt chafed at her diminished role and at my mother's implied presumption that she had the right to manage Yasha's family. My mother was the sister, not the wife. Boundaries would have to be set somewhere down the line. My aunt could not even appreciate my mother's gifts of furniture. She did not choose the sofa, and it was not to her taste. As welfare mothers have taught the world, dependency produces more resentment than gratitude.

From her vantage point, my mother would come to the apartment she unearthed and for which she had prepaid six months' rent and see things that made her palpably fume. Watching television, the three children were nestled on the couch with their shoes embedded in the expensive Sloane's fabric. On top of the mahogany TV console was a glass of milk, leaving its round, wet imprint. My aunt, my mother carefully noted, was puttering dizzily around with no concern for protecting the furniture my mother had paid for.

At times, my mother tried to overcome her own vexations. She invited the refugee crowd to our home to meet Yasha and his family just as she had done to let them eye my baby sister. At each event, she served hefty platters of food, as if the food would make up for any discomfort in the fact that my aunt was not fully one of us. Nothing worked. Yasha, jovial and loquacious, was warmly taken in, but my aunt, no matter how hard she tried to be genial and sprinkle her small talk with Yiddish and wear a Mogen David around her neck and contribute a Jewish dish like stuffed cabbage to a family feast, proved an insuperable hurdle.

And what could have been done differently? How easy could it have been for Polish Jews, bred in the bone to distrust Gentiles, to smother their hurt and accept Anne as Yasha's ineluctable wife? How easy could it have been for Anne to overcome whatever defensiveness she felt at being German? Slowly, the suspicion must have arisen in her that she would never be treated as her own person, that in this crowd she could never win. Not all bruises can be healed, even by kindness, and in those postwar years the refugees' reservoir of kindness toward outsiders, let alone Germans, was of a very shallow depth.

Things went downhill. Yasha still could not find a job. When the hat season started my mother returned to work and cooked up what she thought was a generous proposal: she would leave Evelyn with my aunt and pay her as a baby-sitter. That would give my uncle's family some wages while he continued to hunt for work. In theory that sounded fine, but overnight my aunt had become my mother's employee. My mother was telling her what food she should cook for Evelyn, how often she should check Evelyn's diapers, what powder to use for rash, what clothes she should dress her in. All this added another layer of pique. The quiet seething more than once burst into open anger.

"I think I know how to change a diaper, Rachel," my aunt said once. "I've had three of my own."

For a time my mother did not talk to my aunt, and my poor uncle was caught in the middle, trying to appease the two women in his life while brokering a truce.

My uncle did eventually find a job—in a shoe factory—and with his friendly disposition and his nonunionized American dedication to work, he became the owner's favorite employee. When the owner, two years later, decided to move his factory to Uniontown, Pennsylvania—near Pittsburgh—he invited my uncle to come along. Was there a shortage of factories in New York City that could use an industrious worker like my uncle? Of course not. But somehow this proposition offered a graceful exit from what was becoming a treacherous situation, one that was threatening to spoil the deep affection between my mother and her brother.

One day, my uncle and his family got into a used clunker they had bought and took with them their belongings as my parents, my brother, sister, and I stood on Sherman Avenue waving a bittersweet good-bye. They would soon be settled nine hours away by car, but they might as well have been in California because we didn't have a car. The Sherman Avenue apartment was emptied, except for the battered sofa from Sloane's that had once held all my mother's great dreams of re-creating the Golant family in New York.

20

By the time I was in eighth grade, my mother had begun hearing rumors along the Grand Concourse of a wondrous school that some considered the best in America—the Bronx High School of Science. It was free and close by, saving her tuition for a yeshiva that was making less and less sense for her earth-grounded sons. With a father who worked on Saturdays, her sons were not going to turn into pious Talmud scholars like her own father. I was coming around to pretty much the same conclusion about myself. Sure, I did very well in my Hebrew studies, but I was enjoying English as well. In third grade, I had won the class writing contest with a story about a visit to a matzoh factory, whose conveyor belts looked to me like a roller-coaster. In fifth grade, I wrote a swashbuckling account of my rescue from a bunk at Cejwin Camps after the grounds were flooded by hurricanes Connie and Diane. The eighth-grade class had chosen me as editor of the yearbook. Yes, the job required not much more than that I keep a list of stories. But my selection, I sensed at cocksure moments, certified that I had swollen my sails with the gusts of a new language and I could glide with it toward the horizon. Maybe it was time to switch out of yeshiva.

But first there was an entrance test to take. In those years Bronx Science had only a small ninth grade, accepting just three classes, most of them students forsaking private schools. Walking into the test room, I saw kids from a muddle of worlds with which I had scarcely any acquaintance. There were students from the East Side prep schools, already showing the first glimmers of a ripening urbanity, and the more rough-hewn Irish, Italian, and Slavic kids from the borough Catholic schools. Even the yeshiva kids from the East Bronx were coarser than my West Side crowd. Sitting at a desk in this flock of strange faces, I tried to figure out words like *abjure, abnegate, inchoate, jejune,* and *truculent,* which, no doubt, the test makers felt were customarily batted around my immigrant household.

A few weeks later, Manhattan Day School's principal, Dr. Herman C. Axelrod, strode into my class and announced the name of the one student accepted into Bronx Science. It was not me. I sat at my desk, crestfallen. Never before had I suffered a failure on this scale. I had actually begun to believe my mother's fancies that I had inherited the intellectual muscles of a Golant and was destined for some rarefied pinnacle. Now I had to get my mind around the idea that maybe I didn't have the stuff to reach that high. What's more, my classmates now knew I didn't. That was mortification enough, but in the yeshiva I inhabited I had also tipped off the authorities that I was a potential defector, someone willing to turn his back on the Torah-learning fraternity. Dr. Axelrod never let me or my brother forget it.

"You're planting the Bronx Science bug, just like your brother," he told Josh two years later when he took the test (and made it).

The hardest part was telling my mother. Her sagging face betrayed her deep disappointment. But, characteristically, she would not accept this door slammed in her face.

"You'll try again next year," she said. "The women tell me it's easier to get into the tenth grade. They take many more children. This time, you hear me, don't tell anybody you're trying. If no one knows, you won't have to be ashamed."

Of course, I was now able to calibrate more precisely how shameful it was that I didn't make Bronx Science. Still, in her own ham-fisted way, my mother was teaching me a salutary lesson as well, one that was to stand me in good stead throughout my life: slammed doors can be pried open again. It was tenacity that had helped my mother survive as a Warsaw urchin. It was tenacity that anchored my mother in this country. What she did now was enroll me in the ninth grade of Yeshiva

University's high school for boys. There I would bide my time until the matter of Bronx Science was resolved.

Still, for the first time in my life I was leaving the feathered nest of Manhattan Day School and classmates I had been together with since first grade. We had never become bosom buddies, but kids like Dickie Hochstein, Howard Moses, Joycie Stern, and Miriam Hausman had become the stable backdrop to my life. I could gauge my successes against theirs, knew where I stood in the hierarchies of learning and social class. Now I would have to reestablish myself all over again, for that September I was on a strange new stage again.

Six times a week, I took a bus across the proletariat ghetto of Highbridge to the proletariat ghetto of Washington Heights and walked up six blocks toward Yeshiva University, a dazzling Moorish citadel of orange stone embellished with towers, minarets, and arches. Here the scholars of the *misnagdim*—the devout but anti-Hasidic movement of learned Lithuanian rabbis—had built their American temple of scholarship, a mission etched into the sober faces of the collegians and their rabbis. The university's high school division was more a grab bag of Jewish youth, some from plush wealth, others from shabby warrens. Some of the East Bronx kids were coarser than any I had encountered at Manhattan Day School. Legend had it that one student had unbolted a toilet at his previous yeshiva, Salanter, and thrown it out the window, where it went crashing onto the sidewalk. This was a felony we had never even imagined at Manhattan Day.

Other kids were also more outsized than any I had ever encountered. There was constant talk about the feats of Hank Resnick, the school's reigning athletic hero. Resnick wore glasses and looked like a taller, broad-shouldered version of the other Talmudic grinds. But underneath the Clark Kent exterior was our Superjew, the star of the winning basketball team who in his spare time was captain also of the swimming and tennis teams. With him as its linchpin, the yeshiva basketball players overran Catholic and public schools. He was better than the goys at their own game, was the way we saw it. Just to glimpse him as he strode down the halls was to feel a brush with greatness. That was the mythic aura he carried.

Here also was Rabbi Macy Gordon, my Talmud teacher, who

delighted in the dazzling disputation of Gemara and made me delight in it too. Yes, the sages were arguing about the fine ethical points of finding a vessel in a dung heap. Does one claim ownership because the vessel is considered discarded? Or must one attempt to return it because it might have been lost or stolen? However mundane the issue, the sages could argue razor-thin distinctions for pages. I began to appreciate how baroque are most of life's significant issues. Questions would not just be solved by a spurt of passion, but had to be finely analyzed and assayed. There were complications and countervailing aspects to everything, and these often made action and decision difficult. At the dawn of the often self-righteous peace-and-love 1960s, a dialectic like the one over finding a vessel in a dung heap became a formative lesson.

Through Rabbi Gordon, I found myself drawn to the rigors of Jewish life. He talked with you as if you were a thoughtful person who needed to understand what you were doing and why, instead of being ordered about like a child. Unlike other Torah teachers, he was not remote and could sometimes be surprisingly freewheeling. He invited the class to his house for Chanukah for latkes cooked by his wife, then asked a few seniors to do their imitations of the school's teachers. Rabbi Gordon himself was not spared.

Orthodoxy could be fun. I had been drawn to it, of course, since I was a young boy, by the families on Broadway, the fathers in fedoras tugging their skullcapped sons by the hand, the stout, overdressed mothers pushing baby carriages. There was a Pietà-like harmony to such tableaux, a cogency of purpose that contrasted sharply with the scattered logic of my own family. My father sent me to yeshiva, but he worked on Shabbos. My mother cooked gefilte fish and stuffed cabbage and flung memories at me of her pious, massacred village, but she had yearnings for Tolstoy and Chopin and Hollywood. I coveted that Orthodox harmony, a life where the paths were clearly laid out, where the boundaries were sharply drawn. This is what you did; this is what you didn't do. Sure, there was endless dispute over the small questions, but the big questions were answered incontrovertibly and forever. I began praying in the morning with *tefillin*—a serpentine contraption of two leather cubes containing Torah passages on parchment, one cube bound to the head and one to the left arm by leather straps. I showed up more often at Rabbi Brodsky's synagogue, and tried to plumb the prayers for their meanings and allusions.

At the same time as the yeshiva world exerted its centripetal pull, I also felt the subversive pull of the secular world. In the yeshiva's English classes, there were daring forays into literature. The *Odyssey* may have been turbid as smoke, but Mr. Cohen, a slender, owlish pipe smoker, had to teach us drama as well, and for outside reading I chose Tennessee Williams's *Cat on a Hot Tin Roof*. I had seen the film version with my mother, who occasionally asked me to be her companion at the movies. (My father, flummoxed by the English of the more sophisticated films, tended to fall asleep moments after the lights went out.) There was something about Liz Taylor wearing bosom-baring lacy slips and spouting tart and cunning observations around her Delta plantation that drew me into the play and made me want to read other plays. I was learning how it really was between men and women.

"Living with someone you love can be lonelier than living entirely alone—if the one you love doesn't love you," Maggie tells the standoffish Brick.

A line like that stirred questions about my own home, and whether either of my parents felt lonely in a marriage of mismatched mates cemented by war, need, and hunger. But inexperienced as I was, I jumped to all kinds of assumptions that didn't account for a marriage's inextricable convolutions.

The play also provided information about what went on in that forbidden Holy of Holies, the bedroom.

"We hear the nightly pleadin' and the nightly refusal, so don't imagine you're going t'put a trick over on us, to fool a dyin' man," Mae, the sister-in-law, tells Brick and Maggie.

"Mae, Sister Woman, not everybody makes much noise about love," Brick replies.

I even learned a word I could use for my next try at Bronx Science: *mendacity*. To train for that assault on that school, my mother was sending me down by subway twice a week to nighttime classes held in a junior high school on the West Side of Manhattan. There, moonlighting teachers coached kids in the kinds of vocabulary words, reading passages, and mathematical riddles they could expect on the entrance test. I spent hours, for example, just deciphering Greek and Latin roots. Where my mother heard of such classes and how she had the confidence to lay out precious cash for such frills, I never knew. But this was another of her providential stabs in the dark and, despite the calculation behind it, it had the serendipitous benefit of deepening my pleasure in English in the way a watchmaker takes pleasure in the geared movement of a fine watch. *Noctophobia* was a fear of darkness because *nocto* was a root meaning "night" and *phobia* a suffix meaning "fear." If you knew the mechanics behind that word you could figure out what *nocturnal* and *nocturne* meant and make a smart guess that *claustrophobia* was a fear of being cloistered in a tight space. Words like *cerebral, pyrrhic, narcissistic, erotic, martial,* and *mercurial* could tie together the other new realms like biology, history, and mythology that I was learning about in ninth grade. This English language that for many years I had been speaking fluently was beginning to make sense. Of course, who could explain why *inflammable* meant something that would catch fire, not fire resistant? But there were exceptions to everything, even in Gemara.

Pumped up like this, I passed the Bronx Science test the next time I took it. More than success, I felt vindication, and so did my mother. Her insistence that I keep trying had paid off. But with some edginess, she must have also realized that I would be cutting the tether of the yeshiva world, and no one could predict what that might mean. It seemed likely that her pipe dream of restoring the Camelot that was Otwock would come to naught. She must have wondered how much of what I had absorbed in nine years—a way of living, not just an education—would stay with me. Would I continue to don *tefillin,* go to synagogue, shun bacon and ham? And if little of that life would linger, which seemed likely, what, dear God, would replace it?

Any chance that I would become a yeshiva scholar was considerably corrupted by my escapes on weekends with Maury from the old neighborhood in Manhattan. Although in the three years after our move to the Bronx we rarely saw each other—my mother shrugged him off as a bad influence who was better left behind—he and I hooked up again once we felt comfortable navigating the city by subway, meeting every few Saturdays and ambling around midtown. Maury had grown into a tall, gangly Dead End kid, one with a sharp nose, thick-lensed glasses, and hair that rambled over his ears. Although he was something of a truant, he seemed to spend all his free time acquiring the offbeat arcana that made him a spellbinding companion. Maury went his own quirky way. Instead of rock and roll, he was listening to Fats Waller, Billie Holiday, and Charlie Parker. He took me along to the record collection at Donnell Library on Fifty-third Street and had me listen with earphones to Oscar Levant's recording of "Rhapsody in Blue."

"Nobody plays Gershwin like Levant," he told me, with the offhand authority of someone who had listened to all the other versions.

While I was up late studying Talmud and binomial equations, he was watching old Bogart and Marx Brothers movies. He knew at fourteen that *Treasure of the Sierra Madre, The Third Man,* and *Citizen Kane* were unmatched gems. He watched the *Jack Paar Show* and dazzled me with tales of Paar's peevish blowups, daring jokes, and the eccentrics like Alexander King who peopled his set. He dared me to try ham, and while under the influence of Macy Gordon, I resisted. But once out of yeshiva, there seemed no reason to do so, and I took a bite of a ham sandwich he had plucked out of a Horn & Hardart glass window. I liked it, and sometime later a lunch of crisp, fatty bacon and eggs tasted better than almost anything I'd ever eaten. The sky did not fall in nor lightning strike from the sky. I could break the chains of my orthodoxy and not much would happen. Why live such an outmoded life when almost no one at the school I was going to, Bronx Science, was doing so?

Maury taught me to smoke. On a bench at Rockefeller Center, he showed me how to light a cigarette in the wind by placing the match between two middle fingers, striking the match on the book, and quickly cupping both hands over the flame, then drawing the match toward the Pall Mall clenched in my mouth. And one raw November Saturday, he brought along a girlie magazine. Nothing as stylish as *Playboy,* it was a cheap pulp collection of grainy black-and-white pictures of women rapturously thrusting some body part or other toward the camera. We looked the women over on the Rockefeller Center bench and I found myself trembling from the cold and the furtive excitement. This was true adventure, nothing that I would ever find in the workaday confines of the Bronx. Maury pulled out a pack of Pall Malls, deftly lit a cigarette, shook one out for me, and reminded me about cupping my hand against the wind. I lit mine well and we launched into a solemn discussion about which parts of the female anatomy we preferred. We wound up our day at a steamy Horn & Hardart on Forty-second Street, eating kaiser rolls and drinking coffee.

"Hold on to the magazine," he said to me, sweeping his hand across the air in devil-may-care emphasis.

It was the kind of generous gesture I could never make so painlessly. On the D train back to the Bronx I stuffed the magazine into a deep pocket of my coat. When I got home to our Concourse flat, I hid it under the steam radiator behind the couch in the living room and completely forgot about it.

A few months later, on a cold Sunday morning, I was sprawled across the living room couch reading the *Daily News*. My mother was hunched over a pair of pants that she was lengthening for me. And my father was squatting in one corner of the room, polishing the family's shoes over a spread of Yiddish newspapers. Suddenly my mother stirred fretfully, looking up from her sewing and sniffing the air in a panic.

"Machs," she said, using the shorthand for Marcus. "I smell something burning."

A chill surged through my heart. I remembered the magazine behind the radiator. The superintendent was sending up steam in full force for the first time that winter and the pulpy pages of the girlie magazine were probably scorching. My father shrugged it off, but my mother's alert blue eyes showed she was not appeased. The war years had finely honed her sensitivity to danger and she was not going to let this premonition pass so easily.

"There's something burning, Machs, I'm sure," she said. "Go check, Machs, go check the whole room."

My father dutifully rose and checked the lamps and electric cords. He looked behind the armchair and the couch I was sitting on, sniffing along the way. I felt the dread of a small child playing hide-and-seek who senses he is about to be caught. I had to act.

"Maybe there's something burning here," I said, sidling over to the couch and reaching under to the radiator.

The magazine was right where I had put it. I yanked it free, stuffed it under my T-shirt, spun around, and headed toward the bathroom with my arms folded awkwardly over my stomach.

"Machs, Machs," my mother said, stuttering with agitation. "Machs, he's got something in his T-shirt. Go see what it is."

I dashed down the hall into the bathroom, swung the door closed, and pressed hard against the door's warped frame, bolting the lock shut a second before my father reached the door.

"What you got there, Joey?" my father said.

"Nothing, Daddy, nothing," I said. "I'm just going to the bathroom. Leave me alone."

I began tearing at the magazine, ripping apart whole sections and tossing the shredded pages into the toilet.

"Joey, open up," my father shouted, pounding on the door. "I know you got something there. Open up."

The torn pages lay in a heap completely covering the pool of water in the toilet bowl. Aware that the operation might turn into a disaster, I nonetheless pressed down the handle. Jets of water surged along the sides of the bowl. The scraps of paper seemed barely to budge for a time, until I could see they were slowly working their way down the trap hole. But the jets of water did not cut off. Instead, the water in the bowl kept rising, slowly, inexorably rising. It scaled the lip of the bowl and cascaded onto the tile floor like a veritable Niagara. A lake of water spread across the bathroom floor.

The persistent flushing sound told my father that something had blocked the toilet and was about to destroy the apartment whose rent he slaved so hard to pay.

"Open up," my father boomed, pounding even more furiously on the door. "I'm going to kill you when I get you."

The puddle was deepening around me and was seeping under the bathroom door, spreading toward my father's feet on the other side. In the midst of this bedlam, I heard the doorbell ringing repeatedly, urgently. It was Mr. Summers, our downstairs neighbor, a prissy immigrant who had come over from Europe before the war. My father strode toward the door and in Mr. Summers grave, distressed tones, I could make out that water was leaking through the ceiling into his apartment.

The jig was up. I sloshed across the floor in my waterlogged shoes and unbolted the door. My father's thick hand grabbed my arm. His eyes looked murderous, Cain-like. He grabbed my elbow with his left hand and brandished his thick right hand menacingly as if he were about to hit me. But he never did. He let go of my arm and moved toward the overflowing toilet.

"I don't know what happened, Daddy," I cried behind him. "The toilet's broken. Why do you want to hit me for?"

Mr. Summers went downstairs to get a plunger. Somehow the toilet stopped spouting water. My father picked up a grimy rag from behind the sink and mopped the floor. He looked up at me several times, glowering, but said nothing. He hadn't handled the situation well and I was embarrassing him in front of a neighbor in a building where we had not won our stripes. He could also feel my mother's fury building behind him in the hallway.

Mr. Summers returned carrying a bright pink plunger and he and my father took turns sucking up whatever was stuck. The plunger wheezed and bellowed and snorted like a sick donkey. I stood at the door waiting for the evidence to surface.

"It's coming up," my father grunted, with a gold prospector's pitch of excitement. "It looks like some kind of paper."

He stuck his hand in the water and showed what he dredged up to Mr. Summers. Even with its distorting wrinkles, my father realized what he was looking at—bare breasts, gartered hips, frilly underwear. His puzzlement quickly transformed into a corrosive scowl at me. Then looking at Mr. Summers, he blushed a timid rosy blush. A faint smirk spread across Mr. Summers's face.

My father tiptoed toward the kitchen to deposit the soggy mass of papers into the garbage can. He was breathing heavily, pulsing with anger, not sure what to do.

"Joey," he murmured, not wanting Mr. Summers to hear. "You're going to get it. I tell you. I don't want you with books like that until you're eighteen. You hear!"

Again, he lifted up his arm, but again didn't have the heart to strike. He moved toward the kitchen with my mother following, and from the end of the dim hallway I heard my mother say, "Machs, if you were a real father this wouldn't have happened."

She stood there fixed to her spot, the daylight filtering through the hallway silhouetting her, a glaring, frightened figure watching the world she had so carefully patched together begin to crumble.

I stepped into my room and closed the door and looked out the window onto the Grand Concourse. I could see the sidewalk gallery bundled in winter coats and scarves and catching the warm sunshine now breaking the morning's grimness. By the afternoon, they would surely learn of this incident through the building grapevine. I had embarrassed my parents. I had splashed mud on the Gimbel's suits, the piano lessons, the yeshiva education, the summer camps, the fancy bar mitzvah. But in the squall of emotions I felt, I also wanted to smash my father and strangle my mother.

What did I do that was so bad? Eighteen years old? How ridiculous! My parents were living in nineteenth-century Poland. They were hidebound greenhorns. They had discovered a part of me I didn't want them to know about just yet, the part that wanted to smoke, that wanted to hear racy jokes on the *Jack Paar Show,* that wanted to escape their bourgeois pretensions and cloistered, small-town Polish outlook on life.

Our plan that we tell no one of my second try for Bronx Science did avoid embarrassment. But it also resulted in a bruising slight. When she found out that I had made Bronx Science, Mrs. Herling, my mother's best friend, felt a kind of betrayal. She had transferred Simon to my yeshiva after fifth grade partly because she liked the idea of her son's going to school with her best friend Rachel's son. Simon had gone on with me to Yeshiva University High School. Now I would be heading to Bronx Science and Simon had not even taken the test. My mother's good intentions had been wrecked by unintended consequences, and the slight put a damper on my mother's relationship with Mrs. Herling.

The chill came at a bad time because within a couple of years Mrs. Herling was diagnosed with ovarian cancer. She went regularly to

Mount Sinai Hospital for treatments and once I went with my mother to visit her. With her belly swollen under the sheets, her skin a greenish pallor, her eyes dazed by morphine, she still managed to crease a smile for her son's best friend. She had always had a genial and attractive plumpness to her face, and somehow the cancer had not yet erased that.

"You like the way I look, Joey?" she said, and laughed with sad embarrassment.

My mother and Mrs. Herling chatted away like two schoolgirls, as if their talk alone would hold off the inevitable. These two refugees who had lost and suffered so much were now getting ready to suffer loss once more, and seemed to take sanctuary in the camouflaging power of reminiscence.

Why was this happening to Mrs. Herling, who had been given more than her fair share of affliction? She lost her entire childhood family to the Nazi killing machine. She had said good-bye to a four-year-old daughter she was never to see again. She had struggled, like us, to build a new life in this country, confining her family to a cramped, single room for ten years while her husband saved tips from his haircuts. Now she and Sam had moved to a sunny apartment on Central Park West with a view of the park and a room for Simon. They had bought themselves a fancy living room set: a couch that wrapped around a curving wall, a bar whose lights showed off their crystal and pink china, a hi-fi made of components. After years of mincing denial, they would finally give themselves some pleasure. And just as they had started to do so, the curse of the cancer came. God could not only be cruel but, it seemed to me, had a particularly malicious streak.

Yet here were these two women laughing at the twists in their fate, at their piddling towns and the goofy inhabitants, at the absurdities of their destitution. They had restored their friendship, and were laughing as vigorously around that hospital bed as they had at several bar mitzvahs where they had been nipping vodka. For a moment or two, one could even believe Mrs. Herling would get better.

She did not, and one day my mother informed me that Mrs. Herling had died. She was forty-six. The funeral would be the next day on the West Side. I took a subway down from Bronx Science, where I was now a junior, but never having been at a funeral, I did not realize that it is the one event in life that always starts on time. When I finally arrived at the funeral home, the cars had all driven off toward the cemetery, and I stood on the sidewalk cursing myself for having arrived so late, bewildered why the doings on the streets around me seemed so normal when something profound had just happened. Mrs. Herling was the first of our refugees who died in America, and her death was to me like the death of a beloved aunt, a death in the family.

21

My mother's younger brother, Yasha, whether he was half a world away in Australia or two blocks away on Sherman Avenue in the Bronx, was a vibrant, breathing presence in my life. Her dead father, Joshua Golant, was also a vivid figure, quickened to life by the stories she would tell and the word pictures she would paint of him. Not so for my mother's half brother Simcha. He was a shadowy figure, unmentioned for many years or lumped together among the barely distinguishable compilation of my parents' dead relatives. Even when my mother began telling me his story, I sensed that something was left unfinished in her relationship with Simcha, that something important was left hanging. Slowly, my mother revealed that he had vanished not in the Holocaust but in the maelstrom of wartime Russia and she did not actually know whether he was dead or alive. How someone could leave such a question unanswered disturbed my journalist's cocky certainty that there was an answer to every puzzle, and I once even made a halfhearted stab at locating him, coming up with the wrong Simcha Warshawiak in São Paolo, Brazil. I never grasped how in a civilized world one could lose track of a brother. But now in my mother's kitchen, as she tells me the story of her years in Russia and as I read her longhand memoir, I learn why holding on to a beloved brother is not always simple.

"It was my sister Freyde Leah who talked me into going to Russia," my mother tells me in our kitchen interview. She has forgotten that at various points in our conversation she has credited, or blamed, Simcha and the wife of her uncle Yossel for persuading her to flee Nazi-occupied Poland for Russia.

"She told me, 'You'll have a better life. You're such a good-looking girl and smart and the Russians will give you a better job and very good treatment.'"

She breaks into a bitter laugh, then hands me her journal.

"Boy, did I get good treatment in Russia."

The train that left Lvov took us for a ride across the heartland of Russia, carrying us a thousand miles east of Moscow to the foot of the Ural Mountains and the smokestacks of the industrial city of Lys'va. The passengers in the car in which Simcha and I were riding were mostly young Polish Jews who, like us, had fled the Nazis. We were desperately looking for work, but at the same time we gloried in our arrival in a land that promised to satisfy our idealistic yearnings. We sang patriotic Russian songs, tried out Russian phrases, and shared the bread and apples we would pick up from peddlers every time the train paused in a station. The gossip and singing made us forget the uncertainties of what lay ahead and our anguish at all we had left behind. Before long we were as friendly as if we had known each other for years.

Much of our gossip concerned a flaming romance between the train's commander and Ruta, a seductive, dark-haired passenger from Lodz. The rumors were that she slept with him in his car at the front of the train. Some heard that he had a wife and children who lived near Moscow; others said he had broken a few hearts on earlier transports. My brother Simcha defended Ruta, admiring her boldness.

"That girl has the spirit of free love," he said to me. "That is one of the great things about the communist way of life."

Such was my brother's rosy outlook throughout the journey. He even argued with a passenger named Rubin, who had already spent two months working in a coal mine in the Ukraine and experienced firsthand the dismal realities of the Soviet system. The work, Rubin said, was grueling, the authorities harsh, and food and basic necessities like shoes and soap were scarce. The society was so corrupt that people had to steal and smuggle to survive. Someone had stolen his boots as soon as he had arrived. But Simcha refused to believe him and disputed every complaint.

"Why would anyone steal boots?" he said. "It's like stealing from yourself. Everything belongs to the people. You can leave gold on the streets and no one will touch it."

I was surprised at how gullible and starry-eyed my brother seemed.

Lys'va's trees and sidewalks were draped in snow for our arrival. One hundred and twenty of us disembarked with our valises and duffel bags. Waiting for us were a half-dozen friendly officials in warm hats and long army coats, their breaths turning to fog as they chatted and joked in the arctic cold. They hurried us to the public baths, where we showered, and then showed us to our barracks. That evening we were taken to a room decorated with imposing red-framed portraits of Lenin, Stalin, and Molotov and treated to a spectacular feast. There were all sorts of smoked meats and fish, herring, and caviar and the vodka was plentiful. The crowning dish was a vinaigrette—a tangy salad of boiled cabbage, carrots, beets, cauliflower, beans, tomatoes, and sour pickles. While we ate with gusto, an orchestra played wistful Russian melodies. We were encouraged to dance, and I reveled in every chance I had to dance with a handsome, blond young German named Hans. My brother, still chafing from his arguments with Rubin, took in the bountiful scene with deep satisfaction.

"We shall see who is right," he told me.

The next morning we returned to the same banquet room to listen to a windy speech by a stout young Russian who was trying to rouse us on.

"Every citizen has the right to work in the Soviet Union," he proclaimed. "But the one who refuses to work has no right to eat. That is what our constitution says."

Unless you were an engineer or a skilled mechanic, there was no possibility of escaping the rugged labor and ash-filled smoke that came with assignment to the steel-smelting ovens. I was used to punishing work, but I was concerned about Simcha. Because of his tuberculosis, he essentially breathed through one lung.

"You must never work hard, and you must surely eat well," an Otwock doctor had warned him.

I could see Simcha coughing nervously as Kirilov, our guide, described the jobs we would be doing. But he steeled himself to approach Kirilov and, with the help of a translator, managed to get an assignment to work as a mechanic on the plant's fleet of trucks and automobiles. I was greatly relieved. Each of us was then given a pair of rough overalls, workboots, and a quilted jacket to keep us warm against the Urals winter. That first day of work at the smelting ovens filled my lungs with a scorching, sour smoke. But nothing upset me as much as a visit by my brother after I returned to the barracks.

"Do you by any chance have my leather boots?" he asked, a deeply worried look on his face.

He remembered very clearly unpacking his valise the night before and placing the boots at the side of his field bed. I went back with him to the men's barracks. It wasn't as if there were many places where the boots could have been. The room was sparsely fur-nished—a bed for each of the four roommates and a hook or two for clothes. My brother kept all he possessed in a valise stored under his bed. The barracks' warden advised us to report the matter to the local police, but she also loudly chided my brother for being so trusting as to leave a pair of boots out in the open. In a Russian win-ter, a pair of sturdy, watertight boots were more valuable than a car.

A week or two later, my brother's salt-and-pepper woolen sports jacket vanished. Then a pair of pants, even though he placed those under his pillow while he slept. We reported the thefts to Kirilov and, with weary resignation, he moved my brother to another bar-racks closer to the center of town.

My brother and his new roommate, Albert, a stocky Hungarian Jew his own age, hit it off immediately. They spent hours listening to music and to news on my brother's cherished shortwave radio, which he had carried with him from Warsaw. Albert, too, was cynical about Soviet communism.

"*Das Kapital* is an excellent theory, but it doesn't work in reality," Albert said. "You can see it right here in Lys'va. The people want food and clothes, but they can't get them through honest work alone."

Albert had already learned how to procure rations of sugar, butter, and soap without shivering on long lines outside the official store. He had bribed the store manager, Shura, and she finessed some privileged party documents that allowed Albert to go right to the front of the lines. He also knew how to work Lys'va's market. My brother and I visited the market and saw that the prices for milk, eggs, butter, and potatoes were prohibitive, but that people, ignoring the law, paid for these goods by swapping their bedsheets, towels, or jackets. Simcha seethed as he reckoned out how much he could have traded for his stolen boots or jacket.

A few days after our market visit, I stopped by at the garage where Simcha worked. He was lying under a truck with a wrench in his hand panting for breath as he tightened some bolts, but he smiled the kind of merry smile I had not seen on his face since our arrival in Lys'va.

"Are you hungry?" he asked. "Because if you are I've got something for you."

How familiar such words were. How often when I was famished or lonely in Warsaw I had heard my brother say "Are you hungry" and see him conjure up a salami sandwich or a plain wedge of bread. This time, he crawled out from under the truck and wiped the grease off his hands with a rag. From his jacket he withdrew a sandwich smeared with lard. I long ago stopped caring whether the food I ate was kosher. I didn't even mind his greasy hands. I bit greedily into the sandwich, relishing savory tastes I hadn't experienced for weeks. He enjoyed seeing my pleasure in eating, and then he whispered his secret to me.

"I sold a shirt on the market," he said, smiling guiltily. "That's how I brought home these good things."

From then on, Simcha and I fell into the same pattern of surreptitious barter as everyone else in our circle. These deals became the main topic of our conversation. They were even the currency of our flirtations. Hans, the kindly coworker whom I fancied, often boasted of his wily dealings in the market to impress me.

"I sold ten yards of muslin and got myself some potatoes and butter," he said. "What did you do with the muslin you got?"

"I never got it," I said. "They ran out of muslin fifty people ahead of me on the ration line."

"You should be up at five o'clock like I was," he said. "I was sorry I had to sell the muslin because you would have looked pretty in a green and lavender dress."

He squeezed my cheeks, and even after I protested, he held my hands in his and gazed longingly at me.

"Next time I'll have to drag you out of bed at five in the morning," he said.

The next morning, my eyes searched for Hans on the way to work. He usually walked with his roommates, but this time he was not with them. A Ukrainian colleague noticed my unease and walked alongside to explain.

"Did you hear the news?" he murmured uneasily. "They arrested Hans. In the middle of the night."

"My God, why?" I said. "What could Hans have done?"

"Nobody knows," the Ukrainian said.

We were soon to learn that Hans was charged with possessing a letter from Israel that was condemned as Zionist. His arrest put an end to my budding romance and sent terror throughout our group of newcomers, but life quickly resumed its necessary rhythms. Simcha, I could tell, was growing envious of all the food his roommate Albert was flaunting in his face. One evening, Albert held up a can of pork stew and, sensing how impressed Simcha was, invited him for a Saturday night out with his two confederates, Shura and Vera, who had slipped him the goods he was showing off. Simcha accepted happily, but when I saw him on the Sunday morning following his big night out, his head sagged as if he were afraid to look at me.

"How was your evening last night?" I asked, trying to be cheerful.

"The girls were a lot of fun," he said. "I couldn't believe how much food there was. They kept filling my glass with vodka over and over. But when I woke up afterward, my watch was gone."

There were tears in my brother's eyes. He had arrived in the Soviet Union with the brightest of hopes and had been knocked down again and again, losing one painfully acquired possession after another. I had never before seen him cry and, as a sister, I felt his despair especially deeply. I returned with him to the militia office. This time a special investigator seemed more responsive. He took down all the details of the party and of the Swiss watch and gave my brother a promising nudge on the shoulder. That evening they arrested Albert for stealing food that, as communist jargon put it, "belonged to the people."

The arrest seemed to make my brother feel worse. He kept wrestling with his conscience, needing to persuade himself that he had done nothing blameworthy.

"What could I do?" he told me, as if I had been rebuking him. "I had to answer their questions about how the watch disappeared."

But he didn't have time to torment himself for long. The day after Albert's arrest, there was a knock at my door and David, a young member of our workers' group, stood there with a key dangling from his hand and a solemn look on his face.

"I am so sorry, but I need to tell you that your brother has been arrested," he said. "He asked me to give you the key to his room."

I asked David question after question, hoping that I might find out that what had happened to my brother was not that alarming. But when I finally made my way to my brother's room and saw that it was in a shambles, my fears were justified. Socks, ties, towels, and shirts were strewn over Simcha's opened valises and over the floor. The shelf where his shortwave radio had stood was bare. On a small table near his bed lay a pink slip of paper, whose large lettering shouted *"Konfiskacia!"* It told me that Simcha's belongings had been seized as part of a state inquiry. On the bed itself, looking orphaned and tattered, lay Maxim Gorky's autobiographical trilogy, which my brother loved to read to strengthen his faith in communism. In a perverse way, the sight of the book gave me some hope. We were in the mecca of communism, and my brother was an ardent believer. Surely, they would not imprison him for long.

I raced to the militia office and found myself standing in front of Niedviedov, the same tall investigator who had appeared so sympathetic when my brother complained about his stolen watch.

"Why is my brother in jail?" I whimpered. "He is sick. He has tuberculosis. He has only one lung. He needs fresh air. He will die if you keep him there one more day."

I kept babbling in my clumsy Russian, as if by the sheer volume of words I could persuade Niedviedov to let Simcha go. I tried to wipe away my tears with my sleeve, but they left moist spots on my blouse.

"What did he do?" I went on, weeping, imploring. "He came to this country for a better life. He dreamed about this country. But as soon as we came here they began to steal things from him. Instead of finding the thieves and putting them in jail, you threw *him* in jail. Why?"

Niedviedov waited for me to calm down.

"Your brother," he informed me, in what he must have felt was a compassionate tone, "will go to trial in a week. I'm sure he will be freed. Don't worry. In our Soviet Union, the courts are fair. If he is found not guilty, he will be sent back to work."

He looked at me earnestly and then started speaking again.

"Tell me, Raisa, what did your brother do in Poland?"

I was touched that he called me affectionately by my Russian name and probably said more than I should have.

"He traded in ladies' lingerie," I said. "He bought damaged goods from the factory and sold them to shopkeepers."

"He was a merchant, wasn't he?"

"Not exactly," I said. "Why do you ask me all these questions? You think that my brother was rich? Well, you're wrong. We were all poor. We were proletarians, not bourgeoisie. My brother was not permitted by doctors to do any hard labor. That's why he traded in women's underwear."

He listened attentively but said nothing to reassure me.

"We'll consider all that in a week," he said. "Meanwhile we will gather evidence."

I dragged myself home and fell into an exhausted sleep. I felt helpless, despondent. But the next morning, I learned some news that, foolish as I was, left me hopeful. My Ukrainian colleague informed me that Albert had been released and had returned home. As I shoved huge spadefuls of ashes out of the smelting furnaces, my heart flared with optimism. If Albert had been released from jail, there was a chance my brother would be released as well. But when I visited the room my brother shared with Albert, hoping to talk to Albert, I saw that Albert's side had been stripped bare as well and his valise was gone. Why did he leave so quickly and where did he go? Did his release have something to do with my brother's arrest? Had he informed? And if so, what could he have told them?

I glanced back at my brother's side of the room. Gorky's trilogy still lay forlornly on his bed. I could not abide standing in that forsaken room any longer and fled. ❧

22

"What I went through with my brother," my mother laments. "What I suffered."

The light is thinning in the room as the afternoon grows shorter. We have been talking now for six hours. This marathon is exhausting me and I feel I have heard more than I bargained for. But I am determined to let her finish her story. What I suffered, she said. I wonder why she phrases it this way. It was her brother Simcha, after all, who went through most of the suffering. But, as she talks to me and lets me read her account of her brother's trial and its aftermath, I realize how much she had risked and sacrificed and immersed herself to help Simcha and how much agony she went through as a result. How many people fight this hard for a brother or sister these days? Who puts themselves on the line this much?

What also occurs to me as I read her composition book is that the story could have seemed far off to me, as if I were reading an epic like *Dr. Zhivago,* about characters in a place and time I have never known. Yet the young woman who is narrating and living through the experiences intensely is my mother, a younger version, perhaps, but undeniably the same unrelenting, indefatigable, impossible yet courageous woman who brought me up.

☙ They came in their Sunday best to my brother's trial, as if they were coming to watch a show. An announcement in the newspaper had informed Lys'va that a Polish merchant by the name of Simcha Warszawiak had engaged in speculative dealings and would be tried on Statute 107 of Soviet constitutional law. Illegal merchandise had also been confiscated. Since my brother's alleged crimes were every-day transactions engaged in by most Russians, what the court would do created enormous suspense. This was a trial not to be missed, and spectators on the long wooden benches of the cavernous courtroom were squeezed hip to hip.

From my second-row seat, I saw a small, skinny military officer escort my brother into the courtroom to face the three members of the people's tribunal—an older, heavyset judge flanked by two indis-tinguishable women, each with a faded gray kerchief on her head. Simcha, tall, lean, and pale, sat in the front row, his deep-set blue eyes communicating pain and terror.

After reciting Statute 107, the prosecutor called his first witness to the stand.

"Ivan Ivanovich Paskov, what did you buy from the accused?" the prosecutor barked.

"A shirt, Comrade Prosecutor," Paskov answered.

"And how much did you pay?"

"Forty-six rubles."

"What kind of a shirt was it?"

"A very fine shirt, somewhat worn, the kind one can't get here anymore. It was definitely worth the money."

"That'll be all," the prosecutor said, and the witness returned to his seat.

Next, a court clerk brought in a box and emptied its contents on a courtroom table. I recognized my brother's shortwave radio, a strip of leather hide, and a dozen pairs of stockings remaining from his Warsaw business.

"Such things," the prosecutor said, "can only be afforded by the bourgeoisie."

And with that, the prosecutor closed his case. Simcha had no lawyer, so there was no cross-examination and no arguments for the defense. All that remained was the verdict. The judge and the two female jurors left the room. The crowd murmured their opinions about what had just transpired while I left my seat and edged over to my brother. He looked at me as if he insisted on remaining hopeful, though I could sense the fear underneath. I could not help weeping. The scowling guard ordered me to return to my seat. After a few minutes the judge and jurors returned. The judge pounded his gavel three times and read the *prigovor*—the verdict.

"After long deliberation, it was decided by the citizens of Lys'va to find the defendant, Simcha Warszawiak, guilty of speculation according to Statute 107 of the Soviet Union's constitutional law for selling a shirt on the market. He will be sentenced to five years in a labor camp in the city of Molotov."

For an instant my brother looked as if he had been struck on the head, then he slumped to the floor and passed out. I flew over to help him but the guard put himself between us. I screamed at the guard and kicked him until he threatened to arrest me. The female jurors admonished me as well, warning me with pointed fingers that I could end up in jail. I did not care.

"Please," I wailed. "Please put me in jail with my brother. I have no one else here." ❧

"Joey, I walked through snow above my knees for five miles to visit my brother when he was in prison," my mother tells me. "I was afraid I would get *farblondzhet* [lost] in the snow so I kept my eyes right on the prison towers. I kept reminding myself of my brother's kindness. He took me to the beauty parlor for my first professional haircut. He persuaded me to join a choir. " 'My sister sings with Orpheush,' he would say to his friends and girlfriends."

Her eyes twinkle as she mimics his enthusiasm.

"That prison was some scene. There was a long line of prisoners and a long line of Russian mothers and wives. The prisoners were all waiting for their packages. Believe me, they wanted these packages as much as seeing their mothers or girlfriends. Breads filled with cabbages, potatoes, meat. I brought Simcha dark bread, which I had to steal from my nine-hundred-gram ration. I dried it in the oven so it wouldn't get molds. When I gave it to my brother he ripped open my package like he never saw food before. But he didn't seem so satisfied with what he saw.

"'Can't you get me some lard sometimes?' he said to me. 'I still have my tablecloth and towels. Maybe you can swap them on the market.'"

"I can see your brother's personality underwent a complete change in prison," I say. "This was not the way he was in Warsaw."

"He was as desperate as a child," my mother answers. "Only food was important to him. He didn't talk about anything else. I couldn't stand to see my brother diminished to this level. When I got back to Lys'va I knew I had to do the same kind of thing that got my brother into trouble. What choice did I have? He would have starved."

～ The tablecloth that my brother kept in his valise was one he especially cherished. Made of fine white linen, it had been colorfully embroidered by Renata, a girl my brother had loved in Warsaw but was forbidden by doctors to marry. She had probably long since married someone else, but Simcha continued to care for her and held on to the tablecloth even when it meant abandoning his other goods. At the market, where an unofficial commerce flourished alongside that of the merchants with official permits, I found a bare table next to a milk seller. I unfolded the tablecloth and I was quickly surrounded by a swarm of curious shoppers. They caressed the cloth tenderly, admiring the fine embroidery. Such quality seemed a reminder of a gracious czarist past. A young woman approached me whose robust features, white woolen shawl, and new woolen snow boots told me she had the wherewithal to make a deal.

"How much?" she asked in a gruff voice.

"I want two pounds of lard for it."

"I don't have lard—I have bread," she said.

"How much bread?"

"More than enough!" she answered. "You'll be able to sell it and buy at least two pounds of lard with the money. I guarantee it."

From a bulging brocade bag, she pulled out a long dark bread that weighed at least eight pounds. Sensing her fear of the police, I swiftly made the swap. The bread was fresh and its aroma tempted me to bite off a piece. But hungry as I was, my objective was to get Simcha some lard.

Soon, another woman appeared who produced a clump of ruble notes from her coat pocket, and gestured that I follow her. I could use the rubles she would give me for the bread to buy lard. In a deserted area behind the market stalls, she counted a number of ten-ruble notes over and over, glancing off to the side as if she were waiting for someone.

"Do you want the bread or not?" I asked impatiently.

"Just let me count it one more time, a little more slowly," she said. "Ten, twenty, thirty."

I noticed her glancing again to her left.

"Eighty, ninety, a hundred," she counted.

Before she could finish, a lean man in a military uniform suddenly appeared. He ordered me to follow him to the market's police bureau. The woman who had tried to buy my bread had been a decoy.

"Where did you get the bread?" the officer asked me once we were in his office.

"I received it in exchange for a tablecloth," I said guilelessly. "I need to buy lard for my brother. He is sick in prison. What else can I do?"

"I'll tell you what," the officer said. "I don't want to put you in prison, so get lost!"

I was momentarily relieved, but my objective of getting lard was as urgent as my freedom.

"What about the bread?"

"It has been confiscated. It's against the law to sell bread."

"But my brother is sick and hungry. I won't leave here without the bread. Please give it back to me."

I was in a kind of delirium. I had gone ahead and sold my brother's precious tablecloth and now I was going to get nothing for it.

"It's out of the question!" he barked. "Get out of here."

He opened the door and pointed to the staircase.

"Get out of here!"

"No, I won't," I said.

Shaking with fear, I planted myself next to his desk, where the bread lay, and refused to move. He looked at me in fury. Then he picked me up by the arms and carried me out the door, shoving me so hard I stumbled down the steps and twisted a leg.

"Give me back my bread," I whimpered, aching from my debacle as much as from the pain of the fall. "I won't leave here even if you put me in jail."

The officer's door was shut but he could hear me sobbing on the stairs. Something must have touched him—he probably needed to feed his family and understood my need—or perhaps he feared I might get him in trouble. But the door flew open and I saw him stride over to the desk, pull out a knife, and cut the bread in two.

"Go home!" he shouted, handing me one half.

I took the half loaf, limped down the steps, and headed back to the market to finish my quest for lard. ✍

"I had so many bad things happen to me in Russia, but there were also some good things. The Russian people are not bad people. I met many who are kind and generous, who have a spirit for living. But one person I will never forget. He was a man named Mikhail Andreyevitch Bykov. He was what you today call . . . oh, help me, Joey, I'm forgetting all my English. He was a representative from Moscow whose job it was to see if the government was being fair with the people."

"An ombudsman?"

"Yes, I think that's the word. Most people would not go near them. They thought they were as corrupt as the rest of the system, but Bykov was the genuine article. Besides, what choice did I have? I had to grab on to the slightest hope. He had a kind face. He listened to my brother's troubles with patience like a father. He told me to come see him in Moscow and gave me his telephone number at his house. And so I took a train ride, all by myself. I was all alone in the universe, but I took that train to a city I'd never been to. You wouldn't believe it. Here I was in this big city of Moscow. I remember the Metro. The subway here is a hole by comparison. There, they have oil paintings, *oil paintings*, right on the station walls. And nobody dirties them with graffiti. I remember I bought myself an ice cream and I got up the nerve to call Bykov. He knew immediately who I was and gave me directions to get to his house. His wife made me feel at home, and they served me a dinner; Joey, I'm telling you, aristocrats don't eat like that. A tasty vegetable soup, roasted lamb, a salad with pickled grapes. I can remember the meal like it was yesterday. There were linen napkins and silverware. I couldn't help but remind myself that just a month before I was fighting with a police officer over a loaf of bread. But to tell you the truth I wasn't that comfortable eating with the Bykovs. Whoever gave me such treatment? But Bykov was the real McCoy. He gave me a pass to the Supreme Court and told me how I should express myself to the officials there. The next day I went to the court—the highest court in Moscow—and I told my story to an official. He must have been entertained by this young, naive girl crying and pleading in front of him. But would you believe it, he gave his secretary a few orders and told me that my brother would get a retrial. This is what I did for my brother. If only it had been enough."

I can see how important it was for her to feel she had done as much as she could, because she still cannot forgive herself that it was not sufficient.

"That was a lot you did for Simcha, Ma," I say.

"I was stupid. The same thing happened to Mrs. Erlich's husband. He was thrown in jail. But she did it one-two-three. She got a few hundred rubles and paid the judge, and they let her husband go and never bothered him again. That's what I should have done. I was stupid. I thought you had to follow the system."

When they led my brother into the courtroom for the retrial, he seemed to me to have deteriorated considerably. The long, dark coat which he had worn on his way to prison the year before now hung loosely on his frame. His shaved head accentuated the pallor of his face and the desperation in his eyes. With his head bowed, he obsequiously obeyed every order of the guard. I had never seen my brother so submissive. He seemed stripped of all dignity as he sat before the tribunal with his large hands resting on his thighs.

The courtroom was filled with as many spectators as at the first trial. The judge was a young man newly arrived from Moscow and so were the two male jurors flanking him. The prosecutor made the same accusations of speculative dealings, but this time Simcha was assigned a lawyer from Moscow, a young, intelligent man who had spent time questioning me in order to prepare Simcha's defense.

Now, arguing Simcha's case before the court, he spoke for forty minutes and laid out my brother's wretched history: his parents' divorce when he was four, his mother's death when he was fourteen, his departure soon afterward to Warsaw to earn his own way, his battle with tuberculosis.

"He began selling women's underwear," the lawyer declared, to bursts of giggling in the audience. "Now, with what sort of bourgeois are we dealing here? If this defendant is a bourgeois than my comrade prosecutor is a czar!"

He pointed to Simcha and turned to the tribunal.

"Please, my dear comrades of the jury, look at his face before you make your decision. Does this face, this physiognomy, look like a bourgeois? Is this the kind of person Lenin had in mind when he attacked the bourgeoisie?"

When the judge and the two jurors stepped out for deliberations, my brother sat stone-faced, not even turning his head to look at my reaction. I too stayed fixed to my second-row seat, begging God in murmurs to let the verdict go in my brother's favor. The judge soon returned. I tried in my mind to shut out the words, so certain was I that the verdict would go against us. But I heard him clearly say the yearned-for words, "Not guilty!" I did not wait to hear the rest of the decision because I raced to embrace my brother.

Still clinging to each other, my brother and I walked out of the courtroom followed by curious onlookers. It was hard for me to digest that all of this was real, that Simcha was finally free from what had been for him a death sentence. But when I glanced at Simcha's face, it was hard to detect any jubilation.

"What's the matter with you?" I asked. "You don't seem at all happy."

"No, I am, I am," he said. "I just don't feel too good right now."

The stresses of the labor camps had aggravated his tuberculosis. In his new room in the men's barracks, he lay down on his cot and began spitting blood. I panicked, but he assured me that he had had several such episodes in the prison camp and that the spitting usually stopped after a few days' rest.

"No use getting a doctor," he said. "They cannot do anything. In a few days, I won't spit blood anymore. Don't worry, Rochele."

The next day, Simcha's lawyer informed me that my brother's fate was more complicated than I had thought. My brother was indeed free, Simcha's lawyer said, but the prosecutor was also given permission to appeal the verdict, though it was doubtful the prosecutor could produce the confiscated evidence of Simcha's illegal market dealings that had been presented at the first trial.

"They did not expect your brother would be around to claim these things," the lawyer said. "They probably made boots for themselves out of the leather hide or gave the stockings to their wives and lovers. And when in their lives did they ever see a shortwave radio?"

He was, however, candid in expressing his concern about how the appeal might go, and advised that Simcha take some action to get public opinion on his side. He suggested that Simcha go to Moscow to tell his story to an investigative reporter for *Izvestia,* the national newspaper.

"It has been done before," he said. "I'm sorry, but I know of no other way to help."

I asked about Simcha's "passport," the identity card that all Russians carried and that he would need if he wished to travel to Moscow. The lawyer told me it would remain in official custody until the conclusion of the appeal.

"He will have to manage to get to Moscow without a passport," the lawyer said.

My brother quickly recuperated and decided to make the trip to Moscow suggested by the lawyer. He gathered his last possessions—the two towels, two Emka shirts, and Gorky's trilogy—and I sold them on the market and gave him the money plus a week's wages so he could buy a railroad ticket and have a few rubles left over for his expenses in Moscow.

It rained heavily that day in June when my brother left for Moscow. Reluctant to go, he slept fitfully the night before and looked frail as he headed toward the train station. He was fatalistic and didn't believe the trip would make a difference.

"Where am I going to sleep in Moscow?" he said. "Who do I know there? And how will I manage without a passport?"

He didn't expect me to answer. He mingled on the station platform with the kerchiefed women weighed down with their bundles and suddenly it seemed as if the force of the crowd was pushing him onto the train. I waved to him once more, but the train let out a shriek and a cloud of smoke and began to move out of the station before he could return my farewell.

I remained standing on the platform long after the train disappeared. I had nothing to turn back to. I no longer even had a brother nearby in prison. I had a strong feeling that I would never see him again. I felt utterly alone. I felt no inclination to return to the empty barracks. Everything seemed hopeless and empty. The drops of rain mingled with my tears all the way back to the barracks. When I entered my room, I slumped on my bed and did not leave it for two days.

When I did, it was to answer a knock at my door from someone who brought startling news; the Germans had invaded western Russia. As distant as Lys'va was, we felt the repercussions within a few days. Activity in the market dwindled until the stalls appeared all but abandoned. It was difficult to obtain a bread ration even a day ahead of time. There were suddenly new faces on Lys'va's streets as scores of evacuees from the Ukraine, White Russia, and even Leningrad fled eastward. Across town there were now posters urging people to be on the lookout for spies.

"Please report suspicious individuals immediately!" the posters read. "They are enemies of our country! Anyone lacking a passport should be reported immediately to the NKVD or to the military police station."

Rewards were offered. The local newspapers devoted full pages to lists of the heroic informers and of the people they named, many of whom, the newspapers later reported, were shot to death. I cried reading the names of the suspects because I could see that my brother Simcha might soon be on such a list.

"It is a war and we cannot allow ourselves the luxury of long investigations," the newspaper said.

Indeed, officials did not waste time on any long investigations into my brother's case. Within a short time, two fateful letters arrived. One was from the court of appeals ordering a third trial for my brother. The prosecutor had been successful in his appeal, the letter explained. Then a second letter arrived from the Moscow Supreme Court stating that "in accordance with martial law, the defendant Simcha Warshawiak must return to prison to complete his five-year sentence." Under martial law, all appeal trials were being put off until peace returned.

The letter was devastating, yet I tried to sustain some hope. My brother would have to return from Moscow, I would see him, and even if he was returned to prison, he would still be alive. Those were the slim threads to which I clung. ◎

As she conveys these stories, my mother's eyes betray her mental absence from the room. She is back in Russia in 1941, reappraising her efforts on behalf of her brother Simcha. Could she have done something more? Did she do too much? Is there still something she can do today to track him down? Though it has only been in recent years that she let her children in on the source of her ruminations, such brooding went on for all the years I grew up in her home. Her distraction is something we all had to cope with; some of us have even absorbed the habit. After half a century my mother still is not at peace.

23

Bronx Science was in the northern reaches of the Bronx, the second-to-last stop on the D train, and traveling there that first year felt as if I were journeying into some exotic borderland. It was not that Science was alien intellectually. Yes, in a school with a reputation for churning out five Nobel Prize winners, there were quite a few hypercerebral virtuosos who spoke their own argot and casually dropped terms like *quantum* and *quasar* that might as well have been Turkish to me. But most of the school's kids, it turned out, were the plebeian Howards and Iras, who pounded a grimy basketball and collided into each other's sweating bodies in the neighborhood school yard on 165th Street. They happened to be bright enough to pass the entrance tests, and by now they had become familiar.

What made Bronx Science seem foreign was that after nine years at yeshivas I was now also going to school with human specimens I had scarcely encountered before. There was an assortment of girls the yeshivas never had, girls who wore skirts above their knees, girls who wore sandals that curled around their calves, girls who, the grapevine had it, were having sex. The school also had Christians—lots of them—and ethnic types I had almost no experience with: flamboyant Russians, ironic Irishmen, Ukrainian toughs, Chinese and Japanese kids whose earnest bookishness struck me as not very different from that of Talmudic grinds, and a sprinkling of black hipsters like Stokely

Carmichael (before a need to charm receptive whites turned to acid resentment and he became the famous Black Power firebrand).

Then there were the Central Park West and West End Avenue kids with whom Stokely often hung out. Worldly and literate, they brought a cocky righteousness to school that was both intimidating and alluring. Quite a few were the children of West Side lefties, parents who had been bruised by McCarthyism, which as late as 1959 had not yet entirely withered away. One was the son of a blacklisted playwright, another the son of a communist lawyer who defended blacklisted writers. They came from the clamorous streets of Manhattan but, brandishing their guitars like weapons, they liked to sing about dogs named Blue scampering around desolate Texas wheat fields. They grieved for the whole spectrum of the exploited and downtrodden: sharecroppers, sweatshop workers, West Virginia miners, lonesome cowboys. The boys let their hair grow shaggy, the girls wore flouncy rustic skirts, and one or two changed their names to Russian equivalents. Ann became Anushka; Natalie, Natasha. They flaunted small buttons on their chests that made stentorian statements about stopping nuclear explosions. They clustered with their guitars around a bench outside the school and sang Weavers and Woody Guthrie songs like "Roll On, Columbia," their faces puckered with tenderness for anyone suffering anywhere, for the wistful possibilities of a world where honest, plainspoken folks shared the same kindhearted visions in simpler locales of fast-flowing rivers and craggy mountains.

Songs like "Roll On, Columbia" meant nothing to me. Rolling rivers, Douglas firs, mighty dams were out in some incomprehensible beyond, far from the cramped intensity of pale-faced boys hunched over yellowed Hebraic tomes swaying to a hoary singsong. Still, there was something in the heartfelt solemnity of these singers that whispered of worlds I myself might one day discover if I only cast off the musty valises of my parents' world. I was beguiled.

I first became aware of this group as a distinct subculture during the school's periodic air-raid drills. All the sons and daughters of the Bronx proletariat dutifully crouched on the hallway floors and covered their heads protectively with their arms, acquiescing even if perhaps some giggled at the exercise's silliness. The folksingers refused. Air-raid drills, they believed, were deluding Americans into the proposition that nuclear wars were tolerable. And so when the sirens went off, the protesters stood ramrod straight, their faces etched in both defiance and fright, until annoyed assistant principals rounded them up.

I felt myself drawn to them. They were unshakably sincere. They treated one another with respect, seemed concerned about significant things. They probably had a place in their victim-detecting hearts for an immigrant like me. But I was not going to let them rope me in. For just as I was intrigued by them, I also resented them. Think about it. Here I was trying to claw my way toward some measure of plain acknowledgment by this country that I had not even been in for ten years, and they were reviling its every blemish. Maybe they had a reason to feel the country had let them down. But from my newcomer's vantage, I still had a long climb up before I could begin thinking about letdowns. Besides, America had been good to my family. It had given my parents steady jobs and some basic comforts. It had taken us to the Grand Concourse, put me in Bronx Science. These babes in the woods equated America with the Soviet Union, but what did they know about the Soviet Union? My parents had spent five years in the Soviet Union and learned firsthand how cruel and corrupt a land it was. Didn't these kids grasp that it was only America's tolerance that allowed them to be so brazen in their rebellion?

OK, mine was a narrow, immigrant's view. But they should have known better. Most of them were not that far removed from the herring boats themselves. Their grandfathers started out as peddlers and tailors, joined unions, tasted freedoms broad enough to let them board the socialist and Leninist bandwagons. Where would their grandchildren be without America's democratic opportunities? Certainly not snug in doormen buildings. It was obvious to me that the cushioning of Central Park West had turned the grandchildren into spoiled innocents.

In any case, for me, the freewheeling sixties took a long time to sink in.

In my social studies class, there was a student named Alan Darion. He was tall, slender, blond, and quietly pugnacious with a small SANE button pinned to his baggy sweater. The button's statement—the white pitchfork on black background urging "Stop All Nuclear Explosions" and thus a halt to outdoor testing of atomic bombs—might as well have come through a loudspeaker. I took him on. The Soviets were intent on world domination, I argued. The United States must brace for a possible war and in this age, that meant nuclear weapons, which the military needed to test, even above ground in Nevada and the South Pacific.

"Ha!" he cackled at my idiocy. "We have enough power to blow the Earth up twenty times over. What do we need all those bombs for?"

"If we allow ourselves to be weak, Alan," I retorted, "the Russians will march into the Bronx just as they did in Czechoslovakia and Hungary."

"And if we keep building nuclear weapons, they'll keep building them, and one day we'll have one hell of a thermonuclear party on the Grand Concourse."

"You mean you'd rather live in a country where they tell you what you have to believe in, what job you're going to work at, where you're going to live?"

Who had appointed me chief defender of the United States, I don't know. But as I argued with Darion, I fortified myself with the pride I was taking in newsreels of nuclear blasts, watching the mushroom clouds snowball above the ocean or the sands, blotting out the sun and the sky. What might there was in those megatons. It was like watching Mickey Mantle, his muscles bulging out of his short sleeves, his body twisted like a giant spring, launch a home run toward the topmost grandstand of Yankee Stadium. The Yankees. The United States. They were all part of a pantheon of power and retribution that I was constructing against the murky forces lurking in my future.

Was I seeking revenge against the Nazis who had persecuted my parents? The forces of life I could not surmount? Who knew then. But in my musings, I was no different from my father. The only show he ever watched on television was wrestling. He would sit in front of the set, his fists clenched, shadowboxing with the wrestlers as they flew off the ropes and pounced on their opponents.

"Daddy, what are you getting so excited for?" Josh would say, chuckling. "Wrestling is a fake. They're not really hitting each other."

But my father seemed lost in the contest, as if he were replaying battles that might have been against sadistic goyim in his hometown of

Borinya or against the barbarians who slew his parents and sisters in some fashion he was never able to learn.

Now I was up against Alan Darion, waging my battle with words, not deeds. He was reading *The Nation*. I was reading Henry Luce's *Time*. He belonged to SANE; I was going to rallies for the new Democratic candidate for president, John F. Kennedy, who was trumpeting the missile gap with the Soviets. The only thing we seemed to agree on was our enchantment with our world history teacher, Mrs. Lanier. She wore tight pastel skirts above the knees and when she leaned back against her desk facing the class, the contours of her hips and thighs came into such tantalizing outline that it was difficult to concentrate on the accomplishments of the Congress of Vienna.

Young men and women like Alan Darion and Stokely Carmichael and the guitar players and the air-raid drill resisters were to become frontline soldiers in the civil rights and antiwar movements that were just sprouting nationwide. One of my classmates, a gentle, gawky, straw-haired boy from Walton Avenue, went on to become a Weatherman, joining Kathy Boudin and Mark Rudd as fugitives. When I heard about him a decade or so after high school, I could not understand why someone from Walton Avenue would want to blow up buildings and give his parents such heartache. What did any of us have to be so angry about, living in uneventful neighborhoods where subways took you where you wanted to go, streets were clean, and schools of the caliber of Bronx Science were free of charge?

And so, while drawn to it, I could never enter the spirit of the left-wing set and I kept my distance. But it seemed like there was no other set with which I could mingle. I wasn't a scientist like Joe Erlichster, who kept an oscilloscope and distilling apparatus at home, or a mathematician like Henry Laufer, who walked briskly through the crowded halls with a slide rule jutting out of his looseleaf notebook. I wasn't an athlete or an actor or a painter or a schoolyard basketball player. I didn't listen to the Shirelles or the Ronettes and live for the Friday-night dances at the gymnasium. There was no club for ex-yeshiva boys. Sure, there were a few of us sprinkled around the school, but we didn't make ourselves known to each other, as if our shared past was a secret.

Not sure of where I belonged in this puzzling public institution. I scorned everything I couldn't or was afraid to belong to. The scientists, I decided, were aardvarks, the rock-and-rollers dumbos, the political types naive dupes. And so I kept myself detached, flailing here and there at a connection and hoping the opportunity would present itself. That first year of high school I was largely lost, saved by the implacable wave of a school schedule that carried me through the spare, clean hallways from world history to biology to gym to lunch to English to mechanical drawing to geometry and so filled out my day. In fact, lunch, with its challenge of finding a congenial table to sit at, turned out to be the hardest period.

The one thing I could do from 8:45 to 3:00 P.M. was show the teachers—and my classmates—my stuff. After nine years of a yeshiva regimen, I knew no other way. For Mrs. Lanier, I took opulent notes about the five causes of the Protestant Reformation and the six reasons for the rise of nationalism. For my biology teacher, Mrs. Ansell, I used colored pencils to draw precise diagrams of an amoeba and the chambers of the human heart. For mechanical drawing, I slid and twisted my T-square to make a cross-section of a screw. After the enigmas, dialectic, and sharp analysis of Gemara, these courses weren't daunting.

For my English teacher, Mrs. Levy, I wrote a Thurberish essay that I called "I Knew a Gnu." Much of the wit was provided by my friend from 102nd Street, Maury, on one of our Saturday outings to Donnell Library. He may have been floundering in school, but staying up nights watching Jack Paar he had heard about Thurber and the wits of the Round Table. We took my first draft in hand around one of Donnell's oak tables and together we penned a funnier version. The teacher liked it. My masterpiece was a sketch of Louis Armstrong and that too had a coauthor, in this case my refugee mother. I liked Armstrong, liked the tenderness of his trumpet, his playful mangling of a lyric, his infectious patter. But I couldn't articulate these things, hadn't found my own voice. My mother's English was uneven, but she had ideas, grown-up ideas, and the teacher liked that essay too.

I began getting 90s. I got a perfect 100 on the biology midterm and grinned with pleasure when Mrs. Ansell announced to the class I was the only student to do so. I wasn't passionate, but I liked doing well, impressing my classmates, pleasing my teachers, pleasing my mother.

Only in English did I feel I wanted to do much better. Doing well in English was a badge of assimilation. And at this point in my life, assimilation seemed a primary concern.

The most effortless place for connections was right in our homeroom class, where for fifteen minutes every day students dashed off any unfinished homework or caught up on gossip while the homeroom teacher, a burly gym instructor named Mr. Allen, took attendance and made announcements about assemblies and team tryouts. Sitting near me in homeroom was a bespectacled straight arrow named Roger Kline, the son of a magazine advertising executive who lived on the East Side. Roger was conscientious, efficient, correct in manners—a grown-up long before he needed to be—although he had an arch side that seemed to want to shuck off all that propriety. He came from upper Madison Avenue and had an earnest desire to make his way in the world, but he was open to disparate personalities like me. Curious about a book that at Maury's urging I had taken out of the library, a Leonard Feather history of jazz, he probed me about what I knew about jazz, as if this were some shortcoming in himself he needed to fill in.

"I've got some great records at home," I told him. "Bix Beiderbecke, Art Tatum, Fats Waller. I even have some Glenn Miller stuff, like 'Moonlight Serenade.' Maybe you can come over to my house sometime and listen to my collection."

I was lying, of course. I had no record collection. My parents did not own a record player. The only records I knew were those Maury and I played on the Donnell Library's turntables. But I wasn't going to admit that to a young swell from Madison Avenue. I must have hoped that saying I had a record collection was as good as owning one. It made me a little more cultivated, American, maybe even a little more Madison Avenue. The invitation to my home was dishonest as well. I did not want him to see my home. Why would I want to show Roger the cramped rooms with the windows facing a gray alley, the refugee father who spoke so little English, the living room without a hi-fi and without all the records I had boasted about?

Hiram, who sat behind me in homeroom, was more approachable. Coming from the North Bronx, he took the same irreverent attitude toward the school that I did and bared some of the blotches on his soul. Dark-haired and lean, he had a chiseled face with deep-set eyes and was lawyerly smart, quick to slam any defects in the details of a story or flaws in an argument, sometimes brutally so. He had an air about him of discernment, good judgment, and confident authority, as if he knew volumes more than all of us. Nothing seemed to rattle him. But he had a saving tender side as well. He too didn't connect to any particular clique. So Roger, Hiram, and I, with some other hangers-on, became our own loose and occasional clique. It wasn't much but it made me feel less alone in the roiling Bronx Science sea.

At some point, I brought my two worlds together, the immigrant gang—Maury, Simon, and Josh—and my new American acquisitions—Hiram and, when he was feeling daring, Roger. None of us had girlfriends, so adventures in sex were not yet on the horizon. But we went down together to Greenwich Village and hung around coffeehouses and took in the gamy scene. Maury was now seventeen, tall and broad-shouldered with a face whose peach fuzz was turning into genuine stubble. He could pass for drinking age. We chipped in and he would stroll into a liquor store as our delegate and swagger out with the goods. At first the bottle was Thunderbird or another cheap wine. Soon it became vodka, which had more of a kick and made us feel more valiant, adventuresome. Josh, blond, athletically built, and now a swimmer on the Bronx Science team, was all of fourteen or fifteen, but since he had been tagging along behind me for much of my life, taking every plunge that I did but at a younger age, I gave almost no thought to whether he was too young to be drinking vodka in Greenwich Village.

One night, in Washington Square Park, we encountered two sailors, wonder-struck, on-the-town Midwesterners, both wiry and flaxen-haired and not much above our own age. They were taken by what they imagined were our big-city smarts and we were captivated by their travels to places like Okinawa and Macao. It was a balmy, moonlit evening and we huddled near the hip-high tubular railing that formed the park's perimeter. We bribed them with our bottle of cheap vodka and Maury's Pall Malls, and the sailors, Walt and Stan, entertained us with their adventures.

"Okinawa is a big rock. Lots of whorehouses, though," Walt, the brasher one, told us. "What the navy makes you do while you're there is take fucking syphilis tests. All the fucking time. They got a fucking line for syphilis tests stretching for a block."

We lapped up this initiation into the craggy actuality of life, life untamed and unrefined, away from the humdrum complacencies and pretensions of the Grand Concourse. But as midnight passed and we kept swigging the vodka, things got a little too untame for us. For no good reason, Walt's buddy, Stan, decided to leap the railing in a head-first swan dive. He landed hard on his scalp and passed out cold, his body motionless, his face a lifeless mask. He had broken his neck, I was sure, and I saw my world unraveling around me—ambulances, police, parents, newspapers, immigration authorities—in a spiral that would end with deportation. His buddy, though, knew him better than we did.

"Give him a few more minutes, he'll come around," Walt said. "He's had too much booze."

And sure enough, after a few minutes Stan stirred into conscious-ness, and soon offered up another bold idea.

"I wanna hear some jazz!" he shouted with a drunken twang. "Some re-e-e-e-e-al New York City jazz."

Why we listened to him, I don't know. But Maury knew that the Half Note was a few blocks east near Astor Place and that Ornette Coleman was playing there. It was this kind of inside dope the sailors were hoping for. So we ambled with them along Eighth Street through shadowy, forlorn blocks of industrial lofts. On Astor Place, the drunker of the sailors walked right into a trash can and sent it rattling into the middle of the street, startling the few nighthawks. The usually unflappable Hiram now seemed to grow edgy too. He was applying to private colleges, and an arrest for drunken rowdiness would not look good on his applications.

We reached the Half Note and peeked in behind the swinging, saloonlike doors at a classic tableau. Ornette was right there to the left of the entrance noodling languidly on his saxophone, he and his backup trio vapored in cigarette smoke and the cheery affection of ine-briated disciples. Before we could decide whether we wanted to pay the expensive cover and minimum, a sharp, crashing noise changed our plans. Stan had collapsed through the saloon doors, falling flat on the floor right in the middle of Ornette's celestial flights of improvisation. I edged away in fear, but Hiram and Maury intrepidly grabbed Stan by the arms and pulled him back onto the sidewalk, smiling apologetically at the bar's patrons. As he wobbled against a wall with Walt propping him up, Hiram gathered Maury, Simon, Josh, and me into a powwow and adamantly told us we had to jettison these sailors before they got us all arrested. So we dropped the two sailors off at a two-dollar-a-night Bowery flophouse and made our getaway.

On the subway train back, we chuckled groggily in reliving our mudbath in experience. This was life at the hilt. Sailors and drunkenness and jazz clubs and Okinawa and syphilis tests. More, we wanted more, and we couldn't wait until next Saturday night for another immersion.

When Josh and I emerged from the 167th Street station around three in the morning, the Concourse was somber and deserted, the purplish darkness broken only by intervals of lamppost light. I glanced up toward the fifth-floor windows and could make out my mother's head and shoulders jutting out the window. Bleary and ashen without her makeup, she had waited up to make sure we arrived safely. A woman whose relatives kept vanishing around her, she had not been able to fall asleep until she knew we were safely home. She would say nothing when we walked in the door, giving us an emphatic cold shoulder. But in the morning there would be a fight. Why did I stay out so late? What was I doing? What kind of big shot did I think I was at sixteen?

She would make me feel childish, puny, unbefitting the company of sailors and beatniks, of well-traveled rogues like Hiram and Maury. But I was determined to escape one day. I saw myself now as an American, hip deep in the American experience. I would no more be the timid refugee boy with one leg planted in the fearful shtetls of Poland, with a mother ever vigilant that no more perils come to the remnants of her kin. I would defy that mind-set, plunge in, take risks, put myself on the line, take a few savory bites of life's dangers.

Sometime later my parents went to Brooklyn to visit some friends, so I gathered my friends in the Concourse apartment for a drinking party, complete with a coquettish female friend of Simon's, whom none of us knew what to do with. I was taking a risk. What would

Hiram and his friends make of my home, and when my parents returned, what would they make of them? I had asked my parents to call before they left Brooklyn. This way we'd have a warning to clean up any evidence of our debauchery. But a short time before midnight, after we were groggy from vodka and were fumbling about for ways to entertain ourselves, the phone rang. It was my parents, they were calling not from Brooklyn but from the pay phone at the corner subway station, a three-minute walk away. We rushed to hide the evidence, rinsing out glasses and burying bottles in a brown-paper garbage bag in the kitchen. When my parents walked in, they seemed pleased to see their sons with a houseful of friends, including genuine Americans like Hiram. Their sons were grafting themselves onto the American tree. As they made pleasant small talk, Hiram noticed the tubular top of a vodka bottle jutting out of the garbage bag. Quicker than me, he snatched up the bag and clutched it close to his chest like a Torah, crunching the bag's mouth tightly to conceal the contents.

"Hiram, you don't need to do that," my father said. "I'll take the garbage down in the morning."

"No, Mr. Berger," Hiram replied. "We made a mess, we ought to clean it up."

"Leave it, Hiram. I'll take it down."

But Hiram was insistent and, smiling, he strolled out of the house with the concealed weapon. No one was the wiser.

Afterward, my father told me, "What a nice boy that Hiram is. He comes here and takes the garbage out. How many guests would do that?"

There were many other such adventures during my high school years. But what were they, this hodgepodge of shenanigans? They gave us a quick jolt of pride in our own capacity for foolhardiness. But there was always a steep letdown. After all, they didn't get us closer to the girls we really craved. No wonder that there were times, before we set out for our late-night adventures, that we soothed our wounded souls listening, on Simon's phonograph, to Frank Sinatra at his most forlorn and brokenhearted. Sinatra embodied the man I wanted to be: tough, swaggering, volatile, yet concealing a bruised soul. He understood the plaintive moments in the wee, small hours of the morning when no one cares and only the lonely understand. I was, it was obvious, wallowing in the pathos of my sorry social life. There were all these girls who knew how the pieces fit in the American jigsaw. These girls listened to Pete Seeger or protested nuclear wars or agitated their bodies to rock music. I was listening to Sinatra and Peggy Lee, their parents' music. What would I tell them about myself? About the way I spent Saturday nights getting drunk? I would gaze longingly at the girls in my school and could only imagine what they were about. I was hesitant to open my mouth and find out.

Then a girl appeared. Her name was Eva Silbermann. She was in my homeroom class. She was pretty, with dark brown hair that hugged her florid cheeks, and dark eyes deepened by the flourish of long, Oriental eyebrows. She had a plucky dignity in the way she carried herself despite what was so obviously a shy nature. I found myself moved by her, by the pride with which she held her loose-leaf to her chest and neatly packed her bag. For months, I would spot her sitting on the D train heading up to Bronx Science when I got on at 167th Street. I noticed how regularly she was seated in one of the middle cars and I positioned myself on the platform to better my chances of seeing her. One day, I smiled at her when I saw her and she smiled back. It seemed natural to say hello and we soon found ourselves talking about watching Dobie Gillis the night before. It turned out we were both charmed by Dobie's beatnik sidekick, Maynard. Over many mornings like this walking the few blocks from the train station to school, Eva told me that she played violin in the school orchestra, that she loved opera, that her father often took her to the Metropolitan. I told her that I found opera histrionic and I preferred American musicals. She squirmed at my crudity, but said she liked Rodgers and Hammerstein's *Carousel*. I sang a few bars of "If I Loved You" and she sang a few bars too. I wanted my song to convey all I was longing to tell her, and concluded as I sang that I must be in love with her.

Then another boy seemed to appear regularly at her side. Steve Rosenbaum was bouncy, cheerful, chatty, no pensive glum-puss like me. He got on at the 183rd Street station, so I had her to myself for only four stops. Once he was on, I had to share her all the way to 205th Street and along the half-dozen blocks to school. He seemed the one she was more interested in. He was breezier, funnier, full of gossip and small talk. I found myself giving way. I wanted to tell her how I wanted to spend the rest of my life alongside her, but instead I talked about Dobie Gillis, and Mr. Allen's homeroom class, and the project I was doing in biology.

As time went on, though, I began to have more to talk to Eva about. With Bronx Science working the magic for which it was created, I was actually acquiring some culture. An English teacher, Arnold Cannell, was training me to savor the delicacies of literature. Short, taut, volatile, and just a tad short of prissy, he was the school's one true eccentric. He was something of a dandy, dressing in tight, neatly pressed suits and vivid neckties pinned so tightly to his collar they highlighted the thrusts of his Adam's apple whenever he spoke. A bachelor, he lived with his mother on the East Side of Manhattan and often mentioned her opinions on the world, as if she were some fount of kitchen wisdom. In a school with a distinctly progressive ambiance, he was a die-hard Buckleyite and to the dismay of his students regularly quoted the *National Review*. But what endeared him to his classes and earned their grudging respect was that he was thoroughly conscious of his own quirks and not afraid to mock them. Even more important was his deep pleasure in the evocative power of the English language, the subtleties of characterization in the hands of a master writer, the stunning turns of the human drama.

After years of such flaccid novels as *Silas Marner* and *O Pioneers!* we were reading *Anna Karenina, Madame Bovary, The Red and the Black,* and *Portrait of a Lady,* novels that delved into irrational passions, labyrinthine motivations, and mottled moral universes where there were no saints and sinners. Could one condemn Anna for her unfaithfulness to a cold stuffed shirt like Karenin? Could one unequivocally detest Emma, restless and selfish as she was, for wanting to run away from her provincial husband and the small-minded concerns of Yonville-l'Abbaye? I would read how Emma as a girl was enchanted by Walter Scott's romantic stories, by heroines like Joan of Arc, by a novel telling of young men clasping trembling women. Did I not too respond like she did to the novels I read that took me out of the banalities of the Bronx?

"Emma Bovary, *c'est moi,*" Mr. Cannell told us that Flaubert had famously said, and I would nod affirmatively.

I too was Madame Bovary, eager for some passionate force in my world, some touch of distinction. And I knew other Emmas. Except for her liaisons, Emma Bovary was my mother, a restless woman whose outsized ambitions exceeded her ability to attain them. And Charles Bovary was in many ways my father, a man of simple needs and no driving aspirations, foolish in his tolerance, yet poignant in his trusting love and devotion.

I was bewitched by the language as well, by the lyricism and shrewd observation of writers like Tolstoy. How skillfully Tolstoy traced Anna's disenchantment with her husband after she met Vronsky, her distaste at her husband's grating, high-pitched voice, even the shape of his ears, as he greeted her on a St. Petersburg railroad platform. Yet Tolstoy does not spare Anna and her selfish blindness. The best writers were merciless, not letting even their beloved characters slip out from under their impeccable eye for the hard truths of human nature.

I found myself enchanted with the possibilities of the language itself, the abundance of words, the flavorful ways of registering so many objects and ideas, the calibrated shadings. I relished their elegance, their whimsy, their tenderness. In my Yiddish-speaking home, I knew a single word for hat—*hittel.* But in English, there was a distinctive word for every variety of headwear—a bonnet, a beret, a fedora, a homburg, a bowler, a boater, a panama, a Borsalino. *Canny* was a little different from *savvy,* which was a little different from *smart,* which was a little different from *perceptive.* There was a whole universe of borrowed and offbeat words—*ersatz, doppelgänger, debacle, cynic, stoic, epicurean, sybarite.* There were words whose origins gave me pleasure when I researched them in the dictionary—*bedlam, assassin, bowdlerize, billingsgate, nomenclature, Pecksniffian.* There were charming-sounding words like *helter-skelter, harum-scarum, molly-coddle, shilly-shally, and willy-nilly.*

I noticed how songwriters like Cole Porter would virtually cavort with a lyric in a song like "You're the Top," rhyming "nimble tread" with "the feet of Fred Astaire," "O'Neill drama" and "Whistler's mama," "You're a rose, You're Inferno's Dante" with "You're the nose on the great Durante." They could tangle with words, and come out being witty and topical, sassy and clever. Porter was not an immigrant or child of immigrants, but it did not escape my notice how many songwriters were: Gershwin, Berlin, Lorenz Hart, who in "Manhattan" could write a lyric like "I'd like to take a / Sail on Jamaica Bay with you." Sometimes when my brother, Josh, who was becoming an accomplished piano player, would toy with a Gershwin melody on the piano, I'd stand behind him singing the lyric and imagine myself as George's brother, Ira, wondering for the briefest moment if possibly Josh and I might one day make it in Tin Pan Alley just as those immigrant sons had done.

How lucky we immigrants were. We had the capacity of astonishment before this great language, could not take it for granted the way its native-born speakers might.

By the senior year of high school, Eva Silbermann and Steve Rosenbaum were still not officially sweethearts. They didn't walk from the subway station to school with their arms around each other. They talked a lot, just as Eva and I did. Maybe I had a chance. And now I was more experienced. After all, I'd had three summers in the bungalow colonies.

24

Those who didn't experience them cannot fully appreciate what the bungalow colonies were. But they deserve some historical footnote because they formed a distinct and colorful world with an all-too-short life span. They came into being early in the century as tenement Jews craved summertime relief from soggy apartments and steamy asphalt; by the late 1970s the plebeian Jewish culture that had nurtured them was all but extinct. Until they were lamented nostalgically, the bungalows were scorned as second-rate even by their habitués. What they didn't get enough credit for was that for people of pinched means—people who could not afford the gaudy Catskills hotels, let alone such lofty realms as the Hamptons—they provided a basic respite of pine-scented air, bracing lake water, and merciful shade.

Most families arrived at the bungalows in cars. My mother improvised our way up. She, Josh, and I, carrying or dragging baby Evelyn, hauled two laundry bags stuffed with ten weeks' worth of clothes and sundries onto a subway train heading toward the Forty-second Street bus terminal. From there we boarded a Short Line bus and spent three bumpy, airless hours until we reached the foothills of the Catskills and my mother nagged or sweet-talked the driver into letting us off right in front of the colony we had chosen that summer. Once the bus had vanished from sight, my mother rested the bags on the ground, took a deep whiff of the country air, and proclaimed, "Aaah, the air is like

Otwock." Her remark had the same ceremonious effect as a champagne bottle smashed on the hull of a new boat. Our summer was launched.

The colonies we summered in, with names like Broadlawn Acres, Silver Crest, and Jay's, were essentially alike. Each had a necklace of two-room cottages arrayed around a broad lawn shaded here and there with oaks, elms, and maples that concealed a few reclining Adirondack chairs. The cottages were built on short, squat stilts and each had a screened porch for evening idling. The rooms were cramped and the tiny kitchenette intended for feeding anorexic pygmies, not the outerborough *fressers* who usually inhabited the bungalows. The colony's heart was the casino, a barnlike social hall where on rainy days children played Ping-Pong and knock-hockey, and at nights the men connived and kibitzed over nickel-and-dime poker and the women gossiped over the clacking of mah-jongg tiles. Occasionally, the casino became the cinema for an outdated, flickering movie, although if the night was balmy the film was projected on the colony's handball court, where the guests, gauzily highlighted by a mix of screen-glow and moonglow, could watch transfixed from their fold-up lawn chairs.

On Saturday nights, the casino had a drawing card, a comedian, magician, or singer whose shopworn outfits and shopworn numbers corroborated what we all sensed: within a few years these entertainers would flame out. Why else would they be playing a bungalow colony? Still, the jokes they told were often lewd and laced with Yiddish bodily humiliations, so the grown-ups, wanting to laugh freely and heartily, would send the children off to bed early. How wonderful it was a few hours later to hear the laughter of our mother and father as they stole into the bungalow trying unsuccessfully not to wake us up. From their whisperings it seemed like the tensions of the week had melted away, and we could reassure ourselves that there was still enough affection between them to hold our family together for another year.

Much of the time was spent near water. We went up to the colonies for three summers with another refugee family, the Coopermans and their two sons, Sol and Charlie, and the four boys raced one another at the pool in a variety of strokes and distances in what we fantasized as our own Olympics. One of the luminous moments of my life until then—outmatching the thrill of acceptance to Bronx Science—came on the day that I set out before dawn to fish. I pushed the rowboat out onto the glass-smooth lake, rose-tinted in the early morning light, and with the warble and chirp of foraging birds providing a tranquil background score, I cast my rod at the edges of weeds and lily pads. While blinking away the stabbing light of the rising sun, I landed a bass, then another, then a third, in such swift succession that I was ready to return before my mother had even started making breakfast. Docking my rowboat, I took the long way around to our bungalow, making sure I showed off to whomever I could those shimmering, stupefied carcasses dangling from a chain. This city boy had versed himself in a country thing or two.

In the bungalows—how did the name of these thatched-roof cottages spawned in colonial India become so familiar to the greenhorns that it entered their Yiddish lexicon?—the wives and children would stay up all week while the men toiled alone in the city. But the men would show up on weekends, an infusion of bottled-up sexual energy that could be felt in the otherwise indolent Friday-afternoon air. By Sunday morning, after reestablishing themselves with their families and reveling in the merriment of Saturday night at the casino, many of the men—mostly the Americans—were ready to play a pickup game of baseball, with youngsters like Josh and me taking in their antics.

My father worked Saturday mornings and so showed up late Saturday afternoons for his abbreviated weekend, bumming a ride from some other hapless stiff who worked Saturdays. He was elated to see us, his wavy black hair setting off a smile so radiant he might have just returned from a two-month trip to the Khyber Pass. On Sunday, he didn't play baseball. He didn't even come to watch. But he was up early, decked out in Bermuda shorts—a pair of worn chinos my mother had neatly lopped off—black stretch socks that contoured over his veined, bony calves, and well-shined black dress shoes. Not owning a pair of sneakers or sandals, he was trying as best he could to look summery. I would sometimes wince at the unfashionable sight of him, particularly those shoes and black socks, but he seemed pleased with the world, ambling through a grove of pines and brushing his hand against the needles as if he needed to test them for sharpness or inspecting the mushrooms at woods' edge for edibility in a habit that must have reached back to his country childhood. For him, this burst of freedom in the Catskills, this break from the unrelenting six-day cycle of predawn risings, obstacle-course commutes, and the evening daze of exhaustion, was all he could have asked for. A vacation for two on the Riviera could not have made him happier. Retreating to a patch of dappled shade, he and the just-as-reticent Mr. Cooperman would attempt a conversation. A great dialogue of Western man they did not have. But eventually their chattier wives relieved them of the obligation to talk, and the two couples whiled away the afternoon warding off the enervating sunshine in the kindness of the shade.

These were people, don't forget, who all the year round never allowed themselves a meal in a restaurant, a take-out lunch, a daily newspaper, a taxi cab to a doctor, a second week of vacation. Six months might go by before they took in a movie. Except for a single shot of vodka when company came, they never drank. Even their splurging on the bungalow colonies—was it $300 for the summer?—was a sacrifice made for their children. But since the children were up here anyway, they could indulge in the colony's cheap pleasures.

Clustered together under an ample tree, they recounted in Yiddish the pathos of their Polish hometowns, exulted over the achievements of their children, and quibbled over the merits of this or that. Mrs. Cooperman liked the tidy modernity of Queens, where she lived, my mother the theatrical liveliness of Manhattan. My mother liked movies with Burt Lancaster; Mrs. Cooperman adored Gregory Peck. Once or twice the conversation got so heated they did not talk to each other for a few days. But stranded together as greenhorns on this bungalow island, they were in no position to sustain a lengthy quarrel.

Sometimes, when the breeze and the shade were just right and she and Mrs. Cooperman had reached an amicable truce, my mother would clear her vocal passages, lean back, and burst into song. She had a full-throated, rich soprano that had never had a day of real training, but everyone who listened knew she was a gifted songbird. She would start off with an American standard like "Autumn Leaves," and you felt in the drifting leaves of red and gold and the memories of a lover's sunburnt hands that she was mourning things lost long ago.

"But I miss you most of all, my darling," she ended the song, her voice cracking with emotion. "When autumn leaves start to fall."

There had never been a lover that we knew of, but in the shattered Otwock of her childhood, there had been autumn leaves of chestnuts and oaks and a father, stepmother, brothers, and sisters, and she let us feel the rueful absence of a place and people we had never seen.

When she felt especially comfortable with her audience, her eyes would twinkle merrily and she would follow up with the plaintive Yiddish melodies of her childhood, songs by wives of penniless scholars too engrossed in Talmud volumes to grasp their families' hunger, songs by young girls trying to assay the virtues of their betrothed, songs by emaciated boys peddling single cigarettes along teeming urban streets. Whatever complicated feelings one had toward my mother, her singing would disarm everyone.

Sometimes my parents and the Coopermans would venture into the lake, my mother executing a decorous breaststroke, my father slashing at the water and twisting his head to breathe in the terrified agony of a drowning man. No one had ever taught these people to swim. No wonder my brother and I felt we had to make up for their shortcomings by developing skillful swim strokes.

We went with the Coopermans each summer because my mother figured that Josh and I would have parallel playmates, Sol and Charlie, and she would have someone to talk with. The way it worked out, however, was that I hung around with Charlie, Sol's younger brother, and Sol hung around with Josh. Charlie and I took long walks while I introduced him to Pall Malls and gave him the benefit of the wisdom I had gathered from the three extra years I had lived. Sol and I, having been infected by our mothers' rivalry, seemed to spend our time together competing. We would try to outdo each other at swimming and baseball and making the bungalow gang laugh at ribald jokes. In the evenings we would compete for girls. One year Sol ended up with the prettiest girl in the colony, and I ended up with someone less so but adventurous, in her own way. Lorraine told me her boyfriend in Brooklyn had a gun and would shoot her if she was unfaithful. But toward the middle of the summer she decided to live dangerously, by the standards of that time. The next year Sol ended up with a plainer girl and I paired off with a girl who lived two miles up the Concourse. In the evenings, Barbara and I would dance in the casino to an old phonograph that came with some rock records, slow songs like "Oh, Donna" and "Blue Velvet," and I would feel her curves and inhale the cloying smells of lipstick and hair spray and long for some forbidden extra. But this was 1960 and we sensed the bounds of our gropings. I didn't deeply care for the girls I ended up with. Both, I felt with adolescent snobbishness, knew little more than the confines of their own neighborhood while I, in my inflated imagination, was on the verge of becoming a rakish boulevardier. These were not the deeply experienced girls I deserved. These romances, I sensed, would end when my parents took me home. And they did.

When I returned to Bronx Science for my senior year, I resolved to ask Eva Silbermann for a date. More than a year had gone by since I first realized how much I liked her and I still hadn't asked her out. One reason for my hesitation was that I wasn't sure exactly how one did that. Should I ask her to a movie? That felt silly. She probably had friends whom she went to the movies with. Why would she need to go see a movie with me? People sometimes went to restaurants, but restaurants were as far removed from my family's experience as cotillions and regattas. She might laugh at my asking her for so intimate an evening, might tell me how obtuse I was that I didn't realize she and Steve Rosenbaum were sweethearts. My father had never discussed dating with me. And what did he know about dating? Had he ever dated in Borinya? I could not imagine his taking my mother out on a date in Russia, although something must have happened to help them converge. Men had asked my mother out in Warsaw. Should I ask her about dating? Frank Sinatra did not ask his mother how to date. My friends were not doing any better than me. That's probably why they were my friends. Roger kept a condom in his wallet, but it had stayed there untouched for more than a year and probably grown brittle. Maury, Simon, and Hiram, as far as I knew, had never paired up with a girl.

Weeks passed and I was still walking with Eva Silbermann from the subway chattering about teachers and what we saw last night on television and never letting her know what was in my heart, how much I loved her but was simply too spineless to say.

But then came the perfect pretext. Roger informed us about a New Year's Eve party that his friend David was having. It would be a crowd of East Side teenage gallants. Eva would be impressed. And the need for a New Year's Eve date would remove any hint of special intimacy. It was the force of the calendar that was prompting me to ask her out. Eva could say no, she was busy, and I wouldn't have to take it as a reflection of her feelings. I would not have to be hurt. One morning on the subway to school, after a half hour of arming myself with the right words and some courage to mouth them, I blurted it out.

"My friends are having a New Year's Eve party on the East Side. Would you want to come?"

Casual. I kept it casual. She looked up at me with a coy, sidelong smile, as if she detected some deeper intentions behind my nonchalance. I loved those naughty dark pools of her eyes that betrayed a mischief lurking in her soul that I was sure I would one day release.

"Can I think about it?" she said cryptically. "I'm not sure yet what I'll be doing."

But she came back a few days later and said she would enjoy going with me to the party. How vindicated I felt. I had taken the challenge and met it. This would be the start to a new life as Eva and I became first lovers, then lifelong partners. What that meant, I wasn't quite sure either, but I was eager to display her to the new circles I was traveling in. I was making it in this more cultivated American world. I was going to East Side parties with pretty girls on my arm. I could say good-bye to the gaucheries of my refugee friends. Any day now I would find myself at one of those bone-white palatial Art Deco nightclubs where Fred Astaire whirled Rita Hayworth across a shimmering tile floor.

Of course, I was terrified I would bungle it. Somehow Eva and I didn't speak much about the date—as if it were some uncomfortable secret between us. But New Year's Eve finally rolled around. I had my tweed sports jacket and woolen dress pants dry cleaned and I bought a new tie. My father, of course, had shined my shoes the Sunday before.

I shaved what little was worth shaving and used a touch of my father's Old Spice aftershave. I took a D train down to Fifty-ninth Street and switched for the Broadway line back up to 168th Street, then walked over to her house near Riverside Drive.

It was not a fashionable neighborhood, a maze of weathered tenements on the borderland between Washington Heights and Harlem. On the corner of Broadway there was a bodega. As I strode down the sloping blocks toward Riverside Drive, I found myself looking over my shoulder. Her building, midway in the block, was a gray stone apartment house with a dingy lobby. The elevator wobbled up to her floor and I rang her bell. Her father opened the door. He was a small, leathery-faced man with the hunched neck of a tailor, which I soon learned he was. His manner was correct and he spoke in a European accent, although his English was adept, far better, in any case, than my father's. He looked at me suspiciously and I saw it as my first goal to win him over.

"I notice you have a European accent," I said. "Where are you from?"

"You ask a simple question that doesn't have a simple answer," he said in a sad, resigned voice. "But as short as I can make it, I am from Poland."

"My parents are from Poland too. They came over in 1950."

"Where in Poland?" he asked, intrigued.

"Otwock," I said. "Or at least my mother is from there."

"Oh, Otwock," he said. "Everyone knows Otwock. It was a famous resort town near Varshaw."

Before I could go much further, Eva interrupted: "We can talk about that another time," she said. "I think Joe wants to get going to the party."

She said it sweetly. I could see she had an almost flirtatious power over her father, that he would do anything for her. He smiled and walked off to a small, cluttered room off the hall that had a narrow bed and a Singer sewing machine, with its familiar curvy black motor housing and the gold Singer insignia. The machine could have belonged to Mr. Weinberg or Mr. Granas. The greeners always dedicated a spare room to the sewing machine, like a writer will outfit a spare room with a desk and typewriter. And the accent could have been theirs as well. Mr. Silbermann, it seemed likely, was a greenhorn, although I didn't yet know enough history to distinguish greenhorns who came over long before the war as immigrants from those who had survived the Holocaust and come over as refugees.

It was possible that Eva, whom I had elevated to the lofty status of our high school's genteel belle, a Scarlett O'Hara of Washington Heights, was a refugee, just like me. We had found each other, through some murmur of our hearts, but neither had divulged who we really were. Apparently, hailing from an immigrant family was not something either of us was entirely proud of. I sensed that her respectful but firm cutoff of her father might have had something to do with that fact. She wanted to play down the connection. Or else—and this was something I had not yet learned that children of survivors do—she wanted to protect her father from the pain the memories dredged up. A simple question like When did you come over? could be a thread that unraveled a weave of unbearable events.

The unsought discovery of her roots must have made it easier for me to relax with Eva, for we chatted without much strain on the IRT subway, which took us downtown toward the East Side party. But the disclosure may have also diminished her. In my distorted subconscious hierarchy, immigrants were not as worthy as Americans, certainly not as good as West Side or East Side Americans. I swept Eva past the doorman posted at the East Side building and through the intimidating lobby with its embossed ceilings and marble floors. We rode up in the elevator with a taciturn uniformed operator whose silence made me worry that he saw right through the absurdity of my presence. Inside the sprawling apartment, I saw my friends Roger, Hiram, Richie, and Joel cavorting with drinks in hand and with their high-toned girls. Somehow it seemed more important to me that I remain one of the guys than that I attend to Eva. And so, drinking vodka tonics, I sat with Roger and Hiram on the couch recalling our bacchanalian escapades in Greenwich Village for the entertainment of the strangers circled around the coffee table. Once or twice I found Eva and asked her to dance. But mostly I would glimpse her wandering through the room or chatting with someone I didn't recognize. I was glad she was occupied and hoped she was taking in the clique of sophisticates I had surrounded myself with.

Then somewhere before midnight, I went looking for her in the rambling Park Avenue apartment and she was gone, vanished. At the stroke of twelve, everyone shouted "Happy New Year" and blew noisemakers and caressed and sang "Auld Lang Syne." I joined in the merriment, but could not squelch the suspicion that she had gone off with someone else and that my friends were aware she had.

"Have you seen Eva?" I unguardedly asked Hiram.

"I think I saw her talking with David's brother," he said with a sly grin.

At twelve-thirty or so, she reappeared and at her side was indeed the brother of the host. They were smiling and talking easily and she had that dreamy remoteness that I sometimes detected when she was around Steve Rosenbaum. David's college-aged brother looked somewhat scholarly in glasses but also had the tall, lean frame of a tennis player and clearly possessed a lot more assurance than I did in handling a seventeen-year-old girl like Eva. She whispered something to him that I was sure smacked of intimacy, and then came over to me.

"Joe," she said, "I think we ought to get me home now. We have a long ride."

That was fine with me. On the way home, I pretended nothing had happened. What, after all, did I know about the rules of a date, and the propriety of taking a walk with someone other than the guy who brought you? But after I dropped Eva off at her apartment, with sleeping parents who like mine did not go out on New Year's Eve, and returned about 3:00 A.M. to my apartment house, with my mother's head poking out the window to establish with scientific certainty that I had come home, I felt under my anger that Eva and I would never really make it. She would run off with David's brother or Steve Rosenbaum or whomever. It seemed we knew each other too well in our immigrant guts and needed to keep a distance.

We continued to walk together mornings from the subway station to Bronx Science, but the walks had less of the consequence they once did. Sometimes I even slipped away to walk by myself to school. Graduation neared and knowing we were both heading for the City College of New York, we wrote affectionate salutations to each other in our yearbooks. Hers cryptically suggested that she still kept some notion of me as a possible fallback somewhere down the line.

"To Joe," it said, in a well-turned ballpoint hand. "I'll be seeing you the next four years. So I wish you patience. Love, Eva."

25

Among my high school friends, plans for college seemed to be a secret more confidential than sex. Perhaps it was because such serious doings would taint their carefully cultivated images of insouciance. Behind the scenes, however, each of them was huddling with his parents and making very distinct plans about going out of town. Roger, diligent and businesslike, ended up at Dartmouth. Hiram headed for George Washington. I too was making plans with my parents, but the intrigue was of a distinctly different sort.

"We don't want you to go away," my mother said bluntly.

First she argued economic practicalities.

"What for do you want to waste money to sleep and eat in the wild somewhere?" she said. "You can sleep and eat here. Make a try for Columbia. Maybe you'll get a scholarship. If you don't make it, go to City College. People say it's an excellent school and it's free."

I had no idea what going away to college might mean, and was a little intimidated by the proposition of striking out on my own. But when I did push the murky idea of going away, she answered with an irrefutable argument.

"Joey," she said, her voice low and sad, with a trace of shame. "We don't have nobody. You and Josh and Evelyn are all we have. We need to stay together. I don't want you going far away."

My father stood alongside her, his doleful, pleading eyes speaking the volumes his voice seldom did.

What did my parents know about going to an out-of-town college, anyway? Not only had they not gone to college, but in the United States they'd never been out of town except for the few summer visits to the Catskills and the trip to Yonah's chicken farm. With my average and SATs, I might have had aspirations for places like Amherst and the University of Chicago, names that floated in the air at Bronx Science and seemed to have about them the whiff of quality and exclusivity. But I knew my parents could not afford the tuition, let alone the residential expenses. *Scholarship* was a word I barely understood and I wasn't sure how one went about getting one. Bronx Science was helpful to those who took the initiative, who formed a relationship with the handful of guidance counselors. But to do that, you needed a fundamental grasp of what college involved.

So Columbia was the only school I applied to. For the interview, I wore my High Holidays suit, but when the interviewer, a lanky blond New Englander, asked me to compare the two recent books my application said I had read, *Catcher in the Rye* and *A Tale of Two Cities,* I clutched. How does one compare a Victorian saga of the French Revolution with the plain-spoken escapade of a tortured Manhattan adolescent? Yet of such moments are lives determined. If I had been more self-assured, I might have finessed my way through. But this was the first time I was coming under what, in my cloistered view, I saw as the full glare of the Gentile Establishment. By my fumbling answer, I figured, he knew me for the refugee misfit I was, dapper suit and all. When I walked out of his office, feeling awkward and deflated, I felt pretty sure I would not be accepted, and I guessed right. So in September of 1962 I showed up for registration at the City College of New York.

As a public institution, City College was something you took for granted, like the subway or the sanitation department. Though respected academically, it was in those years becoming less precious to many of its patrons. Top colleges had begun to open their doors to Jews and other ethnics. City College, for many, was the fallback school, wrapped in the disappointment of a consolation. I took the subway to 145th Street in Harlem, in a faded but still handsome black neighborhood cheered by some lovingly tended brownstones, and melded into the largely white-faced masses of New York high school graduates streaming along Convent Avenue toward the campus. Except for the cluster of stately Gothic buildings on the northern end, everything about the college bespoke public bureaucracy: the crowding, the tumult, the long waits, the sullen clerks. Most disquieting was my sense of anonymity. No administrator or teacher at the school knew or cared that I was there. I had no idea how I would discover a place for myself within this undifferentiated swarm.

So I found myself on orientation day joining whatever I could. I signed up for a fraternity, a college-organized neighborhood club called a house plan, the drama society, and one of the two school newspapers. A towering recruiter from Army ROTC, with a crew cut whose hair shafts stood at ramrod attention, looked me in the eye and strong-armed me.

"You wanna be a mama's boy all your life?" he said.

So I joined ROTC as well.

Just as in my first weeks at Bronx Science, I was swept up and saved by the force of schedule and routine. There were, it turned out, some wonderful teachers. Edmund Volpe and Marvin Magalaner in literature, George Schwab and Aaron Noland in history, Stanley Feingold in political science. They had personality, passion, and a shimmering intelligence and they quickened William Faulkner, Charlemagne, and Sam Rayburn to life.

"Kill them all, God will know his own!" Schwab used to proclaim, quoting the Christian Crusaders in his European accent, the mockery in his voice and smile deepened by his own bitter encounter with the Holocaust.

Unfortunately, I absorbed only a small part of what he and every other professor had to offer because I was skipping more than a few of my classes. It turned out I had found a very snug place for myself at one of the college's two newspapers, the *Campus*.

Not that I got a friendly reception the moment I walked in. A burly guy in an army uniform named Mike Katz scowled at me and a hard-boiled Lois Lane, Sue Solet, seemed aggressively disinterested. But soon the room lit up with a spellbinder like Vic Grossfeld, who quoted

Joyce and Mann and Lawrence Durrell, and a skinny, dry-witted joker, Ralph Blumenthal. Even Katz emerged from his curmudgeonly crust. They needled one another, and mocked officials like President Buell Gallagher, and told mesmerizing yarns like the one about a *Campus* editor named Lou Egol who in disgust hurled a typewriter across the room at a colleague named Ralph Danheiser. They remembered a story in an April Fools' issue about college administrators clamping down on the campus whorehouse. The accompanying photograph of the madam, the face of a prim old lady borrowed from the dusty photo files, turned out to be that of the oldest living alumna at Hunter College. Grossfeld recounted how embarrassed college officials did not take the joke in stride and flailed about trying to react, just like the bumbling administrators in the April Fools' story. They suspended the five editors, only to retreat sometime later.

"It could have been a Marx Brothers movie," Grossfeld said.

And, bang, I discovered that these editors liked the Marx Brothers and W. C. Fields and Humphrey Bogart and Billie Holiday and *Citizen Kane* and *The Third Man,* all the tastes I had acquired through Maury's corrupting influence. The *Campus* looked like it was going to be my place.

Our clubhouse was Room 328, a long, narrow room on the third floor of the college's social center, Finley Hall. Here we came between classes, after classes, and too often during classes, to schmooze, gossip, rib one another, and work on the two newspaper issues we turned out each week. The room was dominated by a long table with several grimy Remington typewriters. Two tall arched windows overlooked a deep and spacious lawn, where students crammed or necked or played guitars or capered with Frisbees. Squeezed against one wall were a battered couch and an armchair. Any stab at being clever or provocative was sure to get a retort from the rotating audience on the couches and window alcoves. A good deal of it was sophomoric, like one editor's quipping that Clyde Haberman—a freshman friend—was so skinny he had to dart around the shower in order to get wet.

Wisecracking and cheeky we were, but we seldom became sour with discontent. Almost no one was a true believer out to transform the world. We saw the clumsiness and silliness in every cause. With that detached stance, we were perfectly suited to be journalists, and that is what most of us became.

Our mission was to get the newspaper out twice weekly, and within weeks of joining I was aboard. We covered speeches fiery and humdrum, sought out professors for colorful quotes, sat through student government meetings whose issues were often of consequence only to the members of student government. We clacked out our stories on rough, pulpish paper on the office Remingtons, and edited one another's cherished phrases, and laid the stories out on page dummies with rulers and primitive calculating wheels, and took joy in the arch or clever headlines we wrote.

The campus gates closed at 10:00 P.M., which on many nights didn't give us enough time to finish editing. So we adjourned to a bar on Convent Avenue, the Moulin Rouge, and continued reworking stories in the smoky, honey light of the vinyl booths. In those days before the heartfelt stirrings of the civil rights movement congealed into racial distrust, we were never made to feel unwelcome by the neighborhood's drinkers, whatever they may have thought of our gang of cocky white kids. We put quarters in the jukebox and played a jivy version of "Deep Purple" and Bunny Berrigan's "I Can't Get Started." The camaraderie and laughter and significance of purpose mixed with an occasional scotch and the lowdown music suffused us in so much sweetness that no one wanted to leave.

As the hands of the bar's clock registered the deepening night, I would sometimes visualize my mother's head poking out of the fifth-floor window, gazing angrily down upon a subway entrance from which her son did not emerge. Who understood then what imaginings must have flitted through her mind? All I knew was that I was feeling in exhilarating command of my life and I was not going to gratify her. Let her stay up all night and worry.

As a result of the newspaper schedule, we spent much of our days walking around in a twilight of exhaustion deepened by guilt that we were missing classes and term papers and sinking into academic bankruptcy. I dropped out of ROTC because I could not abide mornings of standing at attention for twenty minutes on an asphalt field, one indistinguishable speck in a column of uniformed men, after coming home the night before at 2:00 A.M. So absorbed was I in our crusade to get the paper out that one morning on the way to school, I paced the 167th Street subway platform while reading a newspaper and walked right off the edge, tumbling onto the tracks below. A woman let out a piercing scream that rebounded across the tunnel, and someone helped me clamber up to safety. When the train pulled in seconds later, I felt the horror of what had almost happened and knew I had to get some perspective on my frenzied life.

We could not let go of one another even on weekends. We went to jazz clubs like the Central Plaza on the Lower East Side and then later Jimmy Ryan's on West Fifty-fourth Street, where stars long past their prime like Tony Parente, Roy Eldridge, and Zutty Singleton played blues late into the night. The first few times I was still seventeen so Ralph slipped me into the Central Plaza on his draft card. Then when I turned eighteen in January, I received my own card, my certificate of adulthood. We drank scotch and listened to "Muskrat Ramble" and "St. James Infirmary" and savored the way Zutty would mischievously freeze the drumstick in midair so that it wouldn't come down on the expected beat. We went out in groups to the Thalia and the New Yorker Theater and saw classic old movies like *Citizen Kane* and *The Philadelphia Story* and *It Happened One Night*.

We spun our own mythology, a pantheon made up of legendary *Campus* editors of the past. These included not just journalists like Abe Rosenthal and Ed Kosner, but people closer to my generation who showed up at some of our parties. In our oral tradition, working news-papermen like Vic Ziegel, Jack Schwartz, Bob Mayer, and Mike Katz became giants who strode across the plains of my impressionable mind. Even without meeting them, they seemed in my imaginings to be wittier, sharper, savvier, more literate, and more levelheaded than the rest of humanity. When I finally got to know them, I came to realize they were young men and women who grew up in the same lumpen Bronx and Brooklyn precincts that I did, rode the same straw-seated subway cars, suffered from the same workaday insecurities and hungers that plagued me. Perhaps we all needed to believe there was a purer, saner, tougher set of characters out there that we could emulate.

One giant who was around a lot was Vic Grossfeld, who had been an editor in chief several semesters before I got to college but hadn't taken enough courses to graduate. He had an elliptical, discursive mind that could sail off on enchanting tangents and a gift for spinning a story that made the characters and worlds he talked about more luminous than they probably were. He had read Lawrence Durrell's Alexandria Quartet, and described it with such verve that, even before any of us read the four books, he had us pining for the dark, enigmatic beauty of Justine and the sensuality of Alexandria itself. Once he returned from Magalaner's class on Joyce and walked into the *Campus* quoting the opening of *Ulysses*.

"Stately, plump Buck Mulligan came from the stairhead, bearing a bowl of lather on which a mirror and a razor lay crossed," he proclaimed, a Jewish kid invoking a renegade Catholic mocking the Mass. "He held the bowl aloft and intoned: Introibo ad altare Dei."

Or at a party he would unearth phrases from O'Neill's *The Iceman Cometh* like "Hickey, what did you do to the booze? It's got no kick in it."

And we would feel the bitterness of disillusionment, not only of the disillusionment of the inebriates in Harry Hope's bar but of Grossfeld's own disillusionment, although no one plumbed too deeply for the source of Grossfeld's melancholy streak.

Gradually and with practice, I learned how to write catchy leads, to shape a story so that the significant points were made at the top, rather than in chronological order, to let all sides have their due. Reporting turned out to be no different from what I had been doing all my life— exploring, unearthing, inquiring, trying to figure out the boundaries and the rules and work within them. I didn't realize it at the time but the detached attitude of my newly adopted vocation particularly suited me. I could be a comfortable part of this newspaper circle, yet elsewhere keep my habitual distance—from the college mainstream, even its organized fringes—and feel justified doing so. We had to be outsiders to retain the impartiality we needed as reporters, even if we were green ones. We were a club of outsiders, of self-proclaimed exiles, and as a refugee I more than fit in.

The *Campus* was not only the center of our work life but also of our romantic life, inchoate as it was. After our nights at the Moulin

Rouge or the printer, the guys sometimes escorted the girls home—girls
like Eva, Batyah, Nancy, and Jean—to their apartments on the West
Side. As time went on, I realized that some of the girls were being more
than escorted. There were fumblings of love going on, and we took our
infatuations as earnestly as our work. The girls in our circle seemed
more intense, insightful, droll than girls anywhere else. And so we fell
in love, although we didn't always get the sequence right. If I was taken
with Nancy, she might be enamored of Bob, who was smitten with
Eva, who was in love with Jerry. It was an intricate square dance.

I was taken not only with Nancy's high spirits but with her West
Side world. I came to her stout, venerable West Side apartment building and there was an awning and a doorman and a roomy, ornate, fur-
nished lobby. An elevator took me to the sixth floor and there Nancy's
cheerful, well-spoken mother welcomed me into a living room filled
with hardcover books, fine prints, and lush plants. More frayed than
elegant, the room gave off the scent of intellectual ferment. Her parents
were not refugee seamstresses and candy-store owners. Her mother was
an editor at Simon and Schuster, her father an organizer in the labor
movement. In their home, they percolated coffee, shunning the instant
brand my parents used. Her mother completed the *Times* Sunday cross-
word puzzle; her father walked a small dog. Nancy kept up with the
ballet and with off-Broadway plays. She knew the charm of noisy, aromatic street festivals in Little Italy and the splendor of the frozen hot
chocolates at Serendipity. How much did I understand of who Nancy
was and what moved her? Probably not very much at the time. I was
propelled by my enchantment with the life I was leading. This sometimes fuels love.

I decided to take Nancy out to a restaurant, the first time I had ever
attempted such a date. Other than Horn & Hardart, what did I know
of restaurants? But Nancy knew real restaurants and suggested Tony's,
a neighborhood Italian spot on Seventy-ninth Street. I hoped I could
carry it off with Hollywood finesse. I offered Nancy a Winston, lit hers
with cupped hands, then lit my own. I tore a chunk of Italian bread
from the napkin-draped basket, savored its crusty texture, then passed
the basket suavely to Nancy. The white-aproned waiter came over and
with his solicitous paisana delivery inquired whether I wished to order

a bottle of wine. I had learned through the cultural ether that red wine went with red meat and asked what red wine he would recommend. He could have said Manischewitz and I would have nodded in assent. He suggested a Bardolino, brought a bottle over to the table, and showed me the label. It looked like a nice label. The Italian writing, after all, guaranteed it was authentically imported. What other significance I was to glean from the label I did not know, but again I nodded my head in approval.

The waiter pulled the cork out with a pleasantly percussive pop, poured a small amount into my glass, and looked at me, waiting for my response. Now I was ready to show off my deep urbanity, that I was truly a man of the world.

"Uh, I'll have a little more," I said.

There was a moment of suspended quiet, broken by Nancy's muffled titter and the waiter's conspiratorial smile at Nancy.

"He wants you to taste the wine to see if you like it," she said, smiling affectionately.

Ah, so this was what I had to do. Yes, I had bungled the classic restaurant ritual. Yet because Nancy was gentle about it, I could laugh at my clumsiness. There was a lot more I would have to learn.

I was finding a craft, a profession, a group of friends I admired who seemed to like and respect me. My life was coming together. I had become a valued member of an American club. And suddenly I felt bold enough to let people peek into my other world, the world of my parents. I could tell them that I was not born in the United States, that my parents survived the war, that my name had been Israel until it was changed when we immigrated. Always the joker, one editor, Ken Koppel, christened me Young Israel of the Concourse. There was a synagogue by that name right near my house. Before 1948 my name had been Palestine, he said. The crowd along the couch and window alcoves in Room 328 rollicked with laughter and I was delighted by the attention.

There were times I must have seemed almost puffed up with my family's background of war and destruction, as if it were a badge of courage that distinguished me from the sheltered Manhattanites and rough-hewn borough types. I might look and talk like them, but I had a dramatic story behind me—and I wanted people to know it, or at least know it in the unthinking, romanticized version I had distilled. There were limits, after all, to what I could say about my family, because I did not grasp many things yet myself. What could I say about the unmentioned sorrow that was the subtext to everything my parents said or did? What could I say about the dread and suspicion with which they encountered a world that had proven maliciously fickle? Their fragility was not something I dwelt on. Better to revel in tales of hurled typewriters and April Fools' merriment. And so I did. That was a mistake. It turned out that several of my *Campus* friends, like Eva and Batyah, were children of refugees, although their families had escaped to America in the early years of the war. We might have given ourselves something more meaningful to chew over, drawn even closer.

By the end of sophomore year, it was the rookies' turn to take the helm. Clyde was chosen as editor in chief, I as news editor, and George Kaplan, the third of our freshman triumvirate, as sports editor. We covered speeches by President Gallagher and antiwar rallies and the consolidation of the municipal colleges into the City University and resignations of deans and we did it in what we believed was a thoroughly professional fashion. We were impudent in our way and figured we were putting out the best newspaper in the country. We could not imagine that Harvard's newspaper could be any better. Clyde, angular, intense, quick-witted, was particularly fastidious and exacting. He labored over copy until he felt it was immaculate, not worrying as much as I did about the time it consumed or about the bruises to a reporter's feelings. He put in long, wearying hours and I felt a traitor if I put in any less. He insisted on putting out two issues per week, no matter how much printer overtime strained our budget. The result was a series of outstanding newspaper issues that showed the care put into them and made us all look smart.

When term's end came along, we ran out of money to put out the last two spring issues. Clyde felt it was incumbent that we find a way to print them. There was a tradition to sustain, a tradition going back to 1907. He was going to help pay for the extra issues with his state Regents scholarship money—about $150. He asked me and the business manager whether we might do the same, and we agreed. Although we did not need the money for tuition, the annual Regents scholarship was a considerable help to our working-class families and did pay for books, subway fare, and the rest. We fortified ourselves in our rash gesture with the flimsy belief that the student government would recognize our sacrifice to the cause of the First Amendment and reimburse us later on.

When I told my mother of our plan, she did not wait a second to scoff.

"No one will ever pay you back," she said. "You might as well throw that money in the garbage can!"

"It's my money and that's what I'm going to use it for," I said.

I did as I had promised Clyde, but my mother turned out to be right. We had the glory of knowing that we fulfilled the newspaper quota for that year, and maintained the *Campus* tradition. But the student government, whose officers we regularly tweaked, turned down our request for supplemental funds. When I became editor in chief, we made a concerted effort to live within our budget. I was not going to squander my scholarship money again.

But maybe that reluctance came from a dawning shift in my feelings toward the *Campus*. After finishing off my term as editor, I would come to the office and hang around, but the legendary old-timers like Grossfeld and Blumenthal and Katz were gone. I had personally gone to a ragtag Brooklyn wharf to see Grossfeld off by merchant steamer for a one-way trip to the Mediterranean. He was heading for Greece, France, Spain, and Morocco to live the life for which he had always been destined—that of an expatriate writer. The trip had no end date. It could last a year or forever. Grossfeld's Grand Concourse parents— his father, I learned, was a school principal—and his attractive sister were there to bid a domestic farewell, but they seemed like they had been placed in the picture by mistake. There was something so otherworldly about Grossfeld that I never realized he had parents or a sister. I preferred to concentrate on his trunk filled with books by outlaw writers like Henry Miller and Nikos Kazantzakis. He was on his way to acquire the tangle of experience he needed to join their ranks, but he was leaving a large emptiness behind.

Clyde and I and the others of my generation could not fill it. We did not seem to have the razzle-dazzle to become deities for the younger reporters. And the younger reporters, it seemed from my grizzled vantage, would never have that razzle-dazzle for those who succeeded them. They were serious about journalism, but did not have the esprit that we had. My disillusionment was partly the result of simply getting older and gradually losing my capacity to worship heroes and institutions. As an emeritus editor, I could no longer sustain myself with the production of the newspaper and had only a tepid enthusiasm for college politics or for the antiwar demonstrations that were making *Campus* headlines. So there was a bygone aura clinging to Room 328, a sense of irrecoverable loss. It was difficult to linger. Soon, I stopped coming around as often, as if the *Campus* were some juvenile folly, and focused on my classes. My grades got better, my interest in literature and history enlarged, and I began to think about who I was and what I wanted to do with my life.

Toward the end of senior year, Nancy and I strolled through Central Park together and I brought my sister along. Evelyn was then a pretty girl of seven or eight, with a fetching pageboy and dark, twinkling eyes that venerated her older brothers (she actually reflected on the fact that neither Josh nor I could ever become president of the United States because we were immigrants). I put Evelyn on the carousel and watched her soar and plunge on a revolving painted horse to the sweet and melancholy calliope sounds. I could not help recalling the scene from *Catcher in the Rye* when Holden took his little sister, Phoebe, on the carousel and lamented the inexorable loss of her innocence in a world contaminated by phonies and hypocrites. I felt a sob welling inside me too at the loss, not really of my sister's innocence, but of my own, at the relentless march of time that was moving me further away from the refugee world I had grown up in and, now, from the tender cocoon that had been the *Campus*. I knew that soon I would be breaking with my sister and the rest of my family, moving out on my own.

Nancy and I, it seemed plain, were not going to click. My other *Campus* friends would be carrying on with their lives on their own. Yes, they would become an anchor through my twenties and thirties, the people around whom I could take whatever chances I wanted, knowing they would be there to fall back on. They would provide companionship and affection. But our crackerjack world, discrete and inimitable, was irretrievably crumbling. And there was nothing I could do to put it all back together.

26

I had always known I was foreign-born, of course, but until I was twenty-one I believed the country I was born in was Poland. There was even something of a yarn surrounding my birth. My parents told me they were hiding from the Nazis in the forests around the ancient Polish city of Lublin, and I was delivered in a barn while my mother lay shrieking in a bed of straw. Just like Jesus. It was a beguiling, even intoxicating story and I was pleased to tell it when someone asked me about my origins. But it was a lie, one I tripped upon by chance.

At the time, I was applying to Columbia University's School of Journalism. I would have preferred to start working for a newspaper right after graduating college. But the Vietnam War was in full swing, my parents were anxious that I not be drafted, and they heard through the grapevine that graduate school enrollment would shield me from the draft. I had done nothing else to make sure I didn't end up in Vietnam. I had only the most amorphous notions of what war might mean, and part of me was intrigued by the idea of soldiering for my nation, by the adventure of throwing my lot among Southerners and Midwesterners and other exotic types, by the chance to explore the country and even the world. Clyde and George were heading into the army, and George was going right to Vietnam. If I was drafted that would not be so bad, I figured.

But for my parents, the possibility that their son might land in the middle of a war was not an abstract notion. They knew firsthand of war's arbitrary savagery. They were not going to let one of their children into a war, no matter how righteous a cause, and saving Vietnam was to them a particularly flimsy cause.

The Columbia application asked for proof of citizenship, so I had to locate my parents' sheaf of important documents, which I knew they kept in the mahogany night table near their bed. There, secreted among the folds of their pajamas and nightgowns, was the weathered vinyl pouch. I came across the life insurance policy that a salesman had persuaded them was a prudent investment for responsible parents. I found the certificates for the AT&T shares they bought in a poignant effort to do something shrewder, more like the Americans, with their savings. There were receipts for the television they had worked so many hours to purchase.

And finally there were the yellowing but still crisp citizenship papers themselves, with the young faces of my father and mother in their insecure immigrant propriety, he in a suit and a cowlick jutting out of his hair, she in a formal floral dress, grinning brightly through the intimidating ritual of an official photograph. There was my brother's bashful eight-year-old face. And there was the certificate with my ten-year-old face, also timorous, betraying some inner wobbliness that I recognized, to my regret, was lingering into manhood.

Among these papers were also four small laminated cards with photographs of our faces looking younger and more hopeful than on the citizenship papers. Since we lacked passports, these cards had been our permits into the United States in 1950, the equivalent of what would later become known as green cards. I hadn't seen these since I was a child and scrutinized them more closely. They gave our names—mine said Izrael Berger, which my mother had changed to the more American Joseph soon after our arrival—our addresses in the Schlactensee DP camp in Berlin in 1949, the color of our hair and eyes, our height and weight and our birthplaces. My card said, reassuringly, Lublin, Poland. I found myself studying my parents' cards as well and, as I did, one detail sprang up and clawed me.

My parents, the card said, were married in 1947. That would have been two years after I was born. It meant I was illegitimate, a bastard.

Initially, I felt a kind of roguish titillation. There was another revelation about my life that catapulted me out of the ho-hum decorum of the Bronx. But the detail also seemed to warp my life story, throwing it out of a sensible sequence. I needed to confront my parents, and when I did they were caught off guard. The 1947 wedding, my mother said at first, was a civil ceremony performed in Berlin in order to confirm the rabbinical ceremony they underwent during the height of the war in 1943, more than a year before I was born.

"Don't worry, Joey, you're legitimate," she assured me.

Her eyes glinted merrily and her tone was coy.

"I'm not worried," I said. "Who cares at this point? I just was curious why you were married in 1947."

There was a long silence. My mother and father looked at each other significantly. And then my mother unburdened herself. The story she had just told was also a lie.

"Joey," she said, "we're going to tell you something but you must promise never to tell it to anyone. It could cause us big trouble. Don't tell anyone. OK?"

I gave her my promise, suspecting she was exaggerating something trivial. She glanced at my father again, hesitating as if she feared she was making a fatal mistake.

"We were married in Russia in 1943, not in Poland," she said. "It was in completely kosher fashion in a government office. There was no rabbi because who could get a rabbi in Russia? There was a war on. But we went to the city hall and we registered. We even had a party for our friends, with a big barrel of vodka that Daddy got from the Russian officers, and plenty of food. In those days, people didn't even bother getting married. There was such a chaos. A man and a woman just announced to everybody they were married and they started sleeping together. But we got married."

"OK, OK," I said, not wanting to hear anything more about their sex life. "Just explain one thing. If you were married in Russia, how did you get to Lublin, Poland, in 1945 to give birth to me?"

She grinned with embarrassment, my father chortling along.

"We weren't in Lublin," she said. "You see, Joey, you weren't born in Poland. You were born in Russia."

"In Russia? While you were in hiding? In a barn?"

"No, you were born in a hospital, a plain Russian hospital, the hospital in Lys'va, which is deep, deep in Russia. Far east of Moscow. In the Ural Mountains. You have to take a train for more than a week to get there. You even had a birth certificate, but we had to destroy it. We made up the story about hiding in Poland because we had to tell the American officials how we survived."

This revelation was convulsive, powerfully disorienting. It was as if I had fallen asleep in one house and been shaken awake in another. However romanticized my birth story, it was *my* story and it gave the rest of my life a particular shape. This new story, with its different starting point, threw the whole life out of kilter.

"I don't understand," I said. "Why couldn't you tell the Americans I was born in Russia?"

My mother vacillated again, so much so I could tell she was struggling whether to continue telling me the truth or another lie. My father waited for her to decide.

"If the Americans knew we had been in Russia during the war, they would not have let us come here," she said. "You know already in 1950 there were—how you say it—suspicions, suspicions of communists, and the Americans did not trust anyone who had been in Russia. A lot of the greeners ran to Russia when the war broke out. That's how they survived the war. Who survived in Poland? Hitler killed almost everyone. Only the skeletons left in the *lager*—the concentration camps— survived. But nobody will tell you they were in Russia. Because nobody could tell the Americans they were in Russia. We all made up false documents. That's why you can't tell."

Even at twenty-one, I sensed that my mother's anxiety approached the paranoid. I could not imagine the FBI disturbing the bourgeois equanimity of the Grand Concourse and arresting us in our apartment, taking us to jail, then deporting us, all for lying on our immigration forms seventeen years before.

"What do you think they're going to do, Mommy, deport us?" I said, mocking her mistrust.

"Joey, you're naive. You think this government is all hotsy-totsy, fair and square. But governments are not like that. There are rules and documents and bureaucrats and politics. You get caught in the machine and—finished."

She paused.

"Don't tell anyone we were in Russia, you hear!"

Her voice was edged with terror. She made it clear how absolutely crucial it was that I remain silent.

"How long was I in Russia?" I asked.

"We left when you were a year and a half. That was 1946, when the Russians let the Poles come back in. What did they call it? Repatriation. That's when we went back to Warsaw. We stayed in Poland a few months and then we heard there was a pogrom, in a city called Kielce, and we left as fast as we could. They killed forty-one Jews."

"Would you believe it," my father interrupted, driven by some mixture of anger and irony. "They blamed the Jews for the war. Jews came back and wanted their apartments and houses and the Poles wouldn't give them back. They are bitter anti-Semites, the Poles. They always were and they always will be."

"After that," my mother said, "we paid some people to take us across to the American zone in Germany."

She looked at me and smiled coyly again.

"Don't worry, you're legitimate."

She went over to the coffee table and picked up a photograph album, leafing through until she found a black-and-white snapshot I had often seen of my parents and me as a round-faced baby posed with two of their friends in front of a picket fence in a park. It was obviously summer, the trees were lush, there were flowers blooming along the fence, and my father was wearing a sleeveless undershirt. My smiling mother was holding me up for the photographer and I had my arms tightly, desperately wound around her neck. My father looked dour, a demeanor that, as I looked at the photograph, seemed to me to express his discomfort with having his picture taken but which many years later I came to recognize as betraying a bedrock melancholy.

"This was taken in Lys'va, in Russia, not in the DP camps," my mother said. "That was a friend of Daddy's, Schulsinger, and his wife or girlfriend. Who knew if they even got married? But we were married. And this shows you. You were in Russia."

Of course, this photograph could have been taken anywhere. It was evidence of nothing. But I doubted they were making up another tale. It all seemed so murky, though. I was Russian, not Polish. I was born in the land of America's totalitarian enemy, yet in this free country I would have to keep the story of my birth a secret, tell people what I now knew to be a fiction. There was also a smidgen of disappointment. In contrast to a surreptitious birth on the lam, my start in life seemed to have been somewhat more ordinary.

Yet the truth was also invigorating. It ignited a curiosity I had never before felt to delve into my origins and my parents' origins. An intriguing mystery had suddenly been thrust in my hands and I had to follow the clues, to unearth the full story. It took years, though, until my parents could tell me much more, until they could overcome their own pain and guilt, and talk with more candor about their dead parents, brothers and sisters, and the youth they were still mourning. And it took many more years, into my parents' old age, before I could listen.

27

Joey, I was depressed," my mother tells me, the word flowing from her lips without the shame she usually attaches. "You know me. I don't believe in this psychology, shmuckology. I'm my own best psychologist. But if you mean by depressed that I could not get out of bed, that I wanted to die, that was me. I was alone. My brother Simcha was hiding somewhere, and I didn't know if he was alive or dead. He was afraid that if he came back to Lys'va he would be arrested. He wrote me one letter. It didn't have his address. I knew from the postmark it was from Gorky. Why he was there I don't know. But he could also have died since he wrote the letter. With his tuberculosis, it was very possible."

We are sitting in her comfortable middle-class kitchen continuing my effort to plumb her story. She pauses and looks around to make sure there is no one besides the two of us to hear. Her eyes, framed by her rumpled silver hair, betray the old terror.

"Joey," she whispers, as if someone were spying. "They threw me in a jail. You don't want to believe that of your mother, but I was in a jail."

"For what?"

"I didn't show up for work. In the Soviet Union, in wartime, they threw you in jail for that. I didn't care about work. I didn't care about anything. I had already a good job. I wasn't shoveling the ashes in the steel factory anymore. I was reading blueprints, I was operating a machine that cut out weapons. They never told us what kind of weapons. But with my meager education I was reading an engineer's blueprints. I can do anything if I put my mind to it. You don't believe it, Joey.

"But without Simcha, I felt despair. Who was there to live for? When I came home, I would go straight to bed. Nothing interested me, not even food, which I didn't have. You can survive on having nothing, as long as you have a piece of bread to eat. I survived on a piece of bread. But despair, you don't care anymore what happens to you. I showed up once late for work so they put me in a jail."

❧ "One who doesn't sit in jail is not human," the Russians like to say.

I sat around each day with a dozen women in a dingy, stinking barred room and at night we slept on the floor's bare wooden planks, with some of the women groaning in their sleep from pain or sickness. After a week, we were marched under guard through the main street of the town and put aboard cattle trains. When we reached the labor camp, they let us sleep for the night, and at 4:00 A.M. we were awakened and marched from our barracks to the side of a river that was jammed with logs. Guards ordered us to jump into the water, fully clothed, and push the floating logs downriver. I tried to explain to one guard that I couldn't swim, but he gave me an angry glare and pointed his rifle at my face. Soon, I was neck deep in icy water heaving the enormous logs forward and trying to keep afloat at the same time. As I worked, my fellow prisoners frightened me with stories of young workers who had drowned when they lost their footing and were swept away. After twelve hours of such toil we marched back to our barracks to dine on nine hundred grams of dark bread and a dish of watery soup where three or four noodles floated—more if you knew the man or woman ladling the soup.

The next week, as falling temperatures made river work too treacherous, they trucked a group of us to another spot along the river where we had to haul logs to a sawmill. Some young men, feeble with diarrhea and with legs swollen legs from malnutrition, simply gave up and died on the job. The women, it seemed to me, were more resilient. There was talk that women who rendered favors to their male superiors procured easier jobs. I learned firsthand how true these rumors were. One evening a Romanian Jew about fifty years old offered me a wedge of raw cabbage.

"I work in the kitchen," he told me amiably. "If you come here tomorrow I'll bring you some more."

The next day he brought me another wedge and on the third day he asked me to follow him to the barn. I did, but became suspicious when I noticed the cabbage lying on the barn floor while the Romanian was poking around the opening of his pants. I ran away and never saw him again. My father's strict teachings remained with me even in such harsh, inhuman conditions.

The work went on like this for four months. In the evenings, the women prisoners passed the time by delousing one another with knives and combs. The destruction of the nits made a rhythmic popping sound and the women seemed to enjoy the activity, a game that passed the time like card playing.

At the end of winter I was released and took a midnight train back to Lys'va. The first person I wanted to see was my younger brother Yasha, the one sibling who shared with me the same mother and father. Although Yasha had made his way to Lys'va like my other brother Simcha, he was immediately drafted into the Red Army and sent off for training in Siberia. He would write me letters telling me of his hunger and overwork and I would send him bread, hiding away slices from my own ration. Just before I went to prison, Yasha had shown up at my room in Lys'va. His eyes were puffy, his legs swollen, and he was so emaciated that he was unrecognizable, looking more like a war prisoner than a soldier. My roommate offered him some potato soup, but Yasha was too weak to eat it, asking only for a bed on which to rest. In a few weeks, with his own bread ration and a daily ticket for a bowl of soup and a job cobbling boots, he began to regain his health. Just as he did, I was sent off to prison.

Now that I was back, Yasha looked splendid in his green army coat, hearty and well nourished. He also had a pretty girlfriend, Natasha, with whom he was very much in love. I was embarrassed that he had to see me in my mangy, lice-ridden prison attire. He gave me the key to his room and told me I could sleep in one of the three beds. I lay in bed thinking how Yasha was no longer the brother he was when we were teenagers. In my months in prison, Yasha had visited me only once early on, even though my letters had let him know how desperately hungry I was. Now he had a woman with whom he spent his free time. He probably spent little time thinking about me. I wanted to sleep forever.

The next day, though, I stirred myself awake, went looking for work at the military affairs office, and came up with a job sewing men's underwear for the army. The job felt like a comedown from reading blueprints, but it gave me a legal ration card for six hundred grams of bread a day. At least I would eat.

In the spring of 1943, the Germans were making substantial advances and were approaching the outskirts of Moscow. Leningrad was under siege as well. Even our city of Lys'va, a thousand miles to the east, was affected by the pandemonium of war, and was now teeming with more refugees, most of them women, children, and the old. Nevertheless, life seemed to proceed in its customary rhythms. One day Yasha's roommate, Mendele, let me know there was going to be a party in our room that night to celebrate a Soviet holiday. Mendele, who left a wife and two small children behind in Lvov when the Russians drafted him, revealed he was bringing a girlfriend.

"Oh, I forgot to tell you, I also invited Marcus," Mendele said. "He is a very, very nice young man. I want you to meet him."

That night, I heard the party approaching from the hallway. Giddy and loud, Yasha, Natasha, Mendele, his girlfriend Maria Fyodorovna, and several people I did not know barged into the room carrying herring, colorful vinaigrettes, breads, cold cuts, and, of course, bottles of vodka. Yasha, with the beautiful Natasha at his side, looked more cheerful and confident than I'd ever seen. He was enjoying life. No wonder he did not remember to visit me at the prison camp.

Crowded around our three beds, we toasted Stalin and the Soviet Union and sang the required patriotic songs. Some of us were drunk and others moody for love, but soon everybody collapsed on the beds in contented exhaustion. Except for Marcus, the young man whom Mendele brought. He sat on a small chair, his arms folded across his chest, his legs folded one over the other, and stared at me with a shy smile. I attempted to start a conversation and he answered my questions with short replies, gazing at me all the time with his large, dark calf's-eyes. He told me he was from a small town called Borinya in southeastern Poland near the border with Ukraine and Czechoslovakia. He had been drafted by the Soviets when they occupied eastern Poland. Although he spent some harsh months in the field, he had escaped combat and now was assigned to the same work battalion that Yasha was in, making shoes and boots. The conversation seemed to lag and, fatigued from the hour and the vodka, I found a spot on the corner of the floor, spread out a cloak, and soon was fast asleep.

I spent the next day in bed, but by the afternoon I was roused awake by a knock at the door. There stood Marcus, young and virile in his sleek-fitting green uniform, with the same diffident smile of the night before.

"Aren't you hungry?" he asked.

Without waiting for an answer, he pulled out a box of cookies from a brown paper bag and spread a handful over my bedcover. I ate them eagerly, feeling a twinge of guilt that I would feel obligated to him. As I finished munching the cookies, he leaned over and kissed me warmly and passionately. He noticed that my response was tentative, and I explained that I wasn't in the mood just then. He was understanding and soon got up to leave, scattering the rest of the cookies across my bed just before he walked out the door.

"I'll see you tomorrow," he said.

Marcus kept his word and showed up the next day, and the next, and the next, always bringing me something to eat. Once he even gave me a sandwich filled with slices of sausage. The foods he had access to tasted wonderful, a delicious contrast to my bare ration of bread and watery soup. It turned out that Marcus—and Yasha—were favorites of the shoe workshop's manager, Hans Manfredovitch, and he was helping them acquire such hard-to-find treats. Marcus also earned his own treats by making extra pairs of boots for Russian officers and exchanging the vodka they paid him with for food.

The shoe workshop soon became my world as well. When the shop's purchasing agent was drafted to fight on the front, Marcus and Yasha arranged for me to replace him. I was given a list of supplies to buy—various cuts of leather hide and tools—a set of traveling papers, and told to make my way to Kungur, one hundred kilometers southwest of Lys'va. Every time I went I had to catch an 11:00 P.M. train, but I never walked through the pitch dark alone. Marcus learned of my schedule and made sure to accompany me to the station. He held my bag in one hand and my hand in the other. He was delighted to be with me, and for the first time in many years I felt someone genuinely cared for me. On the platform he looked tenderly into my eyes without saying a word and embraced me. As the train arrived, he put several ruble notes into my coat pocket.

"Buy yourself something nice," he would say. "And don't forget to eat well."

In Kungur, a gloomy industrial town packed with shoe factories and leather stores, I would order the list of supplies, tour the town's market, and have something like a potato knish and a glass of baked milk. When my train steamed into Lys'va early in the morning, there was Marcus, greeting me with fervent excitement.

"Were you able to eat?" he said, and just to make sure I was well fed, he pulled out a roll with salami and I chewed it voraciously while he stood there watching.

I enjoyed Marcus's generosity, but I also found myself growing wary. Who besides someone who seemed to love me and nourish me was Marcus? One night, with some of Marcus's money in my pocket, I wanted to go to Lys'va's one theater and see *The Great Waltz*, a movie biography of Johann Strauss that I had seen years before in Warsaw and that I felt would take me away from my miseries. But Marcus cringed at my suggestion, spoiling my enthusiasm. After he grudgingly consented, he entered the theater looking confused, uncertain of where to go, as if he had never been inside a theater before. He seemed uncomfortable sitting in the dark in front of a large screen, and after the movie had been on for a short time, I heard the sound of snoring. Marcus, with a dull, groggy look, was fast asleep. I wanted to wake him up and tell him to go home and let me enjoy the movie alone, but I let him sleep through the whole two-hour story. As we strolled home, I felt there was no sense in sharing my thoughts about the movie.

"Tell me more about yourself," I finally demanded. "Did you see movies at home?"

"No," he said half angrily.

"What did you do there?" I asked.

"We lived on a farm in a village," he said. "We raised cows. We used the milk for cheese and sour cream. We sold the cheese and sour cream to the people around us."

"Wasn't there a big city or town nearby?"

"The biggest city was Turka."

"Did you see movies there?"

"No."

He seemed to surrender every detail piecemeal and with reluctance. I found out that he was one of seven children. All the rest were girls and one was already married and out of the house. His father was a pious peasant who diligently worked his land but seemed, as far as I could tell, to have no other remarkable traits. The picture of his mother was even vaguer.

That night Marcus stalked off in anger. He must have sensed I was beginning to grow uneasy. I was. I could not understand his possessiveness. I felt I had never given him any signal that I was drawn to him. I felt guilty taking his money and food. Yet I found it hard to refuse because he was very sensitive. The next time I had to make a trip to Kungur, I was lost in thought aboard the trains there and back. I saw our relationship as a trap. I wished I could run away from it all and even schemed of ways of fleeing Lys'va, impossible as that was. I would tell him the truth, that I could no longer go out with him. The truth is the best lie, my stepmother used to say. I would tell him that I needed time to meet other people, to do the singing, dancing, flirting that I used to enjoy so much in Warsaw.

"Why do you look so gloomy?" he asked me as he greeted me on my return home.

I took out two hundred rubles he had given me before I left and put them in his hand.

"Please don't give me any more," I said.

"Why not?" he said, glaring angrily. "What did I do to you?"

"Nothing, you did nothing. I can't go out with you anymore. I am not interested, that's all. Please forgive me."

The murderous expression on his face scared me so that I raced home, feeling even more guilty about how I was treating him.

In the weeks afterward, I looked around for other opportunities. I heard about a dance for workers who were heading for the front. I washed and ironed a blue dress from Warsaw that I had managed to hold on to and shined my shoes. The orchestra played waltzes, polkas, tangos, and fox-trots that carried me back to the best days of my teenage years. Someone asked me to waltz and whirled me around the vast ballroom until someone else broke in and also swept me across the floor. During a break in the music, my girlfriend Lusia and I found ourselves surrounded by young, chatty soldiers, intelligent and funny, and we laughed along with them, realizing that these young men were trying to snatch a last bit of happiness before leaving for the front.

It was great fun, but the dance made it crystal clear just how impossible it would be to find a companion in Lys'va. The fact was that in the spring of 1943, with the army drafting everybody it could, there were hardly any young men, let alone Jewish men, in Lys'va. The work battalion consisted mainly of married men like Mendele who had left wives and children behind in the Ukraine or Poland. Many of these had found themselves Russian women, sometimes widows and wives. Hunger was deepening across the country and old and young were starving to death. I was eating pancakes that my friend Nadia had made out of potato peels and getting sick. I even received a proposal of marriage from Misha, a redheaded roofer, who let me know through a go-between that if I said yes he would give me canned milk and meat and a promise to wash the floors throughout our marriage.

I began to realize I had to deal with the realities of life, not my girlish fantasies. I was twenty-three years old and needed to think about bearing some children. Who knew if the war would ever end? Marcus was a shoemaker. Everyone in Lys'va knew how prized an occupation this was in wartime, offering opportunities for food and privileges. And he was warm and generous. One could tell in Marcus's pained smile how much he loved me.

The next time we ran into each other, he invited me and Yasha for a dinner in his room of potatoes and oil cooked by a mutual friend, Zajev. The potatoes and oil tasted delicious, even if Zajev told us later that the oil was the same as that used in the machine shops. Marcus showed up the next day at my apartment with a pork stew, a canned American aid product that was supposed to be reserved for soldiers. As he ate, Marcus never stopped looking into my eyes. His love was so honest and simple that I found myself yielding, even liking him. One could tell in his wounded smile that he had made up his mind that I belonged to him. ❧

I read these passages with almost childlike discomfort. This is my parents' courtship I'm reading about and, for a son or daughter at any age, it is slightly embarrassing to realize that your parents courted and kissed and caressed. Yet, at the same time, it is wonderful to see my father in the role of paramour, ardent, aggressive, in hot pursuit of the woman he loved. My father has always been deeply devoted to my mother. I don't remember a single time he showed any interest in any woman in my parents' circle. His eye never followed a shapely Grand Concourse enchantress nor seemed drawn by the Jayne Mansfields on television. But I have always tended to look on his devotion as slavish, not the passion of, as my mother herself suggested, the virile young romancer. My mother's memoir is therefore corrective.

At the same time, there is also something touching about this love blossoming in the mire of war. My father was the same shy, inexpressive man then that he has been my whole life. My mother showed the same skeptical, suspicious streak. They are people from very different backgrounds, and there have been times I wondered how this rustic from a Galician shtetl managed to pair up with a woman who had at least tasted cosmopolitan diversions, such as they were, and developed an affinity for some finer things. My mother's writing helps me understand and I think of a saying that was common among the refugees I grew up with. "Hitler married us," they would declare with irony. But the irony was seldom laced with scorn. Rather it signified a wise tolerance for the caprices of fate and the blessings that come out of even the most incongruous encounters.

"Your father was kind and generous" is as much as my mother will say. "I was hungry, exhausted, without any spirit, going crazy about what happened to my brother Simcha. Your father gave me food and he cared about me. I had nobody who cared about me."

We both tacitly agree that enough has been said.

◆ Marcus and I were married on December 5, 1943. We picked that day because it was a national holiday and a day off for our shop's workers. Musicians from the work battalion orchestra provided the music for the wedding party. A friend of Marcus who worked in a slaughterhouse supplied sandwiches of cold meat. Marcus, with the connections he had made by making boots, procured the vodka—more than enough for everybody. My only regret was the room was not large enough for dancing. Still, Marcus looked handsome in his new green uniform. And I felt gay in a white satin dress that the dressmaker Shira had tailored from a fabric Marcus had bought for me (along with woolen snow boots and a winter coat).

The next day we strolled over to the SAKS, a government bureau, and registered our marriage. I moved out of the room I shared with Yasha into Marcus's room. Marcus's army coat, trousers, and shirt were dangling from a nail on the door and on another nail was his green towel. There was nothing else in the room except a large bowl of potatoes and a chipped dark pot on the stove. Where were the shelves full of canned milk and meat that I had imagined he would be loaded with?

"Don't worry," he said to me when I confronted him. "We will eat!"

I had been living off bread for so long that I didn't know how to cook, not even to boil water. Marcus showed me how I could tell when water was boiling and when potatoes were soft enough to eat.

The next time I went to Kungur, Marcus handed me six hundred rubles and told me to shop for honey, butter, any provisions I could find on the black market there. Instead of buying food I was intrigued by a sheet of wine-colored calf leather. On the train ride home, I was terrified that my illegal purchase would be discovered and that I would wind up like my brother Simcha had, in a labor camp.

"Guess what I'm carrying in this bag?" I told Marcus when he picked me up.

"A chicken!" he guessed, laughing.

Marcus showed my purchase to Mendele—the broker for all lawless dealings in Lys'va—and Mendele concluded with a pleased smile that there was money to be made. A few hours later Mendele returned with orders for a pair of boots and two pairs of ladies' shoes and we were able to quadruple our six-hundred-ruble investment.

But after a few tense months of such business I lost heart, and so did Marcus. Besides, I had to start taking things more easily. I was now pregnant.

By the fall of 1944, the Russian army had reversed the course of battle and seemed poised for victory. They had held off the Germans at Stalingrad, although at the cost of tens of thousands of lives. Still, to solidify its gains, the army needed more soldiers and it began drafting many of those who had been left behind to work in essential industries. Yasha was taken to the front lines without my even saying good-bye to him. Marcus was put on the list of potential draftees and it was only a matter of days until he too would be called. I would be left alone to give birth in a strange country. What if I should die? Women died giving birth all the time in Lys'va. What then would happen to my baby?

There was something even more dreadful on my mind. Word was filtering in about the horrors that had befallen the Jews of Poland. Marcus had received a letter telling him how in February

1942, Gestapo agents, assisted by Ukrainian policemen, raided the Jewish homes of his village of Borinya and took scores of people away, including several of his cousins. The Jews were marched, naked and barefoot, through the winter night to the edge of the village where, at gunpoint, they were forced to dig three large pits. As if in some dark ritual, a name of a Jew was called out, the person approached the grave, and shots were fired. One person was left alive to fill the graves with dirt. The only saving news was that the letter did not mention Marcus's parents and sisters.

One night Marcus and I went to a movie to get away from our worries, but the film we saw, which started out as standard Soviet anti-German propaganda, contained newsreel footage of what was probably Babi Yar, the notorious killing ground outside Kiev. We could see for ourselves what had happened to our families. The newsreel showed men, women, and children, shrieking and sobbing in terror, as German soldiers and their dogs chased them across a field. The victims were forced to strip off their clothes and stand in front of a vast pit. We saw puffs of gunsmoke and men and women dropping into the pit. I will never forget the screams of a mother fleeing the dogs and calling "Abrasha!" to the small boy who couldn't catch her.

That night I dreamt that my father was trying to rescue my sisters Esther and Chana Leah and my brother Shimele from flames that raged through our house in Otwock. He was screaming for help and I stood and watched the flames, unable to move. Years later, I wondered if what I had dreamed had been only a nightmare whipped up by the film or a vision I had been given of what had probably happened to my family in Treblinka.

Marcus was not drafted—his skills with fine boots were too prized by the city's army officers. On January 17, 1945, he was in town when my first child was born. Lying in an isolated room on a hard wooden bench, ignored and forgotten, I suffered through three days of excruciating labor pains. No one paid attention to my screams and no one was permitted to visit me. Yet, on the day of the birth, Marcus came in to see the baby and he was so happy he started to cry. I told him that I had just heard on the radio that the

Red Army had captured Warsaw. This was delightful news because it meant we could begin to think of returning to our homes. But even more delightful was the simple sight of my baby nursing at my breast. It made me feel as if heaven's doors had been opened to me to compensate me for all the suffering I had endured. ⟨⟩

28

W e named you Yuri," my mother tells me. "You know already you were named after my grandfather—Israel Zelig Olszewski, yes? He died of a stroke right after he visited us in Otwock."

"I knew about 'Israel,' I never knew of 'Yuri' before."

"Sure, what did you think we called you Israel right in the middle of Russia? They would have accused us of Zionism. No, Yuri was the closest name to Israel in Russian."

Yuri. This is indeed something I have never known. A person, I suppose, should accurately know the name he was born with. I knew that my first name was the Yiddish diminutive of Israel-Srulek—but it never occurred to me, even once I resolved the mystery of my place of birth, that I must have had a Russian name. I think of Yuri Gagarin, the first human to fly in space. I was in high school at the time and I remember how troubled I was that we had fallen behind the Soviets in the space race. It was important to me as a new American that we surpass our chief rival, in the Olympics, in missiles, in space, in everything. Had I known I was born in the Soviet Union, I might have had a softer spot for the achievement of an astronaut who shared my name.

"Remind me again," I say to my mother. "Why did you name me after your grandfather? Why not your father or Daddy's father?"

She strains in concentration.

"I forgot already. Don't wait too long if you want to write down this story because my mind is going."

"That's why I'm interviewing you, Ma."

"Oh, yes, I remember now. We didn't know yet for sure my father is dead. You know Jews don't name their children after someone who's living. We didn't know Daddy's father was dead either. When Josh was born, we kind of knew already, so we named him after my father and his middle name is Solomon after Daddy's father."

"So you brought me home from the hospital. Where did I sleep? What did I eat?"

"Daddy found a crib in the house of an old Russian woman. We put it in our barracks room. No one could walk across the room, so crowded the room was. But we were very happy. Then I remember you got sick. I was stupid, what did I know? I was nursing you, but I wanted to give you something special to eat. This is the kind of mother I was. I found two tangerines in the market that had come from Turkey or Egypt or someplace like that. Nothing was too good for my baby, so I bought them and I let you suck on the juice. The next day you were cranky and you had diarrhea, and the next day too. I got scared. So I asked the other women around where we were living, and one of them told me I should stop nursing you and give you juice from cooked rice. She was from Leningrad so I figured she must know something, And I listened to her. Would you believe it? That's how young and stupid I was.

"I gave you the rice juice. You didn't want to eat it and you got thinner and thinner. I was afraid I would have to take you to the hospital. In Russia, if you went to a hospital you never came out alive. I was crazy. I left the baby with Marcus and I ran around the streets like a crazy woman looking for someone to help me. God must have been watching out for me because I met the mother of the woman who made my bridal dress. She was an experienced woman. She came to the house and the first question she asked me was 'Are you nursing him?' When I told her I wasn't, she got angry and ordered me to nurse you. You drank the milk hungrily and in a day or two you were completely better."

"Yes, that's a story you told me."

"You could have died," she says, laughing with relief. "I was so foolish."

"Thank God for that woman."

"This was the same woman who persuaded me to get you circumcised. Where could you get a *mohel* in Lys'va? There was no such person. It was wartime and everything was chaos. And it was already late. You must have been two months old. But on the next trip I made to Kungur I asked around and I found a *mohel*. He was an old, wrinkled Jew—I didn't see someone like him since Otwock—and I found him to be a distasteful personality. But I remember the *Bris*. The streets were covered with snow. All of our friends squeezed into our little room and he made the *Bris*. I remember how you cried. I was in tears myself. Everybody else enjoyed the sandwiches and vodka that Daddy got. Oy, that *mohel*. I had to feed him cheese because he was kosher and he wouldn't eat my meat dishes."

Although I have heard this story before, there are fresh details and I find myself touched by the tableau of a dozen Jewish refugees huddled in a warm room with snow blanketing the streets performing this age-old rite in the anarchy of war.

"That's when they called Daddy to the police station," I say, trying to keep the story on track.

"Oh, was I scared. I was sure I would never see him again. He got a letter telling him he had to come down to the station for questioning. We thought it was for the food and vodka he was getting from the officers. I remember he kissed me and you like he was going to jail for a long time. But he came back after a few hours. They learned about the *Bris* and they wanted to know if he was involved in Zionistic activities. They wanted to know who performed the circumcision. And they told him to come back the next evening with the name of the *mohel*. We embraced each other again as if we would never see each other anymore. Marcus told them it was Uncle Yasha who made the *Bris*. It seemed to work. They couldn't question Yasha because he was away on the front. They called Daddy in again for questioning, but they never threw him in jail. Maybe they didn't mind if an uncle did it, only if it was someone from a Jewish organization."

꙳ In the spring of 1945, the war finally came to an end. There was talk among our crowd that Poles like us would now be permitted to return to Poland. Most of our friends looked forward to repatriation with great enthusiasm, but I was not so eager. We had established ourselves in Lys'va. Marcus earned enough for us to eat regularly and was liked by his superiors. We had grown fond of the Russians, most of them plain, hardworking folk. And what, after all, was so attractive about life in Poland? Most Jews there were confined to a life of dismal poverty. Only the fortunate could proceed beyond grade school. At least in the Soviet Union everyone worked and went to school.

I was also tormented about my brother Simcha. As far as I knew, he could be alive. How could I leave him behind? And what about Yasha? He was still in uniform. Could I leave him behind too? Besides, who was there in Poland to go home to? Had anyone come through the war alive, my father and my little brother and two sisters? Were there even any graves to visit?

By 1946, everyone, it seemed, was repatriating. They were forced by a registration deadline to make a decision. Shira and her mother packed their valises to return to Romania. Mendele said good-bye to the Russian woman who had been his girlfriend and took off to see if his wife and children in Poland were still alive. One day before the deadline, we too packed our belongings and followed the herd returning to their ravaged homelands.

The Soviet authorities put us aboard the very same freight cars that had brought us over five years before. This time, we carried babies, pots and pans and bedding that we could spread out on the car floors to sleep on during the weeklong journey. As the train entered the Ukraine and Poland, it made unscheduled stops to let people off at points from which they could reach their hometowns. Everyone was aware these travelers would soon find out what happened to the families they had left behind.

At the last transfer point, a tall, husky border guard pointed his finger at us and bellowed, "Aren't you ashamed? You're leaving the country which took care of you through the war!"

He was drunk, but no one summoned a reply and I found myself agreeing with him.

Most of us were not sure where in Poland we wanted to settle. Marcus had no desire to return to Borinya, where there were no Jews left and where he feared the vicious Polish peasants among whom he had grown up might kill him just for sport. His fears were aggravated by the greetings we received in the Polish stops we made on our way.

"Jesus Maria!" a man in one mob roared with a laugh. "So many of them survived? I thought Hitler had killed them all."

After a week or so, we reached Wroclaw (Breslau) in Silesia, a German-held territory that had just been returned to Poland and where we were told there would be housing. As we gathered our belongings to disembark, who should enter our freight car but my brother Yasha in his Red Army uniform. He had been checking each of the trains arriving from the east to see if I was aboard. It had been two years since I last saw him and we hugged in tears. Tears also glistened on Yasha's and Marcus's cheeks as they embraced. We had survived the war and we were each other's family now. Yasha picked up Yuri, whom he had never seen before, and threw him in the air until Yuri wrinkled a smile.

Yasha told us there was no more housing available in Wroclaw and urged us to make our way to Warsaw. He also told us that my aunt Sheindele—my mother's sister—had survived the war and was living in the Zoliborz section of Warsaw. At least two people had survived from my childhood family.

Warsaw was devastated by the war, with much of the central city, the lively streets on which I had spent my teenage years, in ruins. In the suburb of Praga, barracks had been arranged for people like us that they now called "displaced persons." Five refugee families had to share a single room, with beds practically next to each other and drying laundry strung from ropes attached to the walls.

Soon after we settled in, we visited Aunt Sheindele. She was my mother's sister, the one I considered my good aunt. During my childhood summers in Parysow, she was always kind, unlike her sister Chana Leah. She married her boyfriend at the time and they had a son, Marek. Yasha had already told us how Marek, then thirteen, was torn from her arms by German soldiers and taken away to a fate she never learned. In tears now, Sheindele, looking far more worn out than her years, told us how she and her husband were put aboard cattle cars heading to a place called Maidanek. On the way, her husband, at her urging, pushed her out the train window. At least, they figured, she might live and be able to search for Marek. As she fell out of the speeding train, she injured her leg and spent the night in the woods in unbearable pain. The next morning she dragged her swollen leg to a town she knew was a suburb of Warsaw. There, she said, she spent the rest of the war like an animal, often hiding in a vat of sewage up to her neck.

"If not for the sewage can, I would never have made it alive," she said.

As she stood up and showed me how deep she had been sunken into sewage, I could see that she still dragged her leg. She also told us the fates of a few other relatives.

"My mother was hidden in a wardrobe by Chana Leah and her husband," she said. "She was carried around in that wardrobe, from one place in the ghetto to another so the Nazis would not discover her. Chana Leah's son, Yurek, was taken from her about the same time my Marek was. Chana Leah tried to save Mother, but both of them were killed when the Nazis put down the uprising in the ghetto."

Yuri was growing restless in his father's arms, but there was more to tell. She revealed that Freyde Leah, my older half sister, had died too. Sad as I was to hear that, I was relieved that it was not at the hands of the Nazis. She had simply succumbed to tuberculosis. ✧

I ask my mother about a story she has told me once or twice before: her visit to an Otwock that had been cleansed of its Jews. This time I want to know details that I must have shrugged off before.

"I didn't have the courage to go to Otwock, but I finally made myself go," my mother tells me. "I took the train—the commuter train, you call it here—and in a half hour we were in Otwock. Just like you go by train from Manhattan to Westchester, that's how far it was. The station was exactly the same. The same big tower. What was different was that in the crowd of passengers I didn't see a single Jewish face. Otwock when I was a girl was full of Jews—Hasidim, socialist Jews, plain Jews. So many there were five synagogues at least. So I walked around the station. I couldn't make myself go into the town. What for? I asked myself. Who am I hoping to find? I ought to face the truth that no one survived."

I want to press her on her reluctance. Wasn't she curious about what neighbors could tell her about the fate of her family, their last days before they were transported to Treblinka, if that is indeed what happened to them? Didn't she want to see her father's house once more? I am a journalist, after all. I never let anyone get off this easy, not even Holocaust survivors I have interviewed. But I flinch. We are approaching the kernel of the pain that is always with her, the speculations she has about how her father, stepmother, and two young sisters and little brother spent their last months in Otwock's ghetto and the suffering those who endured probably experienced in Treblinka. I cannot probe any further. Maybe it's because those events are the kernel of whatever pain I feel as well. I let her spin her story at her own pace.

"In a station office," she tells me, "there were big bowls with photographs of the Jews of Otwock. The Nazis were so twisted they took photographs of people they sent to Treblinka. I looked through the photographs. I recognized some of the faces and it was heartbreaking because they were now dead. But I didn't find any pictures of my father or my two little sisters and my brother. Maybe they starved to death in the ghetto. That's what I'm afraid happened.

"While I was looking through the photographs, someone tapped my shoulder. It was the milkman, the man who delivered milk among our neighbors when I lived in Otwock. He knew only what happened to my stepmother. He said she died in the ghetto from tuberculosis. He didn't know what happened to my father and the children. He told me that many Jews starved to death. Anyone who survived was shot when they liquidated the ghetto or else they were taken to Treblinka. 'There's no use leaving the station because no one is here anymore,' he said.

"I no longer wanted to go to the town. How could all the Jews of Otwock have disappeared? Otwock was half Jewish. I thought about my father, not just how he must have suffered, but how he couldn't protect his little children, Esther, Chanele, and Shimele, from harm. He loved those children, all his children. I never left the station. I crossed over to the platform on the other side and waited for the train back to Warsaw."

29

Telling her story has left my mother emotionally spent. I pick up her composition book once more and leaf through it until I find the last few pages, the ones that bring her life in Europe to a close.

❧ There were other opportunities to search for relatives. American Jewish groups and the Red Cross collected lists of survivors and we pored through those. But there was not a recognizable Golant or Berger name among them.

Meanwhile we had to deal with our own lives. We were subsisting on powdered milk and eggs and other dried foods shipped over by Allied relief agencies, and we needed to supplement that. Through the authorities in Warsaw, Marcus found a job as a shoemaker and we were promised a two-room apartment, something that would put an end to our vagabond life. Perhaps we would settle after all in Poland, we thought. But we never took that apartment. One morning outside our barracks, a refugee was cooking powdered eggs over a campfire and there was a strong explosion. Someone had placed a bomb in the stove the refugee had rigged together. The man was instantly killed and another person nearby was maimed. Yuri howled and howled and we could not console him for a long time. We too trembled with fear because it was obvious that whoever planted the bomb was aiming to kill Jews who survived the war.

A week after this incident, a radio broadcast told us of a savage pogrom in the Polish city of Kielce. Forty-one people—Jews who had survived the death camps and returned to their homes—were stoned to death by local Poles. The Poles claimed they had been whipped into a fury by a young boy who told them Jews were murdering Christian children. The broadcast added dryly that help had been slow to arrive. The next day we took every piece of clothing we did not immediately need and our pots and pans and sold them on the market. Smugglers in the Baltic seaport of Stettin were helping refugees cross into American-occupied territory in Germany. We would use the money we earned in the market to leave Poland forever.

Our bundles seemed lighter as Marcus, Yuri, my brother Yasha, and I started our journey toward Stettin. When we got there, Yasha and I tracked down a gang of smugglers. Getting to Berlin, it turned out, would cost us more money than we had. The next day I took our every possession, every item of clothing not on our backs down to a pair of shoelaces, and sold it at Stettin's market. Yuri and I would go to Berlin in one truck; Marcus and Yasha would follow the next day in a second truck. With Yuri on my lap or sleeping in my arms, I spent hours in the dark hollow of a truck packed with women and children. It shook and bumped so badly that I vomited. We reached a checkpoint and I heard loud Russian voices and curses outside the truck and hoped our journey was over. But the truck soon rolled on and at some point we had to get off and climb aboard a second truck. I panicked, wondering if I would lose track of Marcus and Yasha. But I prayed to God to protect us just a little bit longer.

It seems he did. We made it to Berlin, to the American sector. Much of the city was in ruins. I located my uncle Yudel, my father's youngest brother. Yudel too had survived the war in Russia and had preceded us to Berlin. With Yudel was his wife, Fela, his young son, Schmiel, who like Yuri also had been born in Russia, and a new baby girl, Blima. Although as a child I had not spent much time with

Yudel, it was relieving to be with someone who had been so close to my father. Still, I was forced to confront the probability that just four people—Yasha, myself, Uncle Yudel, Aunt Sheindele—had survived out of a family that had numbered more than twenty-five before the war. With Yudel was my uncle Jonah Feigenbaum, the husband of my father's sister Sarah. It was to the home of Jonah and Sarah that my father brought me when I was fourteen so I could earn my own way in their hat workshop in Warsaw. I had been a bother to Jonah and Sarah and left their home after a week, but I never forgot the slights I received there.

Yudel and Jonah took Yuri and myself by subway to the Schlachtensee neighborhood on the outskirts of Berlin. There the Americans had converted German army barracks into housing for displaced persons. This DP camp, with blocks of long, low wooden buildings arranged around a sandy field, would be our temporary home, we were told. Jonah, a husky man with intense eyes, invited me for lunch to meet his new wife, Kyla. My aunt Sarah, he told me, and their two teenaged sons, Samuel and Abraham, had been killed along with twenty thousand other Jews in the village of Ponary outside Vilna, where Jonah had moved his family years before the war. Only Jonah's daughter, Rachelke, survived. Sarah had hidden her, a twelve-year-old, with a Gentile woman. Jonah told me how he had been able to track Rachelke down after the war.

"She is my only reason for living," he said, his voice choking.

To my relief, Marcus and Yasha arrived the next day and the four of us were given our own room in Block 11, with a window that faced the camp's entrance. We had four olive-green American army cots, four olive-green blankets, four olive-green sheets, and four olive-green pillows. I began thinking of this room as my home. With a borrowed sewing machine, I stitched curtains and a tablecloth and a bedspread. Who knew how long our stay would be?

When I opened the door to the long hall, I heard the voices of small children, all belonging to young mothers who had survived the war by fleeing to Russia. Our Russian, though, was now useless, and we began calling our babies by Yiddish names. I changed "Yuri" into "Yisroel," calling him Srulek, or Srulkele for short. Srulek had lots of children to play with and I let him toddle across the sandy field outside my window in his knit cap and heavy pantaloons.

The young men and women in the winter of 1946 to 1947 included the still-frail survivors of the concentration camps, those who had spent the war hiding in forests or basements, and the Poles like ourselves who had fled to Russia. It began to dawn on me that in our camp there were few middle-aged and elderly people and only a handful of children over five. Hitler had killed off those too old to work and all small children. Spread among the camp's Jews were many Christian Poles, Latvians, and Estonians who did not want to live under the new communist regimes. Some of these, we suspected, had helped round up or kill Jews. From them, we kept our distance.

As harsh as our own lives in Russia had been, the stories we were told about Auschwitz and other camps made us shudder, not only because they were so inconceivable in their brutality but because we had to face what our own kin had suffered. I had to imagine how my father, a man of such dignity and pride, must have been degraded by the Nazis before dying, how powerless he must have felt, unable to protect his three small children, how he must have ached in the moments before his death that his older children—Yasha, Simcha, and myself—were probably suffering the same fate. This pious man must have torn himself apart wondering what was in the mind of the God whom he had spent his whole life worshiping.

Yet among all of us DPs, as they called us, there seemed a desire to get beyond the horrible past, an eagerness to get our lives under way, to do some meaningful work, to reestablish ourselves after so many years as helpless vagabonds and victims, to create new families and bring Jewish children into the world. A *cheder* was set up in what had been a German army barrack, and Jewish children began studying again, learning Hebrew and even the Five Books of Moses. Some refugees put on plays, and others performances of opera and Yiddish songs. Some days, I would head to downtown Berlin, to the Kurfurstendamm. A few shops had survived the bombing and there were dressmakers who were willing to sew stylish dresses for little money. I let a street photographer snap my picture so I could record a carefree moment. I wanted to remind myself of the optimistic young woman I was in the spring of 1939 in Warsaw just before my life as I knew it came apart.

Meanwhile, Yasha and Marcus did not just idly wait to live off the hardtack and Spam we were doled out by the United Nations Relief and Rehabilitation Association (UNRRA, as we called it), and by the American Joint Distribution Committee (which we knew as the Joint). They began doing what most of their Jewish acquaintances were doing: dealing with German farmers and merchants who were trying to sell their goods to the displaced persons. Farmers pulled up to the camp's gate and Yasha and Marcus would haul in boxes of plump red and yellow cherries. There were so many boxes, we had to pile them up on Yasha's cot, forcing Yasha to sleep with Srulek on his cot. Later on Yasha and Marcus latched on to other foods—pears, apples, and buckets of herring. Throughout the day, refugees eager to taste something beyond the rations would come to our room to buy cherries by the kilogram or herrings. Russia had given us an elementary education in trading and deal making.

Marcus and Yasha soon progressed from the messy business of fruit to the cleaner commerce of cigarettes and chocolates. They did not ask their source—a DP himself—too many questions about where his goods came from, but everyone suspected they were obtained from soldiers who were filching them from an army PX. Yasha and Marcus would drive their cargo of cigarettes and chocolates over to the Russian-occupied zone. For a small tip the Russian guards let them through the checkpoint. On the other side, Germans were famished for treats like cigarettes and chocolate. They paid in cash or in meat, milk, eggs, toilet articles, and clothes. One time Marcus noticed the Russian guards were questioning the German driver of his truck, and he leaped out of the back and fled out of sight. He lost the entire truckload of cigarettes, but was back in business in a short time. ✎

As I read, I am tickled by this story of my father in the DP rackets. This is a side of my father I scarcely saw—resourceful, risk-taking, reckless.

This is not the man who stayed with General Textile Company for twenty-five years making ironing board covers, who could not make a decision without checking with my mother.

"How do you explain it, Ma?" I ask, as I look up from the composition book. "When did Daddy lose that nerve?"

"Who knows? He was younger and foolish. I was frightened also when I heard of some of the crazy things he did."

"Ma, how do you explain that the survivors were able to go on after all they had been through? They lost their families, their towns."

"This I cannot answer, Joey. You have to ask bigger people than me. I know for me and my friends, the children probably helped us. Seeing you run around in the field outside the barracks with the other children of my friends gave me a kind of hope. You didn't know anything about what happened. You were just children exploring the world for the first time. You were another generation. There was something to look forward to. This gave me hope for the world, for myself."

❧ On April 7, 1947, another son was born to us. We named him Joshua Solomon after both of our fathers. By now we had begun to reconcile ourselves to the fact that our parents did not survive the Holocaust. Joshua—whom we soon called by the nickname Sheealeh—was a very robust, bubbly baby and I attributed his health to the cherries from the boxes piled on Yasha's cot that I kept eating during my pregnancy. When I came home from the hospital with Joshua, there was Srulek sitting on the floor with a hammer smashing a toy train that Yasha had given him. He hammered away at the train until he shattered it into small pieces. Something was making him very angry, and the answer I now realize lay in the bundle in my arms.

After a few months, I hired a German baby-sitter, just as many other refugees did. It seemed peculiar that we would hire the people we despised to watch our children, but when a grandmotherly woman desperate for money came to your door and offered her services for a few marks, it was irresistible. Elsa was a good-natured, affectionate grandmother and I could not understand how such simple goodness could have tolerated the hateful atmosphere of the Hitler years. She hugged Sheealeh and made Srulek call her *Oma*, as German children call their grandmothers.

For most of the time, I felt quite prosperous as a refugee. That might seem odd to say, but life in the Schlachtensee camp was better than any I had experienced since I left home at fourteen. I had never lived in such a cheerful room. I had all the food I needed and Marcus was making money in his dealings. Yet we knew we would soon have to make decisions about our future that might cause my new family—Yasha as well as Marcus and our children—to break up once more.

Then came a political crisis that turned us into refugees once more and postponed any permanent decisions. In June 1948, the Russians blockaded all the autobahns and rail lines into Berlin, a city that was entirely in the Russian zone of occupation but, like the rest of Germany, had been divided among the four Allied powers. Stalin was attempting to seize the entire city for himself. In response, America airlifted food into Berlin to feed its soldiers and the DPs. One morning, the camp loudspeakers told us to pack all our belongings as soon as possible. The camp was being closed down and we would be transferred to a new refugee camp, at Landsberg, near Munich, that was wholly in the American zone. Yasha, for reasons he didn't make clear, wanted to remain in Berlin. So as the refugees boarded the huge military cargo planes, I could not stop tears from running down my face as I gave a farewell embrace to Yasha, whom I loved so much, and watched him embrace my boys, whom he loved so much.

There were no seats inside our plane. We squatted on the floor and gripped our children tightly to our laps. Srulek and Sheealeh seemed to enjoy the bouncy ride. After we landed, we sat on our valises and bundles and watched our children scampering about, glad to be free of the plane. That was the day Joshua took his first steps and, despite all the turmoil, his eager walking was a joy to see. ✖

"Why did you choose the United States to go to?" I ask my mother, wanting to hear in more precise detail a story she has told me before.

"I didn't want to go there," she tells me. "I wanted to go to Israel. It had just declared its independence. The refugees were buying refrigerators, stoves, sewing machines to take with them. I wanted my children to grow up in a Jewish country. They would be self-assured, not like the majority of Jews in Poland. In Poland, if a Pole got drunk or angry, he would spit on the first Jew he saw, and he didn't have to worry that he would be arrested. But Daddy's friend Moshe Granas advised him not to go there. 'In Israel the new immigrants sleep in tents,' he said. 'There is not enough milk for the children. There are no jobs for tailors like myself.' Daddy listened to him, and I was too scared about Israel to argue. I was afraid there would be another war with the Arabs.

"Besides," my mother continues, "Daddy said he had an uncle in New York City. Before the war this uncle had sent over money for his oldest sister's dowry. Maybe we would have a little something to start our lives in America. I was tired of struggle. Israel would be more struggle."

   No country was eager to take in the Jewish refugees. In 1948, the American Congress had made an exception to the annual immigration quotas and agreed to admit tens of thousands of DPs, but the law was written in such a way that it rejected most people who had spent the war in the Soviet Union. We got rid of our Soviet papers and were easily able to get false documents that said we were married in Germany.

I wanted Yasha to come with us to America. But he was making a life for himself in East Berlin. He had become involved with a German girl and, after she converted, they had been married in a Jewish ceremony. They already had a baby boy, Benjamin, named after my father's father. Yasha wrote me that he was not ready to join us just then. I would have go to the United States with only my husband and children. In fact, Yasha did not come to America. He accepted immigration for his family into Australia.

The American authorities questioned us closely to see if we were spies or communist infiltrators. They checked our health, making sure we would not be importing any diseases. Srulek, a test discovered, had at some time been stricken with tuberculosis. To me it seemed probable—and the doctors agreed—that it must have been while he was weak with pneumonia in Russia. The new streptomycin drugs must have cured his tuberculosis as well. At the end we were all approved for a voyage to America. We left behind the DP camp at Landsberg and made our way to the port of Bremenhaven.

At the dock, we had to sit on hard benches inside a cavernous waiting room and endure speeches from representatives of the American agency that was supposed to help us acculturate. Talking in German, a woman informed us that American table manners were different from what we were accustomed to, showing us how Americans spoon their soup from the back of the bowl rather than the front. She even showed us how American men rest their feet on a cocktail table when sitting on a living room couch. I decided they were just trying to kill time until the ship was ready for boarding.

The children were running wildly inside the terminal when we heard the shriek of the ship's whistle. As we walked up the gangplank I realized how colossal the ship was and I was able to see spelled out in large block letters across its hull the name General Greely. As the ship pulled out of the dock, we stood on deck and from the railing waved good-bye to Europe, which had been my only home.

Enormous as it seemed, the *General A. W. Greely* was not a fancy liner. It was a transport ship that had been used by the merchant marine during the war to carry soldiers overseas. I was seasick for an entire week and threw up much of the time. When I finally overcame my nausea and felt like eating, the oranges were dry and the hard-boiled eggs were rancid. Still, we began to enjoy our ocean cruise. In the morning, we would rush to secure deck chairs for the day. We breathed in the salty air, soaked up the winter sunshine, and gazed at the beauty of the heaving seas. When in my entire life had I ever had a moment to simply relax in this manner? I had the sense that the voyage's pleasant atmosphere would cure my battered soul and restore my energy. I began to appreciate my children, my husband, this ship, and the prospect that we would soon arrive in a peaceful and prosperous country.

Then one morning we glimpsed the shoreline. Soon someone who had binoculars screamed out: "The Statue of Liberty! The Statue of Liberty!" As we got closer, other voices joined in and shouted: "The Statue of Liberty!" Finally, even I with my nearsighted eyes could see the statue and I began to cry. To this day I do not know why. I knew nothing about this solemn woman with a torch, and I had so many concerns about how we would earn our livelihood in a strange land and where we would live and whether we would be isolated and lonely. But I also felt in my soul that my family had finally reached its true refuge, and I cried the tears I had denied myself during so many painful moments of my life. ◆

30

I t was time to leave home.

"What for do you need an apartment?" my mother exclaimed when I told her of my decision. "I cook for you, I clean your clothes, I give you clean bedding. Why should you throw away money on rent every month?"

But I was resolute. The pressure of home was strangling me. It wasn't just my parents' meddling immersion in my life. It wasn't just a desire for my own sovereign space, the standard college graduate's craving for freedom, or a need to escape the prosaic Bronx. I was tired of the whole refugee burden, tired of my parents' fumbling need to rely on me, tired of their living their lives through me. Yes, I was tired of them, tired of their fright, their flailing, their sorrow, their whole history. I wanted to start over again, as my own person, to lead a more light-hearted life.

The centripetal pull to stay within the refugee orbit was relentless, however. Sometime during those years, Uncle Yudel, my mother's only surviving uncle and a person we at times treated as our éminence grise, was holding court at our dinner table. I might have said something glib about the variety of friends I had or mentioned a Gentile girl I had dated, but whatever the catalyst, Yudel launched into a jeremiad about the perilous lot of comtemporary Jews.

"You think everything in America is sweet and wonderful," he said. "But Jews should never feel safe here. When the right moment comes, the goyim will turn on us."

My mother listened to him and her dazzled, delighted eyes seemed to endorse what he said. This, after all, was her father's brother, a man who came from the same lineage of scholarly, pious Jews. His face was as close as she would ever come to recapturing her father's sainted countenance, his memories a remnant of that splendid spirit snuffed out by the barbarians. And Yudel knew of what he spoke. He had tasted malice toward Jews first in Poland and then in his travels across the Soviet Union. Through famine and anarchy, he had kept his family alive and together—his wife, his two children, his wife's parents, her sister, and her family. They were the only ones he could rely on. Maybe a few other Jews might be trusted. But the goyim, never.

Who, having known Yudel's life, could condemn such attitudes? Even after American GIs opened the concentration camp gates and saw the shriveled patchworks of knobby bone and skin covered in striped rags that once were animated human beings, even after such horrors the United States refused to expand its national immigration quotas until 1948. Although some concentration camp inmates had expected a repentant world to open its generous arms, the army let the DPs languish in the squalor and sometimes filth of refugee camps for months, sometimes in barbed-wire enclosures next door to the Nazi camps where they had been brutalized. General George Patton called them "lower than animals." An exacting observer of international politics, Yudel had seen how the British allowed the DP camps to fester by closing the doors to Palestine. Yes, Yudel knew of what he spoke.

But his fatalism did not encompass the world I knew. True, my friends were largely Jewish, but I had worked with Italian editors and printers in college, with Greeks, Irish, and WASPs as well. We took pleasure in one another's company and needled one another about ethnic idiosyncrasies. At Columbia University's School of Journalism, there were congenial Midwesterners and Southerners. As a country, America had been good to me, providing me with a free, high-caliber education and no barriers to anything I might want to do professionally. I did not see the world in his way.

"Yudel, I can understand that given what you went through, you would feel that way. But that has not been my experience."

"Joey, you're young and so you're foolish," he said. "You will see."

"Your life is not my life," I said. "I don't want to live with bitterness and distrust."

Uncle Yudel reddened with insult, although none had been intended; I had not shown him the proper respect. For some time afterward, he kept aloof.

Such conflicts only deepened my resolve to leave home. Everything would be solved, I was sure, by getting my own apartment. It wasn't a wild-eyed decision. I was earning money now, teaching English at a junior high school in the Bronx, although even that decision had been mired in my parents' history. As I finished up my classes at Columbia University's School of Journalism in May 1967, the Vietnam War was still dragging on, and after graduation I would again be subject to the draft. I wanted to search for a newspaper job, but my mother's unyielding argument that her children were the only family she had was hard to buck.

I had never given any thought to working as a teacher, but teaching got you out of the draft because there was a national scarcity of teachers. Teaching felt like a diversion from the career I really wanted, but Vietnam would divert me far more tumultuously. So in September 1968 I began teaching English at Wade Junior High School right off the Grand Concourse and about a mile from my home. Working with jumpy, fidgety adolescents was difficult that first year, but once I learned the knack of maintaining an orderly classroom I was able to captivate my students with lessons on novels such as *Huckleberry Finn* and *Catcher in the Rye* and plays such as *Raisin in the Sun* and *The Diary of Anne Frank*. (I was startled to discover that in one of the Anne Frank classes, made up of black and Puerto Rican girls reading below grade level, many students knew nothing about the Holocaust or even World War II. I gave the class a capsule account, and they eagerly entered the world of the play, reenacting the play's clandestine Chanukah, complete with the lighting of the candles.) I began to feel a sense of my own authority, and sometimes even charm, and toyed with the idea of making a full-time career as a literature professor.

Working full-time meant I could afford my own apartment. I was unfamiliar with how to go about finding one, but I knew enough to check the newspaper ads. Greenwich Village was the neighborhood that most enticed me, just as it had generations of young men and women who sought to escape suffocating families and provincial communities. I too was drawn by the human scale of the buildings against an ample sky, the meandering streets and hidden alleys, the gnarled and twisted trees, the incongruous mix of artists and bohemians among Italian shopkeepers and Jamesian matrons. And so, on a sunny fall morning ideal for imagining oneself as a Villager, I found myself in a real estate agent's office off Sheridan Square. Nothing that he showed me matched my conception of a filigreed and wainscoted brownstone apartment dominated by bookshelves, tall, arched windows, and a fireplace. But I was nervous that I might forever lose the bargains I was seeing, and my thoughts converged on a railroad flat on Perry Street. It was in the heart of the Village. The rent was eighty-seven dollars, cheap even in those days, and a sum certain to win over parents who suspected I was a spendthrift. The building was a neglected gray-stone tenement with fire escapes, but the living room actually had a working fireplace and a shelved niche for the books that would testify to the writer I would surely become. The bedroom and kitchen were dim, but there was some light streaming in through one end of the living room, light that seemed to contain all the hope and eagerness I was bringing to this new start in life. It would do.

"Great," the agent said. "Let's go back to the office to sign the contract. You'll leave me a month's rent and a month's deposit, and you can move in on the first."

"A month's deposit?"

The agent explained that in addition to the first month's rent I had to leave another month's rent as security against damage or breaking of the lease. I was taken aback. I had only enough cash with me for a month's rent, and the suspicious nature that had been cultivated in my home wondered if the month's rent as a deposit was some kind of scam.

"What if I give you the month's rent now and bring you the deposit this afternoon?" I ventured. "Can you hold the apartment?"

He thought this over for a moment and said, "I'll give you until two o'clock. Then I have to start showing it again."

I would never get to the Bronx and return to the Village by two, but I figured I could have my mother fetch me the money. Even as I dialed the number for my Bronx home, I suspected this was a formula for disaster, like asking a Vietcong guerrilla to deliver grenades to the American command in Saigon. But part of me must also have needed to show my mother the apartment, to have her realize that her son was proceeding prudently.

"Ma, I'm in Greenwich Village," I shouted into the pay phone. "I just saw an apartment I like. Can you loan me eighty-seven dollars so I can put a deposit on the apartment—and, I'm sorry to ask you, but can you bring down the money by subway?"

"So you're going ahead with this? Well, I'm not giving you eighty-seven dollars of my money so you can do a stupid thing."

"Look, I'm moving out, no matter what you say, so there's no point in starting the whole discussion over again. If you go to my bank, you can withdraw the money. The account is in trust for you, so they'll let you do it. I'm just asking you to do me a favor. Otherwise I'll lose a good apartment."

"Joey, you're throwing away money. You're grabbing without thinking. But if you want to be foolish, I can't stop you. You're a man already. I'll bring you the money."

An hour and a half later, I was standing in front of the agency when I saw my mother, with my sister, Evelyn, in tow, striding emphatically down the street as if she were out to tell someone off. Her white sandals marched purposefully forward, her dress swished back and forth in rhythmic fury. Evelyn, who was then nine, had to take quick little steps to keep up. As my mother drew closer, I could hear the shouted disapproval she was hurling at the neighborhood. Words like *garbage* and *drek* and *loch*—the Yiddish words for "shit" and "hole in the ground"—were prominent in her curses. I was embarrassed, imagining that my prospective neighbors would associate this woman with me, and fail to discern the stylish spirit that I hoped to impress them with.

"So you like living in these old houses with garbage cans right on the sidewalk?" she sneered as she pulled up.

"Look, Ma," I said. "Thank you for bringing down the money, but I made my mind up. Can you give me my money?"

She was fuming, but she handed it over.

"You're throwing away money in the garbage just like you did with the scholarship money you gave to the newspaper," she said. "I told you they would never pay you back and they didn't. You don't listen, and you're not listening now."

My sister stood close to my mother's side, smiling inscrutably. I could not tell whether she was embarrassed at our mother's behavior or actually seconding her view. I was about to head off to the agent, but something—perhaps some need to patch up the wound I was causing—prompted me to offer to walk them back to the subway stop at Sheridan Square. On the way we happened to pass Perry Street and I found myself making an impulsive, fatal suggestion.

"Look, Ma, the apartment is half a block away. Why don't you take a look and see that I'm not moving into a hole."

Grudgingly, she agreed. When we stood in front of the gray-stone building, I could see in her dismissive face that she thought it no better than a hovel. After we entered the dark first-floor hall, climbed the steps to the second floor and opened the door to the apartment, she made her feelings unimpeachably clear. She broke into sobs.

"This is what I worked for all these years, so you could end up in a *loch* like this," she said, gasping in between her cries. "For this, you're going to give up our home? You're pretending that night is day and day is night. This is a *loch,* and nothing you can tell me will make me see it any differently."

We left the building and walked off in opposite directions, with me heading toward the real estate office and my mother and sister toward the subway. But something about my mother's tearful reaction, the misgivings that I had acted unwisely before, the sense that she had always had an unerring eye for value, made me lose heart. By the time I reached the agency I realized I was not going to take the apartment that day. The agent scowled contemptuously.

What I didn't realize that day nor for many years afterward—though I knew it in the quick of my being—was that what was to me a bolt for independence was for my mother the breakup of the family she had painstakingly knitted together. That had been her mission in America, nothing else. This was not a woman who had well-defined aspirations for a career, for wealth, for friendship, for fun. She had emerged from the war with one objective: to grow a new family and watch with pride as it flourished. And now the first of her offspring was breaking off, leaving the ambit of her powers.

What she hadn't bargained for was that her success would not produce the close-knit family of her Otwock shtetl, that as she provided her children with the means to become self-reliant, she was unwittingly sowing the seeds for the family's disbandment. She must have wistfully imagined that everybody would stay together in one happy cluster, like atoms within a molecule, in close quarters if not the same house. But her children were endowed, like all young people, like she herself when she left Otwock for Warsaw, with the urge to test their wings.

It took me a week or two to collect the shreds of my resolve and begin scanning the newspaper ads once more. This time, I found myself wary of the Village altogether. My mother had lost but had had an impact. The next apartment I looked at, and took, was on the East Side. It was tidy and presentable, with carpeted floors and a modern kitchenette—something more in line with my mother's expectations—but it was bland and colorless and I never loved it nor the neighborhood. Still, I was out. I could now do what I wanted, when I wanted, with whom I wanted. I was so on my own that I was frequently lonesome, particularly in a neighborhood of singles bars whose culture I had no taste for.

Within a year, I moved to the West Side, to a town house on West Eighty-sixth Street that had once belonged to Bernard Gimbel, whose family founded the very store my mother dragged me to repeatedly to buy my suits and sports jackets. It also tickled me that I was back on the West Side, one block from the hotel we had lived in when we first came to America and sixteen blocks from the neighborhood where I had capered with Maury and Simon, Sol and Charlie. I had taken a long way around by way of the Bronx to return to my roots. But I was now undeniably an American, on my own terms. I was teaching junior high school kids how to speak English, the language I had learned from scratch as a frightened five-year-old boy. I was bracing for a newspaper career in which I hoped I could fashion English in my own style to take readers into some engaging corners of life. I made friends at the school I taught in and together we succumbed to the sixties and seventies haze of music and pleasure where you could get it. I did not feel good about many of the things I did, but I was young and forgiving of myself.

Of course, there were the old pulls. My parents, to whom I gave a key, telling myself they should have one in case I was locked out, would from time to time steal into my apartment, snatch my laundry, and return it a few days later washed, dried, and pressed. It was nice not to have to worry about laundry, but the price was their right to comment on my apartment and my life. So after a year or two I put a stop to that.

My parents were getting used to the reality that I no longer lived at home. My brother too was out of the house, studying in medical school in Brooklyn and dorming there. The little *pisher* had succeeded where I had not even tried. He was on his way to realizing my mother's ambition that one of us become a doctor. Only my sister was at home, but it was a finer home than the one Josh and I grew up in. Coming along in 1957, Evelyn had been spared the precariousness and turbulence of immigration and acclimation, although she sometimes regretted having missed some of the bungling adventure that those years provided. By the time I left home, in 1967, she was living with my parents in another Grand Concourse apartment building, but this was one of the Art Deco buildings the Concourse was famed for and had a doorman. My parents had made it into the vaunted American middle class. Within a few years, Evelyn was at the High School of Music and Art, and in her junior year was accepted to Barnard College, the first of the siblings to attend college at Columbia University. Still, she was bereft that her two venerated brothers had left her alone and turned a spirited home into a hollow shell of itself. She remained hurt and angry about that for years afterward, although it took her a long time to tell me.

With all their manic fumbling, my parents had succeeded in restoring a life for themselves. They had created a new family in this world that was not quite as large as the one they had lost, but large and bouncing nonetheless. Maybe, I mused, they had even vanquished Hitler's

Holocaust and could put it to rest. I was wrong, of course. The reach of
the Holocaust extends throughout a life, to the grave and beyond,
informs the generation that experienced it and the generations that follow. But they had planted a substitute life in a different soil, American
soil, and it had taken hold and put out tendrils that were now taking
hold not too far away. And it was up to me to make of my life what I
could. To surrender to the past was fatal. To throw it away entirely was
futile. Whether I knew it then or not, I would have to acknowledge my
parents' tormented history, grapple with it, understand its subterranean,
subversive force, and live my life with it as a steady companion, unwelcome but undeniable.

31

POSTSCRIPTS

I am in Israel in June of 1981, at the first World Gathering of Jewish Holocaust Survivors. I am here as a journalist and as a son. More than seven thousand survivors from around the world have come for a week of memorial events, speeches, and even entertainments, and among those seven thousand are my parents, Marcus and Rachel Berger. After thirty-six years, the survivors have finally gathered the self-respect to insist that the world look squarely at what it did to them. After decades of diffidence, they are ready, finally, to celebrate their own triumph, bitter as it is.

This gathering is in large part a reunion. Survivors, most of them over sixty years old, are running into people from their European hometowns whom they have not seen since the war or since the concentration camps and DP camps. In the swank lobbies of the hotels of Tel Aviv and Jerusalem, with their marble counters, soft carpets, and Mies van der Rohe chairs, the survivors gather in knots late into the night, catching up on what has happened in their lives, boasting about the achievements of their children, laughing at the incongruities they lived through, sometimes shedding tears. These greeners, with their ill-fitting suits, their dated ties, their odd Ivy League caps, their ragged speech, their jittery, panicky manners, have taken over these stylish, expensive hotels, and I love them for it. The event has the kind of tumultuous disorganization of all the greenhorn bar mitzvahs and weddings I have been to—raucous and full of inelegant behaviors—and I would have it no other way.

Several of the survivors have come with business on their minds. They show up wearing specially printed T-shirts inscribed with the names of missing relatives and the places the relatives passed through before or during the war. "Simcha Gorevitz, my brother. Janowska. Sobibor. Auschwitz," reads one T-shirt worn by a tall woman in her late fifties. The T-shirt seems like some macabre résumé, with Sobibor and Auschwitz her brother's Harvard and Yale. Perhaps someone in the crowd had been in the Sobibor camp and will recognize the name Gorevitz and give her a scrap of valuable information, a tip to help her search further, maybe settle a small but nagging mystery. Many survivors, though, never having adopted the American fondness for marketing, probably see such efforts as clever but uncouth, and they try more restrained measures.

In one of the larger rooms of the Tel Aviv Hilton, the gathering's main hotel, organizers have set up a bank of a dozen computer terminals where survivors can search for vanished relatives or friends by scanning various lists stored in the computer's memory, such as membership rosters of survivor groups and DP camp registers. Survivors stand in higgledy-piggledy lines and reel off names, addresses, hometowns, and concentration camps as American and Israeli volunteers, with their youthful faith in technology, punch in the data.

It soon becomes apparent that the glitches of life are defeating these computers. Survivors have adopted new nationalities and languages, streamlined their names, married more than once. "Motele" in the Yiddish of Polish Jews became "Morris" in America. "Bikalchik" became "Bacall." Polish and Russian towns have also undergone name changes. The computer program has not been designed to account for these inconsistencies and the searches produce very little. No one can be certain whether that is because the vanished relatives are still unaccounted for or because the technology is simply flawed.

Along the walls of the computer room, bulletin boards have been set up where survivors can leave personal messages. At first the habitually skeptical survivors post only a few, but as news spreads of a handful of implausible reunions, reunions of fellow camp inmates, of neighbors from the same towns, even of a distant relative or two, a fever takes over the survivors. The bulletin board is soon crowded. The notices on them are heartrending.

"I am looking for my brother Moishe Spitalnik. I last saw him in 1943 at the railroad station in Cracow. He lived on Yarmolinsky Street," says one.

"My sister was Rosa Carnovitz of Breslau. She was in Auschwitz and I never saw her after. Call me at the Sheraton, Room 1454."

My parents pass through this room many times, and I wonder why they do nothing to seek their lost relatives. At first, I do not press them. I am here as a dispassionate, detached reporter. It is just a coincidence that my parents are at this event. I am a grown man of thirty-six and my wife, Brenda, is with me. I did not come intending to entangle myself with my parents. Indeed, when my father two years before asked me to join him, even offering to pay for my trip, I refused. This was their life, not mine, I told myself. Only when I saw the gathering as a compelling news story, one I would be able to cover with an edge of personal experience, did I ask my newspaper to send me. But when I spoke to survivors in the United States, hoping to find good subjects to follow in Israel, I began to absorb what they had been through in ways that I somehow had not before, began to see their lives with an impartiality I had never granted my parents. For the first time, I was able to slice through the distancing cloud of youthful resentments and disappointments and see not just my parents but living people who had suffered and been shaped by that suffering.

Somehow, though, at this gathering, I still hesitate to help them. It is almost as if I feel it would be a violation of my reporter's detachment. But in the gathering's closing days, after I have been deeply moved by several encounters among survivors, by the sadness and loss evoked by the Yiddish melodies they sing among themselves, by the survivors' spirit and their pride, even by the ability of the organizers to have put this gathering together and gotten worldwide attention for it, my objectivity has broken down. I am as much a participant as an observer. In the hotel lobby, I ask my mother why she does not punch information about some of her missing relatives into the computer, particularly her brother Simcha, the idealistic believer in communism who coaxed her to leave Poland for what he was sure would be the Soviet Union's benevolent society.

"Maybe somebody here has some information," I say.

"For what?" she replies. "Nobody here knows anything."

"How do you know that? Maybe somebody was with him in prison. Or maybe he got out and lives in Australia or Brazil."

"You're naive, Joey," she says.

The word is my mother's pet insult. It nullifies the fact that I am in my mid-thirties, that I have a wife, a home, and a good job. It reduces me to her little boy Joey. She is telling me that my modern American's creed of a caring, bountiful universe is foolish. Her experience, after all, has taught her that life can be cruel and that some things are not fixable.

"Look, what do you have to lose? It takes five minutes to fill out the computer form. I'll help you."

I forget about deadlines and scoops and hope my journalistic colleagues are not watching. We move down a narrow hallway toward the information room and midway my mother suddenly stops.

"I feel very cold, Joey. I can't stand this air-conditioning. I can't breathe."

Her voice has a startled quality. Her blue eyes seem to be shivering. I take a light sweater she had slung over her arms and drape it around her shoulders. We walk over to a table so my mother can fill out a data card for the computer operators to enter. My mother seems baffled by the form's demands, but with my help she writes down the name of her brother, Simcha Warshawiak, the town in which he was born, the country in which he was last seen, and the years spent in each. I watch her crabbed European handwriting, and I realize that I have forced her to relive something painful. For me, her search is a factoid of personal history. For her it is a brother she loved and never saw again.

She completes the data card, and at one of the computer lines a pleasant young woman cheerfully types in the information. We wait. If there is no revelation, my mother will not be disappointed. She expected nothing. But what if there is information and it turns out he is alive and she finds him? What will this elderly man mean to her, a man whom she has not seen for forty years, who has had a life, perhaps a wife and children, that she has known nothing of? And what will she mean to him?

The data puncher comes up with an S. Warszawiak. We hold our breath. But it turns out to be the wrong one. He is the wrong age and was born in the wrong Polish town. My mother walks away and, to my surprise, she is relieved. She has fulfilled her obligation. She has stilled the doubts raised by her son, smothered his challenge. The world can return to its accustomed order. She is no longer cold.

During this time, my father has not been idle. He has found himself a sheet of paper and has begun writing a message to post on the bulletin board. He asks me to read it to make sure it is spelled correctly. It says:

My name is Marcus Berger and I am missing my six sisters. Gittel, Rivka, Sura, Chava, Leah, Miriam. We was living in Borinya, Poland. If you have information, I am living in Riverdale, New York.

This time, I find myself choking, the feelings flooding over me. It is not mostly because of my heartache at hearing again of the six missing sisters. It is set off by something more mundane: it is my father writing a message. In my whole life, I have never seen my father write anything longer than a mailing address, unless it was dictated by my mother. I did not know he had the capacity in English to even compose this. But something has pushed him to this effort, some emotions that have been wakened by this gathering. He has reached into his mess kit of skills and put together this note. With my American-schooled know-how, I want to tell him to capitalize each letter of his sisters' names so that the names stand out. I want to tell him to write it with more punch. But I do not even correct the grammar. The message has more force than I can bear.

"It's a beautiful note, Daddy," I say, using the name I still call him. "Just pin it up."

I watch him with his awkward, hip-swinging gait march up to the board, find a small free space, and thumbtack the note to it. After thirty-five years, my father is still searching for relatives, just as he did in that first week of our arrival in the United States, when he dragged me by subway to Brooklyn to find his uncle Morris. Does he believe that finding his kin now would greatly brighten his life, would reclaim some old familial love, restore the lost home in Borinya? It is more primitive than that. One never stops searching for relatives that have vanished, even if one burrows only in one's soul.

Although her public school education stopped at the seventh grade, my mother always struck me as a bright woman—not just instinctively bright in the way she sized up a situation or a person, but in a hard-earned practical understanding of much of life.

By the time she was thirty-five, destiny had forced her to master five languages—Yiddish, Polish, Russian, German, and English, and she did. She could read a sixth, Hebrew, because her father had taught her the *aleph bet* so she could attain what was then regarded as a Jewish girl's simple-hearted relationship to God. Just as she could correctly judge *Anna Karenina* a splendid novel, she had a keen eye for what was phony or trashy in movies. She had a brutal cynicism toward politicians, businessmen, and doctors and homed in on the financial calculus for each. By reading newspaper columns about health and finance she figured out what symptoms of disease she needed to watch out for and how prudently to invest her savings. She reckoned on her own that welfare would destroy those who received it by stripping them of the human craving for self-reliance, and she was right.

But there was something stunted and choked about my mother's intellect. She could not vent it in full-throated fashion. She lacked words, she lacked concepts, she lacked basic information. It was as frustrating as if she had been blessed with a natural ear then plunked down untutored in front of a piano and told to play for an audience.

While her children were growing up, she felt compelled to work and could not do much to enlarge her mind. There was no one to relieve her of the chores most other women were spending their whole days doing. She seldom had time to read. Yet she was gnawed by ambition, knew she was meant for something nobler than what life had thus far doled out.

Sometime after I was in college, she managed a significant breakthrough. She passed the civil service test to become a postal clerk, a backroom sorter of mail. It did not sound like much to the rest of the world, but for a half-educated immigrant, passing that test certified her mastery of English and gave her bragging rights with her refugee friends. It allowed her to give up the foul, grueling work of a hat factory for the merely humdrum staleness of the post office. It was a step up in class. But the pleasure of her success proved short-lived. She grew resentful at the indolence of her coworkers, their insistence on doing the bare minimum, their suspicions of anyone with drive. In some ways, garment work was more honorable. She seethed with discontentment and let us know it, every time my brother, sister, and I visited her.

"Ma, rather than complain, why don't you go to school, take some high school courses," I said one day. "Maybe you could move into some other field."

"Maybe you could even go to college," Josh said with a laugh.

Evelyn quickly jumped on the bandwagon. Having been through college, the three of us knew the courses would not be all that formidable. Dull minds got through college, and my mother did not have a dull mind. After a year or two of this kind of prodding, she seemed flattered enough by our confidence in her talents to take us up on our idea. My sister was through with Barnard, ensconced in graduate school, so my mother no longer needed to be at home every evening to fulfill her first responsibility—raising children. She enrolled in a course that promised her a general equivalency diploma, studied subjects like American history and trigonometry, and passed the test. Armed with that certificate, she enrolled in Hunter College in Manhattan and began taking college courses, courses far from the bedrock concerns of her roots in Otwock, courses in James Joyce and Schopenhauer, astronomy and calculus.

On days she had to travel to Hunter, she went first-class, with a chauffeur: my father. Two evenings a week he would start up his light blue Ford Maverick—a used car but cherished nonetheless—and drive her from Riverdale, where they had moved in the mid-1970s, down the Major Deegan and FDR Drive to the East Side of Manhattan.

While my mother sat in class, he would park the car on Park Avenue or along a darkened side street and wait, keeping the engine running on cold days to keep himself warm. He read *The New York Times* or caught a nap until my mother appeared for him to drive her home. I shuddered at what I saw as another sign of his overly doting nature and let him know. But he never seemed to see it that way. It gave him pleasure and pride to be able to make my mother's life easier (and driving his Ford Maverick, topping up the gas tank, finding a convenient parking space were some of the few pleasures he gave himself). It also relieved him of the anxiety he would surely have felt about her safety, since in those years taking subways at night to the Bronx was a risk. It was, in short, an act of love. But I was too busy wrestling with my own notions of manhood to appreciate this at the time.

On my visits home, my mother would sometimes read us the stories she wrote and surprise us with her eye for an evocative detail and her innate narrative ear. Students in her class, it was clear, were moved by her recollections of the poverty of Jewish Otwock and by the hardships of a girl sent out on her own at fourteen. She wrote a story about a refugee friend, a taxi driver, who came up to our apartment in the Bronx one day on the pretext of a friendly visit and made a fumbling pass at her. We never knew such things had happened among the refugees, but in writing class my mother confided them. She wrote an expressive story about her homeless days in Warsaw and how her feeble-minded cousin Motche tried to embrace her one night in bed and how touched she was by his gesture.

She tried to talk to us about Schopenhauer, but since none of us remembered what Schopenhauer had thought we were in no mood to have my mother impress us with her interpretations. Rather than take her seriously, we needled her with the kind of banter that made up so much of my family's dinner table conversation.

At bottom, though, she knew we were indeed impressed by her march toward a degree. More important, she herself was tickled by her achievement. It allowed her to recalibrate how she measured up against the world of learned folks. People well into college were no longer as daunting as she might once have imagined. And she was no longer as inferior as she might have feared.

Eventually she accumulated all 128 credits and put together a B-plus average, higher than my own in college. It was time for the graduation ceremony. Josh, Evelyn, and I and our three spouses made sure to take off work and show up, just as she had shown up in full regalia at each of our graduations. In the appropriately workaday hall of the Felt Forum, in the swirl of Irish, Italian, African-American, Caribbean, Indian, Arab, Chinese, and Japanese faces in black gowns and mortarboards, I spotted my silver-haired mother. This woman from a shtetl where Jews seldom went to high school let alone college, where her father used to sit up at night patching bindings of dog-eared books so she could keep up with the class in elementary school, was also attired in black gown and mortarboard. I hadn't quite expected it. It was always Josh or Evelyn or me who was dressed this way and my parents who stood alongside beaming. Now it was the children who had to do the beaming. My mother seemed a little uncomfortable in her outfit, as if she were dressed for a costume party. There beside her, chuckling at his oddly attired spouse and not quite sure of what it all meant and would mean, was my father, his back a little warped and aching from the war years and the decades of sweat work, but still handsome in a gray sports jacket. Nobody quite knew what to say.

We went inside and dutifully listened to the graduation oratory. But when they began handing out the diplomas and called Rachel Berger, loud cheers went out from the left side of the auditorium where my family was clustered. My mother, her shoulders held high and cocky to hide whatever insecurity she was feeling, strode up and claimed her diploma. How we disguise our world? I thought to myself. Here is this stately ceremony, diplomas being equally handed out to scores of indistinguishably garbed graduates, yet each graduate has a distinctive story, utterly his or hers, some perhaps prosaic with middle-class milestones, some like my mother's, a veritable Scheherazade of affliction and redemption. Yet who would appreciate the distinctions in this indistinct mass? But maybe the point of a graduation is to wipe the slate clean, even of the Holocaust, to let everyone begin anew with the same slate.

Not one to dwell on pomp, my mother laughed off much of the ceremony when we joined up with her on the sidewalk outside the hall, and we conspired in the banter. In my family, we had a need to make light of the successes of life, perhaps as a way of balancing out the way we often shrugged off the misfortunes. We quickly adjourned to Lou Siegel's restaurant at Thirty-eighth Street, the La Caravelle of kosher, where we ate a lavish lunch of pastrami and broiled flounder and chicken soup and merrily toasted my mother with glasses of seltzer and Dr. Brown's Black Cherry. That day our small family felt mighty and important, at the center of the action. Amid the immigrant food smells, we felt something noble had happened to us.

I am sitting in the *New York Times* newsroom waiting for the announcement of the Pulitzer Prizes for 1995. There is a hum of excitement because word has leaked out that we have won three prizes, one for a Metro colleague of mine, Bob McFadden, the legendary rewrite man. Of course, these kinds of events also have a deflating undercurrent. They force reporters to stare at the flaws in their own talents and career decisions that keep such prizes elusive. In my own muddle of feelings, I nervously check my voice-mail messages and one, to my annoyance, is from my mother. As I watch editors and reporters patting one another on the back and chatting cheerfully, I hear her insistent voice: "Joey, call me. I just found out what happened to my brother."

The words are portentous. The shadow of the past has fallen again, pulling me back from the jauntier world I cling to into the refugee world of sorrow and bitterness. I postpone the return call, knowing that talking to my mother about that subject can only stir feelings unrelievable in the setting of a *Times* newsroom. When I call her at home that night, she tells me the story of Simcha, her brother, as if I had never known a single detail, winding out his arrest, trial, and disappearance like a mystery novel, withholding the story's resolution. It seems like an hour before I learn his not at all surprising fate.

My mother finally informs me that five years ago she had visited the International Red Cross office in New York and inquired if there was any record of his death. A clerk warned her that it might take a long time to trace his whereabouts. But this week, she received a letter from the Red Cross. Simcha, her brother, my uncle, died in 1942 in Gorky. She speculates that he turned himself in at Gorky, a town for people "denied freedom" but permitted movement they would not be allowed in a labor camp. The refusenik scientist Sakharov had been similarly confined many years later. But with his tuberculosis and the famine of wartime, Simcha did not survive. My mother tells me she was given no other details except where his grave is. She asked me if I would go visit his grave. She would pay for the trip.

On the telephone, her voice clutches once and she weeps briefly, then resumes the tale of their years together as if rushing forward would leave her grief in the dust. Who is this man she is weeping for? To her he is alive in the intensity of the experiences they shared when she was a waif in Warsaw and he a street-smart apparel seller and together they made the fateful journey to the Soviet Union. She will never forget his generosity, his tenderness, his misbegotten idealism, his flair. I try to visualize him, but I can't. My mother never salvaged a photograph. Yet, in telling me his story, over and over, adding details with each telling, she has kept him alive just a little bit longer. I cannot picture his face, but I can grasp his spirit, the spirit that saved her life but doomed his own, and I can retell his story. That is my consolation, a consolation shared with other children of the Holocaust refugees. By unearthing and telling the stories of those whose lives were cut short, we give them the breath of life for just a while longer.

Mr. Weinberg's funeral is a refugee funeral, slapdash yet eloquent. In the morning, I am still not certain what time it will start nor where it will be. When my parents finally pass on the details, they tell me the wrong time and give me the wrong directions. Thinking I am late, I rush up the West Side Highway from work, nearly colliding with a truck, then get lost in the northeast Bronx looking for the funeral home. When I find it and race to the mourners' room, I see only Mrs. Weinberg and her daughter, Betty, and Mrs. Weinberg's daughter-in-law and I think to myself: "Poor Mr. Weinberg. A simple warm man. He made a few close friends. And most of those have died off. Simple men do not have large funerals." But I soon find out that the reason there are no other mourners here is because I have arrived an hour early.

In fact, within the next hour maybe 150 people fill the room: friends Mr. Weinberg made in the displaced persons camps; chess players he sparred with as a fresh immigrant trying to make his reputation at the stone tables in the parks alongside the Jerome Avenue El; spectators who sat with him after he caught the American baseball bug and watched Babe Ruth League games in the fields behind Yankee Stadium; neighbors from Pelham Parkway, where he moved after Jews fled the South Bronx; a whole delegation of elderly refugees who have driven down from the Catskills bungalow colony where the Weinbergs spent their summers. It seems that Mr. Weinberg folded many people into his embrace.

In the hour we wait for the funeral to start, I talk with Betty and tell her my memories of her father.

"He had a zest for life," I say.

It is entirely heartfelt. I remind her about the Passover seders he would conduct and her father's skill as a dancer, when he would waltz my mother across the floors of refugee bar mitzvahs, that dwarfish man with the shriveled face swirling a woman who seemed a head taller than him with Astaire-like panache. Betty remembers that it was her father who taught me how to play chess, and I remember how passionate he was about chess—*schach* he called it—willing to play even novices like me for the pleasures of sifting possibilities and seeing them play out, relishing both the brilliant moves and the blunders.

I look around the room and there is Yonah the egg man, who owned the small chicken farm in Lakewood, New Jersey, that briefly beguiled my father. Once a week he would drive his DeSoto station wagon two hours to the city to sell fresh eggs to a string of customers, including my mother. Tall, lanky, intense, with steel-wool hair, he would walk into our house with a triumphant smile, as if he had just delivered the loot from his latest bank robbery. Yonah simply enjoyed the routines of living. To be alive, when so many others he knew had perished, was a gift in itself, and if the given life was peddling eggs, so be it. He was grateful. Besides, to people like my mother, raised in East European poverty, eggs were gold, and Yonah knew it. My mother would buy two, maybe three dozen eggs, and offer Yonah a cup of coffee, and they would spend half an hour trading gossip. The stop may have earned him a dollar, but the chance to unburden his heart to someone intimate with the world from which he emerged, someone who understood the ghosts that steadily haunted him made the visit more than worth it.

Yonah has thickened now and lost much of his hair and his face is deeply creased like a well-traveled leather suitcase. He is talking with Moishe Granas, the tailor, whom I have also not seen for ten or fifteen years. Moishe was my father's friend, the man with all the angles, wiles, and shortcuts, the man who had the goods on this riddle of America. What Moishe said, my father repeated with respect and my mother ridiculed because of that respect. In the years I did not see him, Moishe had a heart attack. "It was feeling like a thick rope around my chest," he tells me with a victorious smile, as if to say this too had not defeated him. Indeed, he looks trim and fit, and that sense of vitality is accentuated by the gold tooth glinting out of his mouth. He has driven down to the funeral this morning from a Catskills bungalow colony in his Honda Civic.

"It takes me a half tank of gas," he says, his eyes almost swaggering with pride at how astute he was to buy the economical Civic.

With the mourners crowding around us, he makes sure to tell me the exact sequence of highways he took—cutting ten minutes at least out of the more popular route—and then he launches off on the pleasures of his Honda Civic, a car he tells me he bought upon the recommendation of a canny customer in the private tailoring and alterations business Moishe operates out of his bedroom.

"I'll give you a card," he says, and pulls out a little white business card with a small picture of a thimble, needle, and thread in the corner that says:

> Morris Granas
> Tailor
> Custom Work

He is proud of this card, an adornment that in his mind declares that he has made it in America. He is proud of his car, proud of his bungalow colony, proud of his suburban children. His angles, wiles, and shortcuts have paid off. He is, even with the gold tooth glinting in his mouth, an American. And perhaps he is prouder of that fact today than he usually is because his old friend Mr. Weinberg is dead, and it is a time of summing up.

The refugee world is shrinking. Mr. Weinberg has died. Mrs. Herling died long ago. Moishe Erlich. Motele Tropper. Mrs. Salzberg. In a few years, my mother's uncle Yudel and aunt Feigele, Mr. Herling, Mrs. Weinberg, and Moishe Granas too. My childhood family is getting smaller.

"We have our wealth, but we don't have our health," one mourner laments, savoring the dark wordplay.

The mourners, my parents and Evelyn among them, begin to move into the chapel for the service, and as I squeeze through the door, Betty says to me: "Joey, would you mind saying a few words? You spoke so nicely about my father before." I hesitate for a second. Who wants the pressure of delivering a last-minute eulogy? But I answer, "Of course." It was often the role of the refugee children to represent their parents before American officials, to talk English when their parents could not. The people gathered in the chapel all knew Mr. Weinberg better than I did, but for a eulogy they perhaps would want to hear someone with more polished English. With no time to prepare, I decide simply to repeat what I told Betty about her father. As I speak to this crowd of refugees, I feel all the childhood feelings I felt whenever I was called to represent the grown-ups. I am unequal to the task; they will think I am a bungler. I will spoil the occasion, get someone into trouble. But I have been taking on senior roles for so long, I barrel my way through, talking easily of Mr. Weinberg's spirit and charms. I have bungled my way toward a funeral for an old family friend and ended up giving the eulogy, but for the most part it feels right.

My brand-new nephew's circumcision is an occasion both festive and jarring, one of those fundamental events that seem to call up one's entire life and draw on long-hidden springs of emotion.

The boy being initiated into the tribe of Israel is Jacob Solomon Hartman, the son of my sister, Evelyn, and her husband, Jimmy, and my parents' first grandchild. Every one of life's rituals seem to bring together so many disparate worlds and create new ones in the process, and this is no exception. As I look around the living room crowded with forty or so relatives and friends, I can discern two distinct species: There are aging refugees, friends of my parents who had to restart their lives in sputtering fashion; and, quite separate from them in manner no less than accent, American Jews, Jimmy's relatives and friends, who may have had a generational leg or two up on the refugees but have also struggled to secure their achievements. Our strain has been grafted to theirs in Jacob Solomon Hartman, and he will be stronger for that union in ways we can only dimly perceive.

The *mohel,* or circumciser, a burly, balding man with a pointy gray beard, takes full command of the living room, shifting a grandmother here and an uncle there like a Balanchine deploying a corps of ballerinas. He explains to the gathered throng that Jacob is entering the covenant of Israel, a covenant stretching back to Abraham, who, incredibly, circumcised himself as well as his sons Isaac and Ishmael. "My covenant shall be in your flesh for an everlasting covenant," God told Abraham, promising he would be the father of many nations and inherit the land then called Canaan.

The baby's grandmother, my mother, brings the baby, swaddled in a blanket, into the living room. The baby's grandfather, my father, cradles the baby on his lap. The *mohel* opens the baby's diaper, probes the foreskin of his penis, and clamps it with a cutting instrument known as a shield. Mumbling Hebrew prayers, he snips the foreskin off in one swift stroke as everyone breaks into the traditional song of celebration: *"Seemon Tov and Mazel Tov"* [a good sign and good luck]. Jacob hollers for a moment, but soon he is quietly sucking on a gauze pad dipped in sweet kosher wine.

As we watch this strange rite unfold, tears stream down my cheeks. My efforts at self-control are not helped by seeing my father. His lips are quivering as he tries to choke back the emotion welling inside him. My sister and my wife, Brenda, are embracing in tears. Why are we reacting so emotionally to a ceremony we have each witnessed many times before? We did not cry when we first saw the baby. Why now at the moment of circumcision?

As I think about it, I sense that we cry because we are all part of that covenant, and that covenant has survived through our tribe's history at some wrenching costs. I do not ask him, but lodged in my father's consciousness at this moment must be the murder of the parents and sisters who were killed only because they clung to the Jewish covenant, parents and sisters who could not be here with him at this moment of his redemption. That tribal identity is lodged deep in my consciousness as well. I remind myself of my own secret circumcision in the Soviet Union, where the Russians had outlawed this ancient rite. The performance of the rite was imperative for my parents, as ingrained in each of them as a bird's instinct for crafting a nest.

As I watch Jacob's circumcision, it occurs to me how lucky he is to be surrounded by so many relatives and friends, to have an open and expansive ceremony, complete with a spread of Nova Scotia, whitefish, and bagels, in a terraced apartment overlooking the Hudson in Riverdale in the marvelously free country of the United States. There is, inexorably, that sense of triumph over all the loss his grandparents suffered. The covenant is alive in plenty as well as in misery, in tranquility as well as in turmoil. Triumph and pain are both worth tears, for so often are they indistinguishably mingled into each other.

I sense also that we may be reacting so intensely because Jacob's birth makes us realize we are all growing older. I am now an uncle, not just a son and brother. My baby sister, twelve years younger than me, whom I have watched grow up from infancy, is now a mother of her own infant. Time is passing unbelievably swiftly, and one day, with the finality of a blade snipping a foreskin, we will be no more.

But there is little Jacob, sucking on his gauze pad of kosher wine. He is our continuation, our wistful stab at eternity. The covenant will go on as it has since Abraham.

It is the *Neilah* service of Yom Kippur, the last opportunity for prayer before the Gates of Mercy are slammed shut for the year, our last chance to implore God to inscribe our names in the Book of Life. I am standing next to my father in the crowded men's section of his Orthodox synagogue, feeling the soft brush of his yellowed prayer shawl against the sleeve of my arm as we sway and rock to the prayers, feeling a communion with him and with the lost world from which he came. My father's yellowed talis amid the garbled singsong of desperate, hurried prayer by stale-smelling old European Jews has always been my touchstone to faith in God. That is why it took me years to grow comfortable with the polished veneer of modern, liberal synagogues.

It has become a personal tradition of mine to forgo my own synagogue for this one prayer service and pray alongside him. It began as a convenient way to attend the postfast dinner given every year by my sister, whose home is a few blocks from his, but now I insist upon it. So does my brother, who is standing on my father's right flank. How many more times, after all, will there be to pray alongside my father? Five? Ten? The Yom Kippur question of who will live and who will die grows increasingly sobering as my father ages and declines.

What mystifies me year after year is why my father is standing here at all. Here is a man whose entire family was slaughtered by the Nazis, who almost overnight lost his home, his town, his way of life. Yet he has never stopped believing entirely in a tender, sheltering God. He grew up in a pious farmer's home and from the age of thirteen daily prayed by fastening to his arm and forehead the straps of tefillin—the contraption of two leather boxes concealing slips of Scripture. I asked him once what happened to the tefillin when he was drafted into the Soviet army. He seemed eager to answer the question, as if he had thought about it many times.

"I had them until 1942," he said. "They sent us out on maneuvers. When I came back they were stolen."

That indignity did not rattle his faith. Sometime after the gathering of Holocaust survivors in Jerusalem, I showed him slides I had taken of my mother and him at a ceremony in front of the Western Wall. One shot showed him sitting solemnly next to my mother in the crowd of seven thousand survivors. I asked him what he was thinking.

"I was angry with God," he said more forthrightly than I ever remember his saying anything. "I was asking him why he killed my mother and father and my sisters."

Yet he has kept his faith, and in the last decades of his life he has become even more religious. He long ago gave up work on Saturday and now refuses to drive. He and my mother have made their home kosher. He walks in his leafy neighborhood with a yarmulke. My mother tells me he prays three times a day and says Psalms in between. In this synagogue, my reticent father may not be one of the more prestigious members, but he is known by everyone, one of the stalwarts who help make up the daily minyanim of at least ten Jews.

I think of a central Torah reading of the High Holidays, the binding of Isaac that is read on the second day of Rosh Hashanah. God asked Abraham to sacrifice his son, his only son, Isaac, on an altar as a test of his faith. Abraham, otherwise a master bargainer, did not quibble, rising early to do God's bidding and leading Isaac to the crest of Mount Moriah to bind him upon an altar, upon which he planned to slaughter and burn him. Only an angel's intercession stopped him from slitting Isaac's throat. Abraham's trust in God was such that he was ready to believe even after God asked him to perform such a horrific act. My father's trust is such that he continues to believe even after the horrific sacrifice of his kin. His grudging, patient faith has brought him a kind of reparation, even a squaring of the debt—his two sons standing at his sides, his wife and daughter and daughters-in-law in the women's section across the dividing curtain, grandchildren capering on the fringes of the service. The Holocaust was a watershed in his long life, but it was only a watershed. His life went on. A new family was formed; other ones will splice off from that. Death did not defeat him. He not only survived, he thrived. For his faith in God promised that there would yet be other days and moments worth holding on for.

I am sitting with my sister in a West Side delicatessen, she with a corned beef on rye, I with a pastrami on rye. She is telling me about something that happened recently between her eleven-year-old daughter and our father.

"Alisa had a project for school where the students had to research their family history," she begins. "She called up Mommy and Daddy. Mommy told her that funny story about the time she fed her baby sister with cow's milk. Then Alisa asked Daddy about his family. He told her that he had six sisters. His father, he said, had two girls with a first wife, who then died. He thinks it was of cancer. Then with the second wife he had five girls and Daddy. The last two girls were twins and one of those died as a baby. He doesn't remember how. That was all he could tell her. On the extension phone I could hear him crying. Then he said, 'I've been alone since I was twenty.'"

I hear this and feel myself choking. I did not know that my father's father had had a first wife. I did not know of the infant twin who died.

Most of all, I was not aware that my father felt so alone, even with my mother, my brother, my sister, and our expanding brood at his side all those years.

I have long wanted to find out more about my father, where he came from, who he is. But my efforts have not gleaned very much. The faces, the stories, even the names of the six sisters and his parents are locked up in my father's heart and he will not let them go. My father remains silent, silent to his friends, to his children, even to his wife. Perhaps if he brings his parents and sisters to life for us by telling us what they were like, he will have to acknowledge that they are really dead. But who knows if this is the answer. I want to bring them to life, just as my mother has brought her family to life. But my father cannot help me. And that is his right, his earned right. His story will never be fleshed out. It will vanish like ashes and smoke.

Thirteen years have passed since the circumcision and there is Jacob, slim, dark-suited, leprechaun-eyed, standing at a synagogue altar in Riverdale splendidly chanting the week's Torah portion in the classic melodies of his tribe while his parents, brother, sister, three grandparents, three aunts, three uncles, and five of his six cousins look on with wonder. Alone among my parents' now seven grandchildren, he has blossomed into a Torah scholar, the heir to the Golant legacy of fervent Jewish learning and observance. Jakey, as everyone calls him, was enchanted by the Torah with his first taste in first grade, pouncing on it the way some boys latch on to the elegance of baseball statistics. By second and third grade, he was gulping the passages down like sweet morsels of sponge cake, not just the stories of Abraham, Jacob, and Moses, but the conjectural commentaries by Rashi and Ramban as well. While his cousins were struggling with the Four Questions, he was running his family's seder. While they had to be goaded to delve into Hebrew, he plunged in with relish. By eleven, he was wearing a small yarmulke clipped to his hair and insisted on eating only kosher food. So protective did my sister, Evelyn, become of her miniature rabbi's spiritual evolution that she stopped shopping on Saturdays, then stopped driving and answering the phone as well. He has, in short, converted his once temporal family into something very close to Orthodoxy.

Knowing all this I am not astonished to hear him performing so flawlessly. What does snare me by surprise is his voice—clear and crystalline. It is the embryonic version, I muse, of the voice of my legendary grandfather, the cantor Joshua Golant, that was passed on in a soprano version to my mother and in baritone to my brother.

Every Shabbos the *parshah* is broken into seven *aliyahs*—seven chances for men to come up and bless the Torah. Since this is Jakey's bar mitzvah, five of the men who mount the altar and murmur or thunder out the blessings are his two grandfathers, my brother and me, and his father. His great-uncle, Yasha, come all the way from Altoona, Pennsylvania, opens and closes the ark's curtain. His uncle Bruce Freyer climaxes the ceremony by dramatically hoisting the naked Torah scroll high in the air for all to see, while his kid brother Benji, another leprechaun, binds and dresses the scroll.

Seeing this unfolding of human generations, the congregation's rabbi, Avi Weiss, displays perfect pitch for its meaning, articulating what everyone cannot help noticing—that a European Jewish family decimated by the Nazis is now bountifully restored here in New York. Without missing a beat, he calls all the men of the Berger-Hartman-Golant clan up to the altar and leads us in a shimmying circle dance as those jammed into separate male and female halves of the synagogue sing *"Seemon Tov and Mazel Tov."* The slow, shuffling dance is Hasidic in flavor but it reminds me also of the circle dances I did among Irish and Puerto Rican schoolchildren that helped me feel at home in my first year in America. My father has brightly glistening tears in his eyes. So does Jakey's rock-ribbed American grandfather. He probably never saw himself doing the musty dances of the Orthodox, but at ninety years old, still tall, agile, and full of kiddie enthusiasms—he even gallops horses on an Arizona dude ranch—he has reconciled himself to the ineluctable wisdom of these age-old ceremonies.

The next day is the party, an affair only slightly larger in scope than the ones my hardworking parents scrimped together for my brother and me forty years before and just a couple of miles away on the now frayed Grand Concourse. What is different, though, are the speeches, with accolades neither my brother nor I heard at our bar mitzvahs. Rabbis from two different synagogues and the principal of Jakey's school have interrupted their Sunday to speak here, and one of the rabbis declares that every once in a while someone like Jakey comes along who is felt to have a blessed, inexplicable gift for Torah.

Jakey's mother, my sister, speaks as well. Just the year before, what would have been her fourth child was strangled in the womb at eight months by a twisted umbilical cord. With Rabbi Weiss presiding, the baby, enclosed in a plain pinewood coffin not much bigger than a shoe box, was buried in a sun-dappled grave in New Jersey. Though it was not born alive, the baby was given a name—Nathan Chaim—two Hebrew words that together mean "to give life." My brother-in-law's brief but heart-tearing eulogy explained that the baby, in its huddled time in the womb, had given considerable life, bringing forth joyful anticipation in the family it was never to know. Now, my sister moves all the bar mitzvah guests by remembering what "a soldier" Jakey had been throughout the ordeal. She also makes us laugh, first paying tribute to the great affection Jakey has received from his grandparents, then tartly taking note of how on a daily basis she has had to fight with those grandparents for the right to raise her children. Knowing my mother's consuming, meddling vigor, I fully understand.

As she winds up her talk, I think of something else: my sister's birth planted an inextricable stake in the bedrock of this country. How ironic that it is she, more than her European-born brothers, who is shaping her family into something of a throwback to the pious Jews of Otwock.

Whatever poignancy is evoked by her speech is soon swallowed up by raucous klezmer music and the wild twirlings and swingings of the yeshiva boys and their teachers, splashes of pure jubilation. In rigorous Orthodox fashion, the women too dance on their own, and while their horas are slightly more demure, they are also exultant. Though Jakey is the focus of this bar mitzvah, a serendipitous offshoot is that the party manages to amount to a recapitulation of my immigrant life. There at one table are my father, mother, and her brother Yasha. They are survivors and refugees, sure, but they have long moved beyond those shorthand labels, with their intimations of marooned castaways or vagabonds, to something more accomplished. At eighty, my college-graduate mother still has a bell-like, soulful soprano and is a Yiddish songbird locally sought out for communal Holocaust memorials. On her own, with random gleanings from radio talk shows and newspaper articles, she has gotten the hang of the American stock market and shrewdly parlayed the savings of a half century of toil and thrift into an impressive nest egg. My father, who after stubborn distrust of doctors and hospitals submitted several years ago to a successful quintuple heart bypass, is a paterfamilias of a widening New York–area clan—fifteen souls and counting—and a mainstay of the senior citizen diversions at the Riverdale Y. My Golant uncle, thickset now with the indulgences of a pensioned shoe-factory manager, is a great-grandfather of two, a grandfather of six, and a general factotum of his synagogue in Altoona. Although to my mother's regret not one of his four children married within the faith, she is nonetheless delighted with them and with her brother's grandchildren, mixing his sweet kindness with the enhancements of more exotic strains and coming up with something fine after all. There also, bubbly as ever, is Mrs. Erlich, one of only a handful of greeners remaining from my childhood, a woman who more than a half century ago wholesaled cherries to my father in the DP camps and then brought her peddling skills to the Spanish ghettos of the Bronx. A widow now, she has melded seamlessly into the flock of comfortable widows who people Riverdale's park benches.

Next to me is my wife of twenty years, Brenda. Is it a coincidence that she too is an immigrant and an exile? She was born in South Africa into a people whose obsolete ideas of human relations stifled not only black aspirations but also made it impossible for a white woman to take up her calling. When we met, she lived by herself in a garret in Greenwich Village and worked as a production assistant for television's *Sesame Street*. Although I was hardly aware of it at the time, there must have been something irresistible about a young solitary woman trying to make a go of it in a new country, feeling herself dangling from a precipice and fated for doom at every turn. And she too must have been touched by something not quite poised and established about me. There were lots of other attractions, of course, but our immigrant sensibilities helped knit together our love. By now, Brenda has more than struggled off the precipice, training herself to become a highly regarded psychoanalyst, pushing herself through the high-wire act of adopting our baby daughter, becoming a tender, beloved mother and a tireless intimate to the friends who form her reconstructed community in America. But there are countless vestiges of exile in her just as there are in me, and we often tease each other about those. Sometimes, when we bicker, as couples do, about the spending of money, I accuse her of frittering it away as if she were back in colonial Africa sitting on a sunny cane-chaired veranda and ordering Pimm's cups. She retorts that I watch every dime as if I were preparing for a pogrom.

At my table there is practically a reunion of my 102nd Street gang. There is Simon, born in a concentration camp, shorn of a sister before he was even born, orphaned of his mother as a teenager, yet, with flinty refugee resilience, he is not only the fifty-four-year-old father of two toddlers and the head of a small law firm but has never lost his childhood fountain of sly wit, his eye for the shrewd move, and his native kindness. There is Sol Cooperman, whose TV set I coveted as a child, my bungalow-colony rival in sports and romance, now a father of three who travels the world to christen new vessels as president of a Norwegian shipping company. And there is my brother, Josh, who weathered my childhood with me, content to trail after me, sometimes in borrowed light, now, to my perennial surprise, completely his own man, a father of three, dermatologist to Riverdale's Jews and, to his own satisfaction, an enthusiast of bicycles and Sherlock Holmes. Whatever our differences, we are bound inextricably. And very much on all our minds is our one missing member, Maury. Maury was a child ahead of his times, a sixties kid trapped in the bland fifties. He recoiled from school partly because he struggled painfully with math and avoided college until deep into adulthood. Now he works as a tax preparer in California. Who could have predicted that?

But as we watch Jakey spinning ecstatically with his friends like a wood sprite, all of us must silently wonder: Who could have foreseen any of this?

It is almost a year later, the first year of a new century, and this time it is my daughter Annie's turn to be called to the Torah, and, oh, what a contrast. Her performance, to be sure, is as fine in its own way. Annie takes the Torah from the ark, opens her lips to sing the Hebrew prayers, and in minutes our relatives, friends, and synagogue acquaintances seem dazzled. She reads her two portions without a fumble and makes a speech full of her sardonic humor and her principled sensibility. It begins: "I remember back in January when it was the rabbi's daughter's bat mitzvah and he stood there and said, 'Your portion, Leba, is a great one. People who have Leviticus would kill for a portion like yours.' "

She pauses with perfect Borscht Belt timing, drawing laughs before the punch line, and says, "I have Leviticus."

For years Annie has been resisting Hebrew school, cynical in her sassy, modern way of much of Jewish lore and literature. When I told her a year before that her haftarah portion would be the shortest of the yearly cycle, she pumped her fist in jubilation. "Yes, there is a God!" she said. But ultimately she wanted to do well, and she has pulled it all together now, commanding the room with her voice and poise and beauty and letting us all know how much she cares for the essentials. She has taken up her part in a religion and a people that has lasted thousands of years and has declared in her own paradoxical way that "Yes, there is a God." Brenda and I are far from alone in having tears in our eyes.

What gives the event such contrast is Annie's world. Her friends clustered throughout this egalitarian synagogue are as Christian as they are Jewish, with several of her friends' parents in the crowd seeing their first bat mitzvah. At the afternoon celebration at a local country club, Annie is not aching to do horas; she wants to dance to 'N Sync and Britney Spears and the Backstreet Boys. And the evening party for her teenage friends is an Orthodox no-no. Boys and girls dance together, with all the awkwardness and uncertainty of thirteen-year-olds on the edge of sexuality. Throughout the day, as I see Annie exulting in a clamor of Yankee, British, Italian, Irish, Latino, and Texan youngsters from our tidy Westchester suburban town, I am struck by how much she is a full-fledged, comfortable-in-her-own-skin American.

Annie has none of the Golant and Berger genes transported here with the remnants of European Jewry. But as her bat mitzvah shows, she has become, and we have helped make her, a Jew. A different Jew from Jakey, but one who understands the Jewish duties of the heart, kindness and sensitivity and an appreciation of the mystique of women lighting candles on a white tablecloth decked out with a honey-colored challah and a glass of ruby wine. Even had she not been our child through adoption, she would not have become a dark-eyed *sheyn meydele,* the classic sweet, decent, and humble Jewish girl. For whatever complicated origins, the pulls her parents feel to swim in the American mainstream are too strong for that. The corner of Westchester we chose is not Riverdale. Public school is not yeshiva. Brenda and I did wish her to have a deep immersion in Jewish life, but we wanted just as much that she feel a kinship with the friends she made in our neighborhood.

Annie is an unquenchable reader but not of Torah, already devouring *Pride and Prejudice, Jane Eyre,* and *Gone With the Wind.* She has her own gifts—for lyricism, for music, for friendship. Most of all she seems happy tooling around our suburb with her pals, kicking soccer balls in the waning days of summer, trick-or-treating on Halloween, playing ice hockey in a clamorous winter rink. She is the acculturated, well-absorbed child part of me always longed to be. But that is the wonder of the democratic American foundry: some turn out like Jakey, some turn out like Annie.

Annie, like Jakey, will keep up the traditions in her own way. But what will she and Jakey and their cousins, Danny, David, Renee, Alisa, and Benji, and the other members of the next generation know of their grandparents' world, really know, not just as a historical legend but with something of the firsthand intimacy that Josh, Evelyn, and I have experienced? Their Bubbe and Zayde have surely spared them. Perhaps their parents and uncles and aunts will do the right thing and teach them about how Bubbe and Zayde lost their families and hometowns in the Holocaust and how, with scarcely any shards left from their old lives, built new lives here. But it will be up to these children to do their own delving, to seek out the dwindling ranks of witnesses or read accounts left behind by those who have already died. They will have to do their own imagining of what racial contempt can lead to and how the victims can have the resilience to go on.

An informed memory is important because the Holocaust, like the destruction of the temples, is a permanent tribal wound, engraved in our souls. Whether we cleave to the ancient traditions or plunge wholeheartedly into the conventional American currents, whether we marry in or marry out, whether we raise our children Orthodox or outlandish, the Holocaust wound defines every day a large part of who we are and how we see the world. Though it would be pretty to think we can escape that past, such flights are futile. Better to look the horror in its face and go on.

Go on the survivors surely do, because in the middle of the crowd of revelers at Jakey's and Annie's bar mitzvahs are Bubbe and Zayde, radiant in the joy of all they have wrought, gleaning their well-deserved *naches*. Yet they are disbelieving too, because who could have imagined amid the human wreckage gathered in the displaced persons camps that one day they could enjoy such bounty? And they are mourning too because the aching for those who perished, for those who cannot be with them to savor such triumphant days, never eases. That is the bittersweet riddle of the Holocaust and its aftermath that no amount of introspection will ever resolve.

ABOUT THE AUTHOR

JOSEPH BERGER was born in Russia in 1945 and came to the United States when he was five years old. He is currently the deputy education editor at *The New York Times*. He has also reported on religion and education for the paper and served as its bureau chief in Westchester. The author of *The Young Scientists*, he lives in Larchmont, New York, with his wife and daughter.